WALTER MOSLEY

Critical Companions to Popular Contemporary Writers
Second Series

Julia Alvarez *by Silvio Sirias*

Rudolfo A. Anaya *by Margarite Fernandez Olmos*

Maya Angelou *by Mary Jane Lupton*

Ray Bradbury *by Robin Anne Reid*

Louise Erdrich *by Lorena L. Stookey*

Ernest J. Gaines *by Karen Carmean*

Gabriel García Márquez *by Rubén Pelayo*

John Irving *by Josie P. Campbell*

Garrison Keillor *by Marcia Songer*

Jamaica Kincaid *by Lizabeth Paravisini-Gebert*

Revisiting Stephen King *by Sharon A. Russell*

Barbara Kingsolver *by Mary Jean DeMarr*

Maxine Hong Kingston *by E. D. Huntley*

Terry McMillan *by Paulette Richards*

Larry McMurtry *by John M. Reilly*

Toni Morrison *by Missy Dehn Kubitschek*

Gloria Naylor *by Charles E. Wilson, Jr.*

Chaim Potok *by Sanford Sternlicht*

Amy Tan *by E. D. Huntley*

Anne Tyler *by Paul Bail*

Leon Uris *by Kathleen Shine Cain*

Kurt Vonnegut *by Thomas F. Marvin*

Tom Wolfe *by Brian Abel Ragen*

WALTER MOSLEY

A Critical Companion

Charles E. Wilson, Jr.

CRITICAL COMPANIONS TO POPULAR CONTEMPORARY
WRITERS
Kathleen Gregory Klein, Series Editor

Greenwood Press
Westport, Connecticut • London

Library of Congress Cataloging-in-Publication Data

Wilson, Charles E., 1961-
  Walter Mosley : a critical companion / Charles E. Wilson, Jr.
    p. cm. — (Critical companions to popular contemporary writers, ISSN 1082–4979)
  Includes bibliographical references and index.
  ISBN 0–313–32022–5 (alk. paper)
    1. Mosley, Walter—Criticism and interpretation. 2. Detective and mystery stories.
American—History and criticism. 3. Los Angeles (Calif.)—In literature. 4. Rawlins, Easy
(Fictitious character) 5. African American men in literature. I. Title. II. Series.
PS3563.O88456 Z88 2003
813'.54—dc21   2002035331

British Library Cataloguing in Publication Data is available.

Library of Congress Catalog Card Number: 2002035331
ISBN: 0-313-32022-5
ISSN: 1082-4979

First published in 2003

Greenwood Press, 88 Post Road West, Westport, CT 06881
An imprint of Greenwood Publishing Group, Inc.
www.greenwood.com

Printed in the United States of America

The paper used in this book complies with the
Permanent Paper Standard issued by the National
Information Standards Organization (Z39.48-1984).

10 9 8 7 6 5 4 3 2 1

For Vincent Maurice Wilson,
whose humor and intellect anchor true brotherhood.

Contents

Series Foreword

The authors who appear in the series Critical Companions to Popular Contemporary Writers are all best-selling writers. They do not simply have one successful novel, but a string of them. Fans, critics, and specialist readers eagerly anticipate their next book. For some, high cash advances and breakthrough sales figures are automatic; movie deals often follow. Some writers become household names, recognized by almost everyone.

But their novels are read one by one. Each reader chooses to start and, more importantly, to finish a book because of what she or he finds there. The real test of a novel is in the satisfaction its readers experience. This series acknowledges the extraordinary involvement of readers and writers in creating a best-seller.

The authors included in this series were chosen by an advisory board composed of high school English teachers and high school and public librarians. They ranked a list of best-selling writers according to their popularity among different groups of readers. For the first series, writers in the top-ranked group who had received no book-length, academic, literary analysis (or none in at least the past ten years) were chosen. Because of this selection method, Critical Companions to Popular Contemporary Writers meets a need that is being addressed nowhere else. The success of these volumes as reported by reviewers, librarians, and teachers led to an expansion of the series mandate to include some writers with wide critical attention—Toni Morrison, John Irving, and Maya Angelou, for example—to extend the usefulness of the series.

The volumes in the series are written by scholars with particular expertise in analyzing popular fiction. These specialists add an academic focus to the popular success that these writers already enjoy.

The series is designed to appeal to a wide range of readers. The general reading public will find explanations for the appeal of these well-known writers. Fans will find biographical and fictional questions answered. Students will find literary analyses, discussions of fictional genres, carefully organized introductions to new ways of reading the novels, and bibliographies for additional research. Whether browsing through the book for pleasure or using it for an assignment, readers will find that the most recent novels of the authors are included.

Each volume begins with a biographical chapter drawing on published information, autobiographies or memoirs, prior interviews, and, in some cases, interviews given especially for this series. A chapter on literary history and genres describes how the author's work fits into a larger literary context. The following chapters analyze the writer's most important, most popular, and most recent novels in detail. Each chapter focuses on one or more novels. This approach, suggested by the advisory board as the most useful to student research, allows for an in-depth analysis of the writer's fiction. Close and careful readings with numerous examples show readers exactly how the novels work. These chapters are organized around three central elements: plot development (how the story line moves forward), character development (what the reader knows of the important figures), and theme (the significant ideas of the novel). Chapters may also include sections on generic conventions (how the novel is similar to or different from others in its same category of science fiction, fantasy, thriller, etc.), narrative point of view (who tells the story and how), symbols and literary language, and historical or social context. Each chapter ends with an "alternative reading" of the novel. The volume concludes with a primary and secondary bibliography, including reviews.

The alternative readings are a unique feature of this series. By demonstrating a particular way of reading each novel, they provide a clear example of how a specific perspective can reveal important aspects of the book. In the alternative reading sections, one contemporary literary theory—way of reading, such as feminist criticism, Marxism, new historicism, deconstruction, or Jungian psychological critique—is defined in brief, easily comprehensible language. That definition is then applied to the novel to highlight specific features that might go unnoticed or be understood differently in a more general reading. Each volume defines two or three specific theories, making them part of the reader's understanding of how diverse meanings may be constructed from a single novel.

Taken collectively, the volumes in the Critical Companions to Popular Contemporary Writers series provide a wide-ranging investigation of the complexities of current best-selling fiction. By treating these novels seriously as both literary works and publishing successes, the series demonstrates the potential of popular literature in contemporary culture.

Kathleen Gregory Klein
Southern Connecticut State University

1

The Life of Walter Mosley

A man of unflappable determination is perhaps the most accurate description of Walter Mosley. Told by prospective publishers that "white people don't read about black people, black women don't read about black men, and black men don't read," Mosley set out to prove this establishment wrong. Though he was unsuccessful in his initial attempts to sell his first manuscript (*Gone Fishin'*), he would go on to write several bestsellers, craft short stories, sharpen his skills in playwriting, and even spark two films based on his novels. That Mosley began writing later in life, in his mid-thirties, probably served him well. As a mature, responsible, and astute black man himself, he knew that the publishers' criticism of black men was simply stereotypical and false, and he also knew that books that showcased hardworking and complex black male characters would enjoy widespread popularity. Refusing to accept exclusion from the world of publishing, Mosley persevered and, in his prolific fashion, has now written fourteen books of fiction.

Walter Mosley was born in Los Angeles on January 12, 1952, to an African American father, Leroy, and a Jewish American mother, Ella. His father was a native of Louisiana and later a resident of Texas; his mother hailed from the Bronx (with extended connections to Russia and Poland). The two met in the Los Angeles school system. Both had come to California during the post–World War II northern and western migrations. Ella worked as a personnel clerk while Leroy labored as a custodian; both would advance over the years and eventually land supervisory positions. Though interracial marriage was legal in California, when Ella and Leroy attempted to marry in 1951, no one would give them a marriage license. Not until a few years after Walter was born did they marry (Jaggi, 26). Self-sufficient individuals, the Mosleys simply proceeded with their lives, always ignoring any circumstance that was not immediately threatening, and they instilled this sense of independence and purpose in their son.

By setting a positive example, Mosley's parents taught Walter to value learning and stressed the importance of a solid education. When he reached school age, they sacrificed $9.50 each week to send him to Victory Baptist Day School, the only black private elementary school in Los Angeles. Mosley received an excellent education and even learned black history, still an unusual circumstance in the 1950s. The Mosley house was filled with books and magazines that both Leroy and Ella read voraciously. And from both his parents, Walter learned how to spin an entertaining yarn. Ella's family shared "old Jewish stories about the czars and living in Russia," and from his father's side he was mesmerized by Texas tales of "violence and partying and eating and drinking" (Gleick, 105). Leroy, in particular, nurtured Mosley's gift for and interest in storytelling. His speech patterns, as well as those of other family members and friends, would serve as Mosley's template for creation. Appreciating the raw beauty and ultimate purity of oral language passed down from his father and others, Mosley has recaptured the rhythms and unabashed clarity of this ironically elegant speech. Mosley insists that when he crafts dialogue, he thinks of having a simple conversation with regular people, or he recalls the language he often heard as a child. Still, he acknowledges the impact his Jewish roots have had on him and his writing. Because he is quite close to his mother and her family (longtime socialists, communists, and intellectuals), Jewish characters figure prominently in Mosley's novels.

Without question, Leroy Mosley was his son's most important role model. He led not only by example but also by instruction. The father's recurrent admonition to his young son ultimately prodded Mosley to realize his dream to write. The elder Mosley often said to his son that in order to live a happy life, a person needs to fulfill two obligations: find something to do to pay the rent, and then find something enjoyable to do (Joyner). For Walter Mosley, the enjoyable is also that highly demanding act of writing. Mosley takes great pride in his father, whom he remembers as being "very gregarious . . . [and] a great storyteller" (Whetstone, 107). That Mosley has dedicated several books to his father, who died on New

Year's Day in 1993, is a testament to the author's gratitude to his most influential role model. In various interviews conducted subsequent to his father's death, Mosley admits to missing him "very much, very, very much." No doubt Leroy Mosley has been instrumental not just in Mosley's ultimate choice of a career but also in the very subject matter itself. Just as Easy Rawlins is a transplanted southerner who was orphaned at an early age but becomes a self-sufficient property owner and landlord, Leroy Mosley was also orphaned (when his mother died and his father simply disappeared) and became a successful landlord while holding down a regular job. And the elder Mosley's death at the time Mosley was writing *RL's Dream*, the novel about a dying blues musician, impacted how Mosley would ultimately treat the protagonist's death. At given creative moments, Mosley's personal life and history have merged with his professional life.

Important as well is the fact that Leroy shaped Walter Mosley's sense of self and purpose. When the elder Mosley purchased, and subsequently profited from, rental properties so that his family might enjoy a more fruitful existence, he taught his son the value of economic freedom. Leroy Mosley never revealed his true wealth to his official employers (he even hid his fine automobiles at home). In this way, he retained and protected his independence. When the younger Mosley later chose a writing career in lieu of working directly for the corporate world, he was emulating his father in a search for freedom and self-determination.

Mosley insists that the most important gift his parents gave him as a child was "a lot of security in everyday life" (Whetstone, 108). Whenever he is questioned about the peculiarities of growing up in the 1950s and 1960s as a biracial child, Mosley responds nonchalantly. For him, there was nothing strange about his racial makeup; he was simply the product of Leroy and Ella, two people who quietly raised their only child in a largely black and Hispanic Watts neighborhood until he was twelve, later moving to the more suburban Pico-Fairfax area of the city. Though others may have considered this family an oddity, Mosley says that such opinions never affected him. If outsiders were disturbed by the interracial family, then they burdened only themselves because, according to Mosley, "[their discomfort] didn't have anything to do with me" (Whetstone, 108). The fact that Ella and Leroy had to live in a predominantly black neighborhood, where they were more readily accepted, helped to ease what would have been more definitive racial tensions in a different neighborhood. This necessity did clarify for Mosley, of course, society's well-defined racial lines. In retrospect, he notes that as a student at Louis

Pasteur Junior High School, which was half black and half white, he was generally in classes made up of all white or all black students, but never equally mixed. Still, the Watts neighborhood where he spent his formative years was a secure enclave where there were also "Mexican families who'd moved to better their lives and launch their children, and Japanese families whose parents had fled the oppressive caste systems of their homeland." And though all of them "had been persecuted and marginalized," they "dreamed of prosperity and equality" (Mosley, "Understanding the Riots," 6).

When asked about his own extended family, Mosley maintains that both sides interacted without incident. He recalls his thirteenth birthday party (it was not an official bar mitzvah, because he was not a practicing Jew), when his maternal and paternal relatives came to celebrate as human beings without any concern for racial or religious differences. However, his maternal grandfather, a doctor whom Mosley describes as "nutty" (Jaggi, 26), was not initially pleased at Ella's choice of a husband, but over time he accepted the marriage. Perhaps Ella and Leroy's successful union resulted from the fact that each brought differing perspectives that complemented each other. While Ella was liberal minded and progressive in thought, Leroy was rather conservative. Mosley remembers that once when his parents attended a party for the Black Panthers, Leroy became so upset that he had to leave. Though he certainly believed in social progress, he eschewed any action that seemed too radical (Williams).

What he saw as his parents' natural complements to each other is still evident. With his father's death, mother Ella, now Mosley's greatest fan, redoubled her support of Mosley's career. Whenever Mosley travels to Los Angeles for a reading, his mother always attends and always purchases a book, making her son feel special with this simple gesture. Though she had hoped he would become a hotel manager, she has been pleased with, and proud of, her son's choices. Because she believes that "Walter is . . . too good at too many things" (Lyall, C1), Ella Mosley is not surprised at Mosley's success.

While Leroy and Ella Mosley provided their son with intellectual stimulation and security, Mosley still recalls feeling an almost unbearable loneliness during his childhood: "I was very unhappy. It seems to me like I wanted something, but the something was intangible" (George, E1). Perhaps this is the reason he has found comfort in books and in his own imagination. His emotional emptiness and pain has made him sensitive to others' suffering. A critical and influential event in his life was the 1965 Watts riots. Though his family had moved to West Los Angeles by this time, Mosley was still affected by the incident. Because no one attended a play in which the thirteen-year-old Mosley was to perform, the teenager was left confused and angry, feelings that were obviously consistent with those of the rioters, though Mosley did not quite understand the similarity at the time. He was simply angry that anyone would ruin his scheduled performance. Nonetheless, these raw feelings would yield the kind of personality suited for creativity and birthing emotionally charged characters. As an adult, Mosley has retained some of his childhood detachment. According to Frederic Tuten, his creative writing teacher and mentor at New York's City College, "There is a kind of elusiveness to his soul. . . . We both have this kind of strange part of us that didn't grow up, so the world is always full of surprises. It's as if the two of us have been condemned to solitary confinement, and when we're let out, we are sort of amazed by what we see" (George, E1). Such wonder is the perfect ingredient for a deliberate and comprehensive creativity.

Luckily, Mosley happened upon an influential mentor when he entered Alexander Hamilton High School. English teacher Arthur Shugard, in whose classes Mosley enrolled at every opportunity, taught the young student how to both read and write critically. He also instructed an eager Mosley on the intricacies of poetry. And though many years passed before Mosley returned to creative writing, he still remembered everything that this favorite teacher taught him (Siegel). While Mosley interacted harmoniously with Shugard, he has admitted not faring as well with other teachers. Because he liked to talk during class, teachers often had to admonish him. Another English teacher, Miss Pearl, gave Mosley a B in class, not because he had not performed A-level work, but because he had earned an unsatisfactory mark in cooperation. Devastated by the grade, Mosley began what has become a lifelong job of defying authority (Siegel). That both his academic successes and frustrations are situated in English classes ironically anticipate his successes and frustrations with the publishing world in general.

In terms of a literary impetus for his interest in writing, Mosley admits to having had a voracious appetite for comic books during his adolescence ("Eavesdropping: Conversation with Walter Mosley and Colson Whitehead," 43), though his father questioned this passion. Before Mosley developed this interest in comics, he read whatever classical works his teachers assigned, an achievement that both of his parents sanctioned (his first favorite book was *Treasure Island*). While his father voiced concern about the comics, Ella was unfazed, arguing to her husband that Walter still maintained broad reading tastes (Steger, 9). Even as an adult Mosley boasts a proud collection of more than 30,000 Marvel comic books while also feverishly working to acquire the first 100 comics in the Fantastic Four series. He believes that comic books provide a perfect outlet and inspiration for boys in general and for young black men in particular. The superheroes featured in these books emulate, in many ways, the black youth experience. According to Mosley, just as these fictional characters must expend superhuman strength to accomplish a task, black boys (and later men) learn that they must perform extraordinary feats to gain even the slightest recognition. Superheroes demonstrate the possibility of success in seemingly impossible circumstances. Without question, these characters anticipated Mosley's own fictional creations. Not until Mosley had written four of the Easy Rawlins novels, however, did he realize that one of his dominant themes was simply the idea of black male heroes. He suddenly realized then that he had clarified for these black characters not only the reality of their existence but also a recurrent principle among superheroes: "even outnumbered, stick to your guns" ("Eavesdropping," 45). What Mosley finds himself creating in adulthood is the culmination of a variety of imaginary explorations beginning in childhood and extending well beyond adolescence.

In addition to comic books, Mosley has had a lifelong appreciation for fantasy and science fiction. From Winnie-the-Pooh to Tom Swift, from Ray Bradbury to Gabriel Garcia Marquez, Mosley welcomes any book "that offers an alternative account for the way things are" (Mosley Web site). And for black Americans, who have historically been made objects of derision, a genre such as science fiction that allows the so-called abnormal to be transformed into the normal is one to be explored and developed. That Mosley would add science fiction to his own canon is no surprise given its relevance not only to his reading taste but also to the black experience.

Even with these early influences, many years would pass before Mosley would apply pen to paper to create his own worlds. Before age thirty-four, he had never considered the possibility of writing fiction. He had long fantasized about writing poetry, though his poetic skills proved inadequate. Even after deciding to pursue fiction writing, Mosley never imagined his rather meteoric rise to fame. He had planned simply to write, get published, land a university teaching job, and publish some more while enjoying the life of a scholar/writer.

After graduating from Alexander Hamilton High School in 1970, Mosley moved to Vermont to attend college. He first entered Goddard College, attracted by its self-styled curriculum. Inspired, however, by the hippie movement and the lifestyle touted by Jack Kerouac and Allen Ginsberg, he spent more time hitchhiking across the country than he did attending class. As a result, Mosley's advisor suggested after a few semesters that Mosley might want to withdraw, given the directionless student's less-than-impressive performance. He later enrolled at Johnson State University, also in Vermont, graduating in 1977 with a bachelor of arts degree in political science. He entered graduate school at the University of Minnesota but decided he did not like it and moved to Boston to be with Joy Kellman, a dancer and choreographer. During this period, the late 1970s and early 1980s, Mosley worked as a computer programmer while pursuing a series of odd jobs, ranging from selling his own pottery to trying his hand at catering. In 1982 he and Joy moved to New York, and Mosley continued to support himself as a programmer. Mosley describes feeling lost during this period of his life. While working as a computer consultant in Manhattan (at different times for Mobil Oil, IBM, Dean Witter, and an insurance company), Mosley yearned to discuss books and movies with his colleagues. Unfortunately, they did not share his passion for such intellectual subjects.

The turning point in his creative life came while he was reading Alice Walker's 1982 Pulitzer Prize–winning novel, *The Color Purple*. Though Mosley had been an avid reader of an eclectic body of works (he especially enjoyed certain French writers during this period), no book had spoken to him in the way that Walker's novel did. Because Walker wrote in a language that Mosley could embrace, he decided that he too could write (Gleick, 106). One Saturday while working at Mobil Oil, a bored Mosley sat down and sketched out the following sentence: "Hot sticky days in southern Louisiana; the fire ants swarm" (Frumkes, 20). From that moment on, Mosley was a writer, working tirelessly at night and on weekends. In 1985 he enrolled in the writing program at City College of the City University of New York (CUNY), where he began to work with his soon-to-be mentor, Frederic Tuten. Mosley and Joy wed in 1987; thus Mosley emulated his parents by entering into an interracial marriage (they would later divorce). In addition, Mosley took a poetry-writing workshop with Bill Matthews, a course he would continue to take every semester while at City College. Knowing that he needed to learn more about concision and figurative expression, Mosley eagerly absorbed as much as he could from the workshops. While in Tuten's class, Mosley worked on the manuscript for the first Easy Rawlins/Mouse Alexander story, the novella *Gone Fishin'*, but after shopping it around to various agents unsuccessfully in 1988, he abandoned that project.

Undaunted, Mosley knew that he wanted to write, so he told his wife that he intended to resign from his computer programming job and devote his energies to his craft. Though an artist herself, Joy was still practical about Mosley's desire, suggesting to him that he save enough money to sustain them for one year. Within a day, however, she pledged her support for his dream.

A second major turning point came when Mosley read Graham Greene's screenplay for *The Third Man*, which, according to Mosley, "made some things so clear to me" (Bruckner, C1). He then reconfigured the Rawlins story and wrote what would become *Devil in a Blue Dress*. While working on this second manuscript, Mosley benefited from the assistance of other City College experts, such as William Matthews and Edna O'Brien, who coached him on how to craft a more compelling and technically sophisticated work. Upon completion of *Devil in a Blue Dress*, Mosley submitted the manuscript to Tuten simply for feedback. Impressed with the writing, Tuten, without Mosley's knowledge, delivered it to his own agent, Gloria Loomis, who in turn offered to represent Mosley. Loomis then shopped the manuscript with Norton, and the publisher soon accepted what would be the first installment of the Easy Rawlins novels. Norton immediately contracted for two more books in the Rawlins series, and Mosley's writing career was launched.

As with most successful writers, however, Mosley's early career was fraught with both disappointment and irony. As noted previously, *Gone Fishin'* was rejected many times in the late 1980s. Not until after Mosley became a famous writer was he able to place it. With good humor, he recounts an early publishing success. Soon into his career, he published the short story "Voodoo" in the literary journal *Callaloo*. One year after its publication, a new staff took the helm at *Callaloo*, and, upon finding a copy of Mosley's original submission, sent him a rejection letter (Salm, E1). Nevertheless, that Mosley was destined to become a successful writer seemed evident when *Devil in a Blue Dress* was nominated for an Edgar Award for best mystery and when it won the 1990 Shamus Award for best first private-investigator novel from the Private Eye Writers of America, and also the John Creasey Award in Great Britain for best first novel in crime writing.

Over the next decade Mosley published almost a book every year. His prolific output is the result of his commitment to a daily writing regimen. In a July 3, 2000, article for the "Writers on Writing" column of the arts section of the *New York Times*, Mosley discusses the importance, the very necessity, of writing every day. Because ideas are precious and most often tenuous, argues Mosley, they must be cultivated consistently. While he admits that there is no rule as to the amount of time one must spend writing, one must honor the responsibility of writing daily. No matter his schedule, Mosley finds time to connect to his writing every day. He generally writes for two to three hours at the beginning of each day, longer if a deadline is approaching. For him, writing "is a kind of guerilla warfare; there is no vacation, no leave, no relief" (Mosley, "For Authors"). Whether he is simply reviewing what he wrote previously, creating a new scene, or planning an upcoming chapter, he constantly "interacts" with his given project. One of his techniques involves reading a whole draft into a tape recorder and then playing it back and listening to the speech rhythms. With pen in hand, he makes the necessary changes while listening to the music of the language (Durrant). Still, Mosley does not consider himself to be disciplined. He defines discipline as completing a task out of a sense of duty or responsibility, like "getting up and shoveling snow every morning" (Applebone, 1Y). But because he loves language and the creation of characters, the act of writing is not a chore for him.

Without question, this philosophy has worked well for the author. Following *Devil in a Blue Dress*, Mosley published, to critical acclaim, *A Red Death* in 1991, which was nominated for the Gold Dagger Award presented by Britain's Crime Writers Association. In the fall of 1997 *A Red Death* was adapted as a play by David Barr for the Chicago Theatre Company, where it received eight nominations for the Black Theatre Alliance Awards. In 1992 Mosley published *White Butterfly*, also nominated for an Edgar and a Gold Dagger. That same year, Mosley received an important nod from presidential candidate Bill Clinton, who mentioned to the press that he was reading Mosley's novels. By the time that *Black Betty* was published in 1994, Clinton's endorsement helped this fourth novel sell over 100,000 hardcover copies, make the *New York Times* best-seller list, and earn Mosley a multi-book contract for further novels in the Easy Rawlins series. In 1995 a now well-known Mosley burst onto the Hollywood scene with the film version of *Devil in a Blue Dress*, produced by Jonathan Demme, directed by Carl Franklin, and starring Denzel Washington and Jennifer Beals.

Even with more than a decade of unprecedented achievement, Mosley maintains his humility and graciousness. Never viewing himself as special, he commented in 1995 that he does not view his life as very interesting in any major way and it is certainly not interesting to anyone other than himself. That people even mention his name, especially after the release of the film, and are curious about his thoughts outside the realm of fiction amazes him. Perhaps his modesty results from the fact that he still lives a relatively normal life. In the early 1990s, he watched quite religiously the popular TV sitcom *Married With Children,* which showcased the lives of a dysfunctional lower-middle-class family (Johnson, E1). Though he no longer has a favorite TV program, he continues to create functional pottery at New York City's 92nd Street YMCA, and he enjoys drawing and regular travel (Applebone, 1Y).

Taking a break from the Rawlins series, in 1995 Mosley published *RL's Dream,* a tribute to the blues tradition and legendary musician Robert Johnson. It was a finalist for the NAACP Award in Fiction, and it won the 1996 American Library Association's Black Caucus Literary Award. *A Little Yellow Dog,* which made the *New York Times* best-seller list, was published in 1996. Also that year Mosley was named the first artist-in-residence at the Africana Studies Institute of New York University. As part of his residency, Mosley worked with the institute to create a lecture series entitled "Black Genius," which sought to bring to campus experts in the arts, politics, and academia to discuss contemporary problems. The series culminated with the 1999 anthology *Black Genius: African American Solutions to African American Problems,* a collection of the lectures published by Norton and coedited by Mosley, who also wrote the introduction and one of the essays.

In 1997 Mosley finally published *Gone Fishin'* (his first completed manuscript). To significant media attention, Mosley, allowed the smaller (Baltimore-based) Black Classic Press the honors of hardcover publication. The year 1998 proved to be a banner one for Mosley, who introduced a new protagonist, Socrates Fortlow, in the collection *Always Outnumbered, Always Outgunned.* One of the stories, "The Thief," which had been published in *Esquire* in 1995, won the O. Henry Award in 1996. Mosley also released his first science fiction novel, *Blue Light.* Because Norton, his longtime publisher, was not interested in Mosley as a science fiction writer, agent Gloria Loomis placed the novel with Little, Brown. *Blue Light* was favorably received in Los Angeles and San Francisco, where it made the best-seller lists in the *Times* and *Chronicle,* respectively. *Always Outnumbered, Always Outgunned* was given the Anisfield-Wolf Award for its sensitivity to the issue of race in America. Translating the book to film, Mosley wrote the screenplay for the March 1998, HBO premiere. Directed by Michael Apted, the film featured Laurence Fishburne, Natalie Cole, and Cicely Tyson. Rounding out his successes in 1998 was the TransAfrica International Literary Prize for his entire body of works. In 1999 Mosley continued the Socrates Fortlow saga with *Walkin' the Dog,* again with Little, Brown. Trying his skills at drama, Mosley wrote his first play, *Since You Been Gone,* which was performed in workshop by the Hartford Stage Company during the summer of 1999. Though it was to receive full production in the fall of 2000, Mosley's grueling schedule prevented the premiere.

Joining with other luminaries—such as Jimmy Carter, Anna Quindlen, Vincent Bugliosi, and Susan Isaacs, among others—who had written for the Library of Contemporary Thought series published by Ballantine Books, in 2000 Mosley wrote the nonfiction monograph *Workin' on the Chain Gang: Shaking Off the Dead Hand of History.* In this book, appropriating America's race history as a metaphor for contemporary social and economic ills, Mosley discusses frankly the dehumanizing effects of capitalism. Calling the book "a nonaligned attack on capitalism," Mosley argues, "Black history is American history. It's mass oppression for mass production and black people have experienced that more than any other people. . . . I think black history is so important because it shows everything that goes wrong, and it shows people who have managed to survive" (McKanic, 1B). Mosley states very directly in this book what he filters more subtly in his fiction. States Mosley, "I've always been pretty political. But I don't think there's any book that I've written—except possibly my book of nonfiction—to convince somebody else of my point of view" (Mudge). In 2000 Mosley also published in *GQ* the short story "The Black Woman in the Chinese Hat," which was honored by the American Society of Magazine Editors.

With *Fearless Jones* (2001), Mosley returned to mystery writing and introduced the title character and his friend, the narrator Paris Minton. This novel Mosley calls *"comic noire* with a fringe of social realism" (Mosley Web site). The author also released another book in 2001, *Futureland,* a volume of short stories that returns Mosley to the genre of science fiction he explored in *Blue Light.* That same year Mosley wrote a monthly serialized volume for *Savoy* magazine; these "Tempest Tales" paid homage to Langston Hughes's serialized "Simple Stories." In celebration of Black History Month in February 2002, HBO aired the U.S. version of *Middle Passage,* a French documentary about the transportation of enslaved Africans from their homeland to the Americas that Mosley adapted and narrated.

In addition to publishing an impressive number of books in record time, Mosley has exploited his celebrity status in the interest of budding minority authors. He not only served as the president of the Mystery Writers of America and on the boards of the National Book Awards and the Poetry

Society of America, but also cofounded in 1994 the Open Book Committee within the highly revered writing organization PEN (Poets, Essayists, and Novelists). The committee was tasked with raising the racial and cultural consciousness of the mainstream publishing industry and encouraging the publication of works by minority writers. Unfortunately, in 1997 Mosley resigned in protest from the committee, charging that the group refused to populate its own board with minority members (Carvajal, D11).

Mosley had already become disenchanted with the lack of minority representation in the publishing industry. In a 1994 op-ed piece for the *Los Angeles Times*, Mosley clarified his disenchantment: "I know that American publishing, the very bastion of liberalism, benefactor of the First Amendment, has kept any hint of color from its halls." This observation notwithstanding, the publishing world in America "has to take its doors off the hinges and let a fresh wind blow through their halls. Because America is going to grow whether we're ready for it or not" ("A Closed Book," E2). In 1996 Mosley pressed upon CUNY president Yolanda Moses the need to establish a publishing institute. With her support and Mosley's $10,000 seed grant, the Publishing Institute at City College, a publishing certificate program aimed at young urban residents, was soon realized. Within this program, Mosley and others in the industry instruct students on the particulars of publishing, providing them with an insider's view of the various aspects of the publishing world (e.g., editing, layout, marketing, employment as an agent). In 1999, commenting about how his frustration had led him to create the institute, Mosley stated, "I'm talking about publishers and people who work in publishing. I'm not talking about writers. You see, writers come and go. You have the snapshot of the writers today, and then years later, ninety percent of those writers aren't around. But the real people who remember are the people in publishing. And it was so exclusive I just couldn't stand it" (Frumkes, 20). Clearly, Mosley wanted to prepare minorities to assume decision-making positions in publishing so that these individuals could also have a long-term impact not only on publishing but on American culture as well.

His political activism extends beyond the publishing industry. Mosley has worked closely with TransAfrica, the organization dedicated to the political and economic liberation of African people throughout the world. He has traveled with the group to both Cuba and Haiti on fact-finding missions to determine the effect of America's foreign policy on the people there (George, E1). At the urging of his close friend, actor Danny Glover, Mosley donated $100,000 to TransAfrica's cause. His activism is also registered in his deep concern about health care in America. Stunned to discover that Cuba has twice as many doctors per capita than the United States, Mosley thinks that America should take radical steps to overhaul the system. A practical man who believes in action and not theorizing, Mosley has suggested that the American government finance the education of students (especially minority students) who have exhibited promise in the field of science. And once they have become physicians, argues Mosley, the government should continue to nurture them by insuring and protecting them (Penkava). Interestingly, Mosley's activism, both in the publishing world and in the real world, stokes the fires of his creativity. When asked how he maintains his creative edge, he easily responds that anyone's edge is "activated" if he or she commits to telling the truth at least once a day.

Appreciative of the power of popular fiction to elate readers and thankful for those same readers who actively participate in the narrative moment, Mosley enjoys any writing that has the capacity to entertain and uplift an audience: "When you're writing, the idea is to entertain people. If you're a storyteller you sit around telling stories and the thing is that you keep people excited. . . . The idea, of course, is that's how you learn. You keep telling stories that everybody's interested in, that they're elated by, that they find ecstatic in some way, and then they might learn something or they might want to learn something" ("Writing About the Universe," 8). Identifying Shakespeare, Charles Dickens, and Mark Twain as the consummate popular writers, Mosley applauds their success in stirring the emotions of their audience (Frumkes, 20). The readers are vital in the creation of any work, argues Mosley, because they really write perhaps eighty percent of the novel. Equating novel writing to the writing of Shakespeare's works, Mosley suggests that just as Shakespeare wrote only two percent of his plays, and "the rest of it we've made up over the centuries" ("Eavesdropping," 45), the readers of a novel, with their various (legitimate) interpretations, complement the writer's initial design. Mosley does not suggest, however, that the relationship between reader and writer is a simplistic one. On the contrary, the two ultimately engage in a *philosophical* conversation, wherein they test concepts on each other. Because "America doesn't have any working philosophers," the "closest thing to philosophers . . . [is] novelists" ("Eavesdropping," 45). Clearly, then, Mosley sees himself as one of American's lucky working philosophers, one who welcomes the intellectual stimulation his readers bring to the discussion. Mosley has commented that readers have often presented their interpretation of a certain line or scene in one of his books, and though the analysis is inconsistent with his intent, more likely than not he finds the assessment plausible ("Eavesdropping," 46). He has been successful just by virtue of the reader's willingness to engage the novel so intimately.

Perhaps the most telling characteristic about Walter Mosley is his resistance to being defined by others, in terms of not only literary genre but also racial identification. This resistance is an extension of his rejection of both external validation and criticism. Mosley has commented that he rarely reads reviews of his works. Instead, he reads reviews of others' works and learns objectively from that exercise. He is not trying to protect a fragile ego, however. On the contrary, he does not want to become dependent on external affirmations that could be misguided, short-lived, or both. So rather than becoming personally, subjectively involved in critiques of his own work (positive or negative), he involves himself only in the general evaluative process and then relates such critique to his own writing.

That Mosley has written detective (or mystery) novels, science fiction, nonfiction, plays, and screenplays is evidence of his refusal to be pigeon-holed as a writer (he is successful not in one area but in many). He insists that he does not initiate a project with a particular genre in mind: "It's not like, 'I'm going to write a sci-fi book or a mystery.' I just try to write a good book. But I write it seriously enough so people who might be interested will read it" (McKanic, 17). If he then does not self-identify generically (as being a writer skilled in only one genre), he defies such external identification. Those who work closest to him understand his unconventional approach to writing. Gloria Loomis, who has represented Mosley since 1988, commented in 1999: "I'm entirely comfortable with the way he switches genres. Very early on, Walter matured as a person, and as a writer I saw that his agenda wasn't the usual one" (McKanic, 18).

As well, he has commented quite frequently over the past decade about being labeled a *black* writer or a *black* mystery writer. While he does not take exception to being identified as a black person (he is quite proud of being a black man), he does find it somewhat problematic when the adjective *black* is linked to his being a writer. He questions whether those engaged in the labeling are, in fact, attempting to limit him in some way—that is, by stating that he is a black writer, they might be expressing amazement that, as a black person, he can actually write. At various times in his writing career, Mosley has battled with this issue. In a 1994 interview he expressed gratitude at being considered a black writer. "If people mention my race, I wouldn't be unhappy," he proudly exclaimed. "I'm using a wide range of black characters and trying to reflect life in America. I'm talking about black life as if it were human life in America, taking the point of view that black people are insiders rather than standing on the outside looking in" (McCullough, 67). Here he reconciles the fact that he, as a black man and writer, has a duty to register black life as an integral component of American life. In assuming this responsibility, he must accept the mantle of blackness as an attribute.

In a 2001 interview, however, Mosley questioned the imposition of race, admitting that this latent concern erupted during the seventieth birthday celebration for Toni Morrison, which Mosley co-emceed with Rita Dove. When a speaker commented on Morrison's being the first black woman writer to win the Nobel Prize, Mosley felt as though Morrison, and any other writer so described, was being diminished: "I didn't want to hear it, and I didn't want to hear someone talk about Toni like that. Damn!" ("Eavesdropping," 46). In that moment, Mosley, as he described, heard only, "Well, you know, but she's a black woman." Without question, this conflict is a manifestation of Mosley's resistance to external definition as he insists upon the right for self-definition. He clearly understands that some who describe him as a black writer are in fact either consciously or subconsciously attempting to devalue him. But such attempts ultimately have little to do with how he sees and identifies himself as a black writer. That he reveres black writer extraordinaire Langston Hughes verifies this proposition. Known for his insistence on writing in the everyday vernacular of black people, Hughes proclaimed in his famous essay "The Negro Artist and the Racial Mountain" that the black writer should never reject racial definition. Instead, argued Hughes, the "Negro" writer must proudly extol his Negro-ness (blackness). Rather than accepting blackness from the white perspective as a sign of inferiority, the black writer must see him- or herself as an agent of rich, vital, and vibrant "Negro" culture, something to be celebrated and not shirked. Mosley's embrace of Hughes the writer is ultimately an embrace of Hughes the *black* writer. As Mosley revealed, "One of the reasons I love Langston so much is that he really liked black people. He loved the foibles and the problems and the dignity of black people, and so do I" (McKanic, 18).

To be sure, Mosley reveals his most intimate thoughts in his nonfiction writing, not the least of which is the aforementioned *Workin' on the Chain Gang*. In this provocative work, Mosley exposes his frustrations with modern society and his concern for wasted human potential. He argues that American society has been stunted by its refusal to live authentically. The crux of his thesis is that most people function in a haze because they do not seek truth. For Mosley, finding this truth involves interrogating the very premises that the society upholds as normal and right. In other words, people must question the very foundation on which they have come to depend but that has also blinded and imprisoned them. For example, they should challenge the assumptions that they, as laborers, should work for the profit of others. They should question the competitive (as opposed to a humanizing) world they are prodded to "succeed" in. According to Mosley, human beings, Americans in particular, are expected to adhere to a certain code of behavior and obey a system that rewards them with a crippling anonymity. As a result, "Our true natures are hidden not only from the prying eyes of the outside world but even from ourselves" (57). If, however, people begin to question their existence and to voice their actual thoughts, they would not only save themselves but also gradually forge social change. Though he admits that his propositions are highly idealistic, Mosley believes that America's long-term survival depends on such romantic initiative.

Mosley believes that Americans need to think seriously about the future and who or what is in control of that future. Insisting that people are being distracted by so-called advances in computer technology, Mosley argues that the only important technology in the world today is the genome. Though he admits to having a weakness for gadgets himself (he boasts that he uses a powerful laptop, a Palm PDA device, and a digital camera [Colker, T2]), he thinks the important technological advances will concern "altering our bodies, altering our perceptions," and such changes will be "based on genetics, rather than on computers" (Salm, E1). To raise their awareness of the world around them, maintains Mosley, people need to read, think, and impart their newly gained knowledge to others: "The most important thing for anyone in America is to figure out what's really going on. And the only way to know is to think about it. I'm reading and talking—and new ideas come up" (Salm, E1). Unfortunately, says Mosley, people have been dazzled and blinded by the Internet, which, though useful for researching basic facts, is ripe with deliberately dispensed erroneous information that anyone can post. If, however, people resume thinking and in turn begin to challenge this new reality, they will at least gesture toward a greater enlightenment.

Mosley still considers himself a Los Angeles writer (but not one who writes solely about that city), though he is now a permanent resident of New York. When asked if he feels disconnected from Los Angeles, Mosley offers a resounding no. Because, in his estimation, Los Angeles is paradoxical, having both a beauty and a craziness and thus no distinct personality, he cannot possibly feel detached from it. Its eclecticism is a characteristic that Mosley considers himself to embody; consequently he is drawn to Los Angeles no matter where he chooses to reside.

Current projects include preparing a series of Easy Rawlins stories. Mosley is also writing another nonfiction book about the black response to terrorism, tentatively titled *Peace Is the Only Defense*. In addition, he is planning another Fearless Jones novel, *Fear Itself*, for release in summer 2003. Mosley is quite proud of the career he has made for himself. His success was truly confirmed when, upon the release of *Bad Boy Brawly Brown* in 2002, he received a letter from one of his childhood idols, the British science fiction writer Michael Moorcock, who congratulated Mosley on his skill and longevity (Gordon). With such praise, Mosley's place in American (and international) letters is secure.

2

Literary Heritage

Although Walter Mosley is best known as a detective, or mystery, writer, now that he has penned works outside that genre, he rejects this limiting label. He has written screenplays, plays, short fiction, science fiction, and essays, and as a result of these accomplishments, he considers himself simply a writer. In a 1997 interview, commenting on genre-driven identity, Mosley declared, "If I had to make my whole life writing mysteries, it wouldn't be as bad as going to work every day, but it would be kind of awful. I'm very interested in a lot of different things. And I'm not interested in being defined by the genre" (Cryer, G11).

Mosley primarily wants to tell the story of the black man's life in America, employing as many literary styles as he can. He has consistently stated for well over a decade now that he writes about black men, whether the story is told in a blues novel (*RL's Dream*), in a coming-of-age novel (*Gone Fishin'*), or in a science fiction novel (*Blue Light*). According to Mosley, "Anyone who knows my work and has paid any attention to it knows what to expect. They know there is going to be a black man at the center of this story, and he's going to be struggling for identity, for redemption, for some kind of comprehension of who he is in a world which doesn't really care about that. And he has to create the tools to do the job that needs to get done" (Rizzo, G1). Mosley's goal, one that he defines unabashedly, has always been not only to feature black male characters but also to present them in such a way that black male readers take pride in their fictional brothers.

It is not surprising, then, that Mosley considers Easy Rawlins ultimately to be modeled after Ralph Ellison's infamous unnamed narrator in 1952's *Invisible Man*. The now classic novel charts the journey of the title character, who begins as a young high school graduate and undergoes a series of initiations that instruct him in the harsh realities of life. For much of the novel, the "invisible" narrator seeks affirmation and definition from various external sources—in academia, in politics, and in the workplace. He ultimately discovers that no one, no other entity, is truly concerned about his well-being; he is merely a faceless pawn to be used and discarded, because no one is interested in knowing him or acknowledging him as an individual. His true lesson comes when he realizes that he alone is responsible for his identity, his self-definition.

While Ellison's novel and narrator function in a highly abstract and metaphorical world, Mosley's Easy, charging his way through the segregated Los Angeles landscape of the 1940s, '50s, and '60s, helps to concretize the black male's struggles as presented in *Invisible Man*. Mosley has suggested that Easy, like Ellison's narrator, is for the most part unseen. The other black characters identify Easy as one of them, and as a consequence, they see nothing particularly special, or threatening, about him. The white characters see him as simply one of a horde of nameless, faceless, brainless blacks over whom they maintain control, and Easy willingly participates in the deception. Invisibility and its twin, silence, characterize the self-styled detective. Easy retains much of his power by keeping his financial holdings secret. No one knows how wealthy Easy is, and no one other than his proxy even knows that Easy is a proprietor. Easy, then, exploits his invisibility and transforms it into a source of power. When he questions unwitting suspects, they, unaware of exactly how shrewd Easy is, relinquish their guard, making themselves easy prey for the preying Easy.

Without question, Mosley wants to empower those like Easy. Instead of treating black male invisibility as merely a condition, Mosley redefines it as a tool. Rather than being restricted, Easy is free to move about and tackle the difficult issues. In addition, Easy accesses freedom when he, in his personal and intellectual space, challenges the "truth" of stereotypical black male identity. While Easy takes pride in his blackness, noted when he insists on speaking the vernacular of his southern roots, he also knows how to articulate standard English. On the surface, he is quintessentially blue-collar, but beneath the harsh exterior, he is a family man, a property owner, a connoisseur of literature, and a shrewd businessman. All of these qualities, however, are rendered invisible from the perspective of the dominant society, because this society does not—cannot—equate these traits with black male identity.

Though Mosley does not wish to be recognized as only a detective writer, he is still a participant, of course, in the well-established genre of detective, or crime and mystery, writing. Mosley has contributed to a tradition that other African American writers before him have also helped to shape. As early as 1901 Pauline Hopkins published *Hagar's Daughter: A Story of Southern Caste Prejudice*, a novel that introduced literature's first black female detective, Venus Johnson. Addressing issues of miscegenation and race passing (the act of light-complexioned blacks passing for white), *Hagar's Daughter* practically exalts Venus's status as a domestic as well as her blackness when both traits assist the detective in solving a case of murder and kidnapping. The themes presented therein anticipate Mosley's *Devil in a Blue Dress*, which also addresses race mixing and passing.

Yet another forerunner of the African American tradition is John E. Bruce, whose 1908 *Black Sleuth* presents an African-born detective whose nationalist perspective militates against prescribed negative stereotypes about blackness. Using detective fiction to celebrate the dignity and inherent nobility of blacks, a literary battle initiated in the slave narratives of the eighteenth and nineteenth centuries, Bruce imbues his black detective with an unapologetic consciousness about his duty to both community and family. Solving his case hinges on solidifying his commitment to black struggle.

Black detective fiction is reawakened with Rudolph Fisher's seminal novel, *The Conjure Man Dies* (1932), the first novel in this genre to be peopled entirely with black characters in a Harlem setting. The protagonist, Dr. John Archer, uses his medical expertise to solve a murder. Highlighting black vernacular and urban traditions, Fisher introduces the reader to various aspects of black life, including rural voodoo/hoodoo practices.

By the time that Chester Himes emerged in the late 1950s to firmly ground the black detective-writing tradition, a slight inroad into the genre of crime writing had been made. With Himes, however, the tradition practically exploded. His canon includes ten detective novels, one published posthumously: *For Love of Imabelle* (1957), *The Crazy Kill* (1959), *Real Cool Killers* (1959), *All Shot Up* (1960), *The Big Gold Dream* (1960), *Cotton Comes to Harlem* (1965), *The Heat's On* (1966), *Run, Man, Run* (1966), *Blind Man with a Pistol* (1969), and *Plan B* (1993). Himes expanded the genre by writing novels that are simultaneously serious and absurd. Focusing on issues of race and class, Himes satirized the social conditions of modern-day Harlem. His detectives, Coffin Ed Johnson and Grave Digger Jones, as Mosley's Easy Rawlins and Mouse Alexander do in Watts, work together to expose criminal intent in Harlem. Just as Easy is more rational than Mouse, Grave Digger is more controlled than the volatile and acid-scarred Coffin Ed.

Ironically, Mosley disputes comparisons between Himes's work and his own, stating that he recognizes no real similarity other than that he and Himes are black. And he emphatically rejects claims that Easy Rawlins is similar to Himes's fictional detective(s). Even when discussing comparisons between Easy and the characters created by white detective writers, Mosley insists that Easy has more in common with the writers than he does with the detectives, in part because Easy is a property owner who has children and middle-class aspirations, and also because Easy "likes to read books, to think. He has an ego to him; he wants to be recognized as important" (Jaggi, 26). Still, Mosley finds himself linked to his black predecessors and his contemporaries because he almost single-handedly authenticates black participation in the genre.

The 1970s usher in a different version of an almost unrecognizable detective fiction. Ishmael Reed, in his satirical novels *Mumbo Jumbo* (1972) and *The Last Days of Louisiana Red* (1974), displaces the detective format in favor of an experimental structure. Featured in the novels is private detective Papa LaBas, a man possessed of so-called neohoodoo powers who uses them to combat white efforts to destroy the black race. In his effort to reconsider, or revise, human history, Reed loses all but the mere trace of detective fiction. Nonetheless, like other black writers, he uses the genre to explore in a more complex way the nature of black struggle in the western world.

In terms of contemporary black detective fiction, by the early 1990s black women began to stake their claim on detective fiction. Perhaps the most well-known writer from this period is Barbara Neely, whose Blanche White series begins with *Blanche on the Lam* (1992) and continues with *Blanche Among the Talented Tenth* (1994), *Blanche Cleans Up* (1998), and *Blanche Passes Go* (2000). Self-styled detective Blanche White is a very dark-skinned (hence, the obvious wordplay in her name) domestic worker who confronts not only crime but also both interracial and intraracial bias. Neely mocks not only "superior" whites but also bourgeois-driven blacks who consider Blanche beneath them. These novels ultimately become more focused on Blanche than on the actual mystery. Blanche's social commentaries provide the unifying thread.

Yet another prolific writer from this period is Eleanor Taylor Bland, whose fictional creation, Marti McAllister, is a black female police officer paired with a white male as they conduct investigations in and around Chicago. From *Dead Time* (1992) to *Windy City Dying* (2002) and a host of others in between, Bland presents a fresh look at African American issues in an urban setting. Writing contemporaneously with Bland is the popular Grace F. Edwards, whose Mali Anderson series includes *If I Should Die* (1997), *A Toast Before Dying* (1998), *No Time to Die* (1999), and *Do or Die* (2000). These novels are set in Harlem, where the unsuspecting Mali, a former police officer turned graduate student, consistently finds herself embroiled in yet another murder investigation.

As popular as Edwards is Valerie Wilson Wesley, who introduced in 1994 Tamara Hayle, a former Newark, New Jersey, police officer and single mother who has emerged as a skilled detective. With seven novels to her credit, from *When Death Comes Stealing* (1994) to *No Way of Dying* (2002), Wesley continues to make her mark on detective fiction that attracts a substantial female audience. Penny Mickelbury has created two sets of crime-solving duos. Mimi Patterson and Gianna Maglione are featured in *Keeping Secrets* (1994) and *Night Songs* (1995), while Carol Ann Gibson and Jake Graham provide the investigative skills in *One Must Wait* (1998), *Where to Choose* (1999), *The Step Between* (2000), and *Paradise Interrupted* (2001).

Contemporary black male detective fiction writers include Gar Anthony Haywood, who produced several novels in the 1990s, writing almost as prolifically as Mosley during this period. Beginning in 1988 with *Fear of the Dark*, Haywood introduced his Aaron Gunner series, crafting five of these novels. In 1994 he introduced the Joe and Dottie Loudermilk series with *Going Nowhere Fast*, to date writing only one more in this farcical depiction of crime solving and domestic confusion. As well, Gary Hardwick's Detroit mysteries, which tackle political, social, and class issues, are *Cold Medina* (1996), *Double Dead* (1997), *Supreme Justice* (1999), and *The Color of Justice* (2002).

The success of these writers confirms African American interest in detective fiction. And with an emergent scholarly interest in either black detective fiction or the black influence on detective fiction in general, the genre is likely to develop further. Critical works on this subject include Frankie Y. Bailey's *Out of the Woodpile: Black Characters in Crime and Detective Fiction* (1991); Paula L. Woods's edition, *Spooks, Spies, and Private Eyes: Black Mystery, Crime, and Suspense Fiction of the Twentieth Century* (1995); and Stephen F. Soitos's *The Blues Detective: A Study of African American*

Detective Fiction (1996). Incidentally, Woods has also crafted two detective novels: *Inner City Blues* (1999) and *Stormy Weather* (2001), featuring Detective Charlotte Justice.

While Walter Mosley has found a comfortable niche in the African American detective literary tradition, without dispute he holds a significant place within the mainstream American tradition as well. The detective story (novel) focuses, of course, on a specific mystery, most often a crime, that must be solved. The bulk of the story is consumed with the detective (and the reader) observing and assessing the various clues that punctuate the work. The detective most often engages in deductive reasoning (proceeding from a general assessment and then wending his or her way to a specific conclusion). The reader is eager to turn each page because he or she will encounter new and more compelling clues that will ultimately yield the climactic resolution.

The American detective story was inaugurated by Edgar Allan Poe in the nineteenth century. Though known also for his Gothic tales (like "The Fall of the House of Usher"), Poe was single-handedly responsible for introducing American readers to tales of ratiocination (or reasoning). Beginning in 1841 with "The Murders in the Rue Morgue," Poe crafted many stories that would help shape the modern detective genre. "The Purloined Letter" (1845) aggressively develops the deductive process in detective fiction by theorizing that when all incorrect possibilities have been exhausted, the one possibility that remains is the right answer. In addition, Poe presented to his nineteenth-century audience the first memorable fictional detective, C. Auguste Dupin, whose seasoned arrogance and contempt for mediocrity anticipate the no-nonsense detectives of the twentieth century.

While American detective fiction enjoyed no noteworthy development after Poe until the first half of the twentieth century, it is important to acknowledge a significant contributor to the genre. In the late 1880s English writer Arthur Conan Doyle created perhaps still the world's most famous fictional sleuth, Sherlock Holmes. When the first Holmes novel, *A Study in Scarlet*, appeared in 1887 and was followed by a series of stories featuring the detective, the cloak-wearing Sherlock and his trusty sidekick, Dr. Watson, were catapulted to fame. So popular was the self-consumed Holmes that in 1893 Doyle was forced to abort the idea of killing off the protagonist. In many ways Sherlock Holmes raised the bar for subsequent detectives with his shrewdness, his intellectual prowess, and his unique style.

Detective fiction was given a significant boost when writers Dashiell

Hammett and Raymond Chandler emerged on the scene. They are credited with popularizing the "hard-boiled" subgenre of detective writing. This label captures not only the gritty, unsentimental atmosphere of the novel but also the persona of the detective, a kind of rogue figure who, in exhibiting passion for his detective duties, also displays characteristics not unlike those of the criminals he chases. Not averse to violence or manipulation, the hard-boiled detective is obsessive in his ultimate pursuit of justice.

Hammett began writing stories in the 1920s (contributing to the renowned pulp fiction magazine *Black Mask*), his interest in the genre growing out of his personal experience of working for San Francisco's Pinkerton Detective Agency as an expert in surreptitiously following suspects. By 1930, Hammett had written some of his best work, including *The Maltese Falcon*. His famed sleuth, Sam Spade, is now considered a classic American detective. Hammett's prose is noted for its Hemingway-inspired minimalist style. The spare dialogue brings the reader into the text as an almost active participant in the interpretation. Hammett further developed the detective story by returning crime and mystery to a corrupt urban environment, salvaging it from the confines of polite (and somewhat sterile) upper-class society.

While Hammett's novels feature different detective figures, Raymond Chandler's novels and many of his short stories showcase the exploits of Philip Marlowe. Chandler began writing professionally in 1933 (well into his 40s), the same year that Hammett's last novel, *The Thin Man*, was published. Most of Chandler's stories and novels are set in 1930s and 1940s Los Angeles, and they depict a very dark, corrupt world marred by violence and paranoia. The first novel, *The Big Sleep* (1939), charts Marlowe's investigation of a missing person, a journey wherein the detective confronts murder, drug addiction, intimidation, and blackmail.

Chandler helped to guide the detective story through the post–World War II period as he continued to write until his death in 1959. Ross Macdonald shepherded the genre into the contemporary (1960s and 1970s) period. Born Kenneth Millar, Macdonald, an intellectual who earned a Ph.D. from the University of Michigan, reconsidered writing as a career after self-publishing his first story, "The Dark Tunnel" (1944). His novels, beginning with *The Galton Case* in 1959, present the unstoppable Lew Archer, the successor to the no-nonsense tradition of Sam Spade and Philip Marlowe.

Mosley credits the Big Three (Hammett, Chandler, and Macdonald) of twentieth-century detective fiction for influencing his writing. Their take on the urban lore of Mosley's native Los Angeles clearly intrigued the author. However, Mosley sought to investigate even further the black urban life that had been given only a passing footnote in the annals of his predecessors. Easy Rawlins and the complex world of Watts, then, is Mosley's answer to this black void. Mosley is loathe to equate Easy with his fictional predecessors, however. Mosley describes the earlier detective heroes as being alienated from many of life's humanizing elements in that they had no families, no friends, no stable home life or jobs (Jaggi, 26). On the other hand, Easy is a property owner, husband, and father with middle-class aspirations. In addition, he is an intellectual, an avid reader and learner. Mosley prefers to compare Easy with the earlier writers instead of their fictional creations. Like Macdonald or Hammett, Easy likes to think and philosophize, and he is possessed of a considerable ego that yearns for recognition. In this way, then, the hard-boiled detective writers of the past have influenced Mosley holistically, in that Mosley has sought to emulate not only the well-established genre but also the engendering forces (i.e., the authors) that created the genre.

In addition to his detective fiction, Mosley has also written two novels that employ the "story-cycle": Though each story can exist as a meaningful unit, the artistic integrity is maintained by consideration of the stories as a whole. This subgenre of fiction developed in the early twentieth century, though it actually was initiated at the end of the nineteenth (one could also easily argue that Chaucer's *Canterbury Tales* is the original prototype). Nonetheless, in 1919 American writer Sherwood Anderson published *Winesburg, Ohio*, a collection of stories that not only sustain an individual unity but also function together to create an integrated aesthetic space. Other notable story cycles that followed include Ernest Hemingway's *In Our Time*, Jean Toomer's *Cane*, Erskine Caldwell's *Georgia Boy*, and William Faulkner's *Go Down, Moses*. Predating all of these, however, is *The Conjure Woman*, published in 1899 by African American writer Charles Waddell Chesnutt.

Mosley's *Always Outnumbered, Always Outgunned* and its sequel, *Walkin' the Dog*, contribute to this tradition. In addition, however, these works defer to the classical tradition represented by Plato's *Dialogues*, which Mosley was rereading just before writing the first book. Clearly Mosley's protagonist, Socrates Fortlow, is the namesake of the great classical teacher. In each of the stories in both volumes, the reader observes as Socrates confronts various obstacles in his postprison life. In each story, he either makes an important decision or comes to some important philosophical conclusion about life in general. In short, each story teaches an individual lesson. At the same time, the reader, assessing each volume of stories (the full story cycle, or novel), discovers a measured and calculated character development that renders the stories also inseparable.

A few similarities exist between Mosley's work and Chesnutt's. In *The Conjure Woman*, Chesnutt features the shrewd and crafty Uncle Julius McAdoo, a former slave now determined during Reconstruction to reap the benefits of his past labor. At once a trickster and resident philosopher who survives as much by wit as by industry, Uncle Julius attempts in every story to outsmart his new employers, John and Annie, a Northern white couple who have come South and purchased the land once held by Julius's owners. Similarly, Socrates Fortlow, an ex-convict, must forge ahead as he gradually adjusts to his new life as a free man. As with *The Conjure Woman*, each story in either *Always Outnumbered, Always Outgunned* or *Walkin' the Dog* witnesses the protagonist a step farther along in his transformational journey. What links both men as well is their perspective on morality in a particularly oppressive world, one where black men like Julius and Socrates are always outnumbered and outgunned (or disadvantaged). Because of this reality, they adopt an amoral stance whereby they justify any action they must undertake to survive. Just as Julius might excuse a poor man for stealing in order to feed himself, Socrates has no qualms about threatening a neighbor who is wreaking havoc on the safety of the neighborhood.

When Mosley has observed that he writes about the plight of black males in America, he confirms that he is contributing to both an actual and a literary conversation initiated generations earlier. What is interesting here, of course, is that one of Mosley's forerunners (Chesnutt) not only participated in the discussion but also helped to create the narrative mode (with the story cycle) that would one day serve Mosley's contemporary agenda.

One cannot ignore, as well, that raising the subject of black male survival automatically invokes the prototype of African American manhood, both literary and real. Frederick Douglass, in his *Narrative of the Life of Frederick Douglass, An American Slave* (1845), established the definition of black manhood. Recounting his confrontation with Mr. Edward Covey, the chief overseer on the plantation, Douglass explains that he is forced to fight Covey when the abusive man threatens him. From 1845 on, black manhood has been defined by civility and self-respect; and it never initiates violence, it only responds to violence. On several occasions, in the Socrates saga, the reader witnesses a mature and decidedly patient man who resorts to violence only when threatened. This response also provides evidence of his development not only within the chronology of the stories, but also inclusive of his entire life (before his incarceration for murder). And certainly, in the detective novels, Easy Rawlins, sensible and respectful of others, never voluntarily inflicts violence.

Another literary predecessor to whom Mosley shows allegiance is Langston Hughes. In his serialized stories published in monthly installments for *Savoy* magazine, Mosley honors Hughes' serialized stories of the mid-twentieth century that feature Jesse B. Semple, or Simple. Like Hughes's common-man protagonist, Mosley's Tempest Landry is a simple man whose observations about life and people, while surprisingly insightful and thought-provoking, both stun and challenge the immediate listeners and the reader. And as is true in all of Mosley's fiction, race and black male survival (issues that also concern Simple) return as major thematic impulses.

In addition to detective fiction, the story cycle, and serialized fiction, Walter Mosley has also ventured into science fiction. Reclaiming his childhood interest in the world of fantasy provided by comic books and the like, Mosley has declared science fiction, ironically the genre least represented by African American writers, the one genre most consistent with African American life. Because science fiction challenges the imagination, expands possibilities, and thus offers hope, it provides the best outlet for black experience. Within the ever-changing space of science fiction, the circumstances of inequity, oppression, or social and economic confinement become almost ephemeral, as does all reality.

And if one adopts the definition of "modern" offered by renowned professor and cultural critic Cornel West, wherein he not only positions black Americans as the most modern of people but also links them to the unknown world of the future, the marriage between African Americans and science fiction is affirmed and solidified. According to West, modern is defined as "newness, revision, and innovation," and because black people, states West, have had to "revamp, revision, and recast themselves" in response to racial prejudice, they are quintessentially modern. And because for generations now, African Americans have altered their intellectual, cultural, and aesthetic spaces to ensure survival, they are forever on the cutting edge of change. As a result of being in this position (of enforcing change), they have also (as popular culture clearly indicates) consistently influenced mainstream American culture, for they anticipate and then initiate the next wave of (pop) cultural domination. Without question, the African American world and the ever-evolving world of science fiction orbit similar spaces.

By definition, science fiction concerns itself with events that either did not happen or could happen but have not yet occurred. Its main objective is to consider the impact of said events on people. The most common themes of the genre include the unknown future, travel through space or time, inhabitation of other planets, problems generated by technological advances, or threats posed by alien creatures and environments. Over time, many writers have contributed to this genre. As early as the fourth century B.C., *The Republic* by Plato considered the possibility of a better society. Its theories were reintroduced in 1516 in Sir Thomas More's *Utopia*. Perhaps the most famous early work of fantasy is the eighteenth century's *Gulliver's Travels* (1726) by Anglo-Irish satirist Jonathan Swift. Nineteenth-century authors Edgar Allan Poe and Nathaniel Hawthorne established American interest in this literature. In addition to his detective stories, Poe also wrote works such as "The Gold-Bug" that subvert the reader's sense of reality and pave the way for later science fiction writers. Hawthorne wrote, among a host of novels and stories, two works of short fiction that helped to shape this genre. In "Rappaccini's Daughter" and "The Birthmark" Hawthorne included as one of his dominant themes the fanaticism of science and scientists.

There is no question, however, that the three early novels that stand clearly as science fiction models are *Looking Backward* (1888) by American writer Edward Bellamy and *Brave New World* (1932) and *Nineteen Eighty-Four* (1949) by English writers Aldous Huxley and George Orwell, respectively. These novels, addressing both the possibilities and the problems to be realized in future societies, introduce the two future-oriented subgenres of science fiction: Utopian novels (which highlight an ideal imaginary society), and dystopian novels (which expose troubled societies).

Defining the genre in the second half of the twentieth century are American authors Ray Bradbury (b. 1920), Harlan Ellison (b. 1934), and Isaac Asimov (b. 1920). Among Bradbury's best-known novels are *The Martian Chronicles* (1950), which theorizes the possibility of colonizing Mars, and *Fahrenheit 451* (1953), which portrays an autocratic society wherein all books are banned and burned and the only information afforded to citizens is screened by the government and presented via television. Ellison has won more awards for the seventy-five books he has written or edited; the more than 1,700 stories, essays, articles, and newspaper columns; the two dozen teleplays; and the dozen motion pictures he has created than any other writer of science fiction/fantasy. Asimov's success in science fiction is legendary. Though he published his first story in 1939, he did not begin his full-time writing career until 1958, when the doctorate-holding biochemist and associate professor retired from teaching to devote himself to writing. Many of Asimov's novels and short stories tell the future of mankind over a period spanning nearly 50,000 years. His scientific background makes his fiction not only engaging but also enlightening reading.

Bradbury is the contemporary writer of science fiction with whom Walter Mosley finds an allegiance. A fan of Bradbury, Mosley poses some of the same questions in his novel *Blue Light* and in his collection of short stories *Futureland* that Bradbury has asked for over fifty years. Both writers are fearful of a society that would rather have its citizens be brainwashed and anesthetized than able to think and question for themselves. And just as many of the negative social impulses Bradbury portrayed in *Fahrenheit 451* (the intellectually debilitating effects of television not the least among them) have actually come to pass, the technological intrusions that Mosley imagines in *Futureland* are already on the horizon.

While *Futureland*, as the title indicates, is concerned with the future and the yet-to-be-determined result of so-called advancement, Mosley's *Blue Light* focuses on another aspect of science fiction writing: alien visitation and alien environment. Initially in the novel, a bizarre blue force, or blue light, impales a select number of people, imbuing them with extra-human insight. Later in the novel, some members of the "Blues" (and some non-members) are transported to a fantastical place where animals interact with humans almost as equals and where plant life becomes extraordinary. With both *Futureland* and *Blue Light* Mosley showcases his ability not only to expand beyond detective fiction but also to craft along the continuum of science fiction narration.

As mentioned earlier, the twentieth century witnessed a dearth of African American science fiction writers. Though some writers have included a few characteristics of science fiction (or speculative fiction, the more general label given to the genre) in their works, only two African Americans before Mosley have been deemed actual science fiction authors. Samuel R. Delaney is a critic and novelist whose highly imaginative works address racial and social issues, heroic quests, and the nature of language. His first novel, *The Jewels of Aptor,* was written when he was nineteen and published in 1962. By age twenty-six, he had won four Nebula Awards; Delaney has written consistently throughout his life, even matching his interest in science fiction with his concern for the AIDS epidemic (in his *Neveryon* series in the 1980s). Mosley's other African American predecessor is Octavia Butler, whose debut, *Crossover* (1971), is the first of many works in which she weaves together African American history, future and past societies, and an exploration of alien perspective. One of her more fascinating and popular novels is *Kindred* (1979), which charts the journey of an African American woman who is sent back in time as a slave to an antebellum plantation to rescue her white, slave-owning ancestor. To date, Butler has written over eleven novels.

Delaney and Butler paved the way for Mosley to enter this genre, and more recently they paved the way for other African American writers such as the critically acclaimed Tananarive Due, whose 1996 novel, *The Between*, enjoyed rave reviews. It was followed by *My Soul to Keep* (1998) and *The Living Blood* (2001). Another fast-rising African American star is Nalo Hopkinson, whose two novels, *Brown Girl in the Ring* (1998) and *Midnight Robbers* (2000), and collection of stories, *Skin Folk* (2001), have received praise from the well-established Octavia Butler. Derrick A. Bell's *Gospel Choirs* (1996) and *Afrolantica Legacies* (1998) are similar to Mosley's *Futureland* in their interrogation of the impact of so-called advancement on black life. And rounding out the list of black science fiction writers is Steven Barnes, whose most recent single-authored books include *Iron Shadows* (2000), *Charisma* (2002), *Lion's Blood* (2002), and *Zulu Heart* (2003). Barnes continues to be, like Mosley, one of today's most prolific writers.

Whatever commercial success these contemporary writers have enjoyed is credited in part to the Terry McMillan phenomenon. Mosley has commented frequently on what he refers to as PTM (pre–Terry McMillan), that somewhat dark period when the publishing world in large measure ignored African American writers. McMillan's market success in 1992 with her best-seller novel *Waiting to Exhale*, however, changed the literary landscape forever. Mosley unabashedly acknowledges McMillan's impact on his own success. That he began publishing his work in the early 1990s was, in and of itself, a fortunate circumstance. While Toni Morrison, Gloria Naylor, and Alice Walker did much to carve out a space for other black women writers in the 1980s, Terry McMillan, with unprecedented popular appeal, created possibilities for both male and female writers. Mosley is particularly thankful to be such a beneficiary of this new wave.

Mosley's first two books, *Devil in a Blue Dress* (1990) and *A Red Death* (1991), enjoyed modest success, as did the hardback publication of *White Butterfly* (1992). After presidential candidate Bill Clinton declared Mosley one of his favorite writers during the 1992 campaign, however, sales of Mosley's books skyrocketed. In 1993, *White Butterfly*, now in paperback, sold over 157,000 copies. The 1995 paperback of *Black Betty* (1994) topped 450,000 in its first-year sales. Hardcover sales of Mosley's books tripled after the Clinton endorsement.

The critical response to Mosley has also been favorable over the years. *Library Journal* praised *Devil in a Blue Dress* for its "unusually refreshing protagonist" as well as its "talented prose, and evocative, realistic descriptions of speech, manners, and social life," all of which combine "[to] make this an exceptional and welcome addition" (June 1, 1990). And Digby Diehl, writing for the *Los Angeles Times*, declared Mosley to have "a confident, perfect-pitch ear for nuances of speech that is astonishing in a first novel . . . a fast-moving, entertaining story, written with impressive style" (August 12, 1990).

By the release of *Black Betty* Mosley had become a critical favorite. Commenting on this fourth novel, *Kirkus Reviews* insisted that "it's high time the Easy Rawlins saga was recognized for the remarkable achievement it is: a snapshot social history of the black experience in postwar LA. This latest installment, teeming with violence, bitterness, and compassion, is Mosley's finest work yet" (April 15, 1994). With this novel, according to Bill Morrison of the Raleigh, North Carolina, *News and Observer*, Mosley proved to be "a writer born, his words like a glorious jazz improvisation, the blues sung with bittersweet humor" (July 3, 1994).

When Mosley decided to write a different kind of novel in *RL's Dream*, he risked not only losing his loyal Easy Rawlins following but also exposing himself to critical assault. However, Lee Bey, writing for the *Chicago Sun-Times*, insisted that "Mosley's prose crackles in [*RL's Dream*], much as it does in his Easy Rawlins mysteries. Laced with on-target metaphors and colorful similes, the novel itself mirrors the blues" (August 13, 1995). Gene Seymour's review for *The Nation* verified Ott's claim: "Mosley works his prose like a worthy bluesman; [the author] has a gift for lyrical violence so consummate that one imagines it can be safely contained only by a gentle, humane sensibility" (September 18, 1995).

The Socrates Fortlow novels have also been lauded as literary masterpieces. "Mosley invests mundane situations with moral peril and concomitant opportunities for growth," stated David Bradley in his review of *Always Outnumbered, Always Outgunned* for the *Washington Post* (December 21, 1997). Still, Lawrence Rungren allowed in *Library Journal* that "while the novel can be a bit contrived or didactic in places, readers will find Socrates an intriguing enough character to overlook these flaws" (October 1, 1997).

Mosley has received mixed reviews for his ventures into science fiction. *Blue Light*, according to *Publishers Weekly*, suffers from a "time sequence [that] is sometimes confusing and a sort of vague poesy that is a far cry from Mosley's typically sinewy prose" (September 14, 1998). Michael Jacobs of *USA Today*, on the other hand, believes that *Blue Light* takes the author "on a mind-bending trip into the brave new world of science fiction, and Mosley proves that good writing is good writing, regardless of genre" (November 5, 1998). And regarding *Futureland*, *Publishers Weekly* said the book will "disappoint readers of that genre who've already seen Mosley's themes of racial and economic rebellion more convincingly handled by authors like Octavia Butler. Mystery fans, on the other hand, are far more likely to embrace this latest example of Mosley's [science fiction] vision, with its comfortably familiar noirish tone and characters, than they did *Blue Light*" (September 10, 2001).

No matter the critical response, Walter Mosley has established himself as a major literary force more concerned with self-definition than with external affirmation. His forays into various genres undermine any attempts to confine him and his artistry. That he continues to be as prolific as he was earlier in his career indicates that he will be a staple of the American literary canon for many years to come.

The following chapters critique Mosley's key works. To avoid unnecessary repetition, whole chapters are not devoted to *A Red Death*, *White Butterfly*, *Gone Fishin'*, *Walkin' the Dog*, *Futureland*, and *The Tempest Tales*. The first three are part of the Rawlins saga, which is analyzed in several individual chapters. The issues addressed in *Walkin' the Dog*, part of the Socrates Fortlow story, are explained fully in the chapter devoted to *Always Outnumbered, Always Outgunned*. And because *Futureland* and *The Tempest Tales* are collections of stories rather than whole novels, a full discussion of them is not merited.

3

Devil in a Blue Dress
(1990)

Devil in a Blue Dress introduces Mosley's protagonist detective Ezekiel "Easy" Rawlins. This first novel establishes how Easy stumbles upon his job as an investigator and lays the foundation for his continued development in subsequent novels as a lay detective and as a man. What distinguishes Mosley's work is the running commentary Easy makes on various social issues, past and present. The crime dilemma is linked specifically to African American struggle and endurance. In addition, Mosley addresses issues such as class, race mixing, and political corruption, among others. This novel also introduces some characters who will reappear in Mosley's later works in varying degrees of importance. In this way, Mosley creates a veritable universe wherein these characters enter and exit as need be as they challenge and assist Easy in his journey toward self-awareness and contentment.

PLOT DEVELOPMENT

As the novel begins, a recently fired Easy Rawlins is having a drink at the bar owned by acquaintance Joppy Shag. Soon entering the bar is DeWitt Albright, a well-dressed white man whose presence in the rundown establishment is odd because of both his dress and his race. After Joppy makes introductions, DeWitt offers Easy a job doing some investigative work: finding Daphne Monet, a young, attractive white woman who enjoys socializing with blacks and going to black clubs. Because this is 1948, DeWitt does not think that he can enter such places without drawing unnecessary attention to himself.

Later that night Easy goes to John's Place, a popular nightclub. Before entering, however, Easy is accosted on the sidewalk by a drunken white man who begs Easy to help him gain passage into the club. Refusing assistance, Easy enters the club and begins to scope things out. He first tries to question Junior Fornay, the robust and always suspicious club bouncer, but with no success.

While Easy is sitting with his old friend Odell, Dupree Bouchard, Easy's coworker from Champion Aircraft, enters with his date, Coretta James. Easy asks the group if they know, or have seen, Daphne Monet, but to no avail. Later, when Easy and Coretta are alone, she divulges more information. It seems that Coretta had met Daphne several days before at a nightclub, and the two, along with their respective dates, had become fast friends. Easy learns from Coretta that Daphne "dates" (this will be refuted later) one Frank Green, a dangerous gangster.

Upon sharing this information with DeWitt later, Easy is paid handsomely and believes himself now free of the situation. Unfortunately, this security is short-lived. On the morning following his meeting with DeWitt, Easy is picked up for questioning by the police. Refusing to tell him exactly why they want him, the two officers, Miller and Mason, ask only enigmatic questions. Ultimately, Easy is released but is made to walk home in the dark.

While walking home, he is accosted again, this time by Matthew Teran, former candidate for mayor, whose chauffeur, Howard Green (distant cousin of Frank Green), has recently been murdered. Teran offers Easy a lift home in his limousine. During the ride, Teran also asks rather cryptic questions, about Howard's murder, about Coretta, and about Daphne. Easy finds the questions puzzling, and he finds Teran particularly disgusting because Teran has a sexual predilection for young boys, one of whom is riding along in the car.

Exiting the limousine at John's Place, Easy soon learns that Coretta has been beaten to death, and he now knows why the police questioned him. After Odell drives him home, Easy tries to sleep, but he is haunted by thoughts of Coretta. During the night Easy receives a strange phone call from Junior Fornay, who now chooses to inform Easy that he remembered seeing Daphne in the club at one time with Frank Green. When Easy attempts to question Junior further, Junior hangs up the phone.

Later that night, Easy receives another call, this time from Daphne Monet herself, who begs Easy to come and drive her to a friend's house so that she can retrieve some of her belongings. She tells Easy that she knows about him because Coretta came to her and told her that Easy was looking for her. Unaware of Coretta's death, Daphne implores Easy to help her. Easy picks her up, along with her battered suitcase, and drives her to Richard McGee's house. Upon entering, the two find McGee dead, with the knife still fixed in his body. Easy realizes that this is the same man who had accosted him outside John's Place wanting entrance into the club. Surprisingly unfazed, Daphne prepares to leave the scene, rushing outside to "borrow" McGee's car. Chasing after her, Easy tries to question her about what they have just witnessed. Daphne impresses upon Easy the necessity of leaving, and immediately. Easy does manage to ask Daphne about the man who is looking for her, the one hired by DeWitt. This Todd Carter is a very wealthy man who is in love with Daphne, but for reasons that she will not reveal, the two of them cannot be together.

Easy returns home to the daylight, this time to find DeWitt and his two henchmen waiting for him. Perturbed because Easy's earlier information yielded nothing useful, DeWitt wants Easy to find out more. Easy then reveals to DeWitt his recent meeting with Daphne. Angry that Easy did not detain her, DeWitt gives Easy only three days to find Frank Green, hoping that Green will lead them to Daphne.

Easy decides that he needs more answers than DeWitt is willing to deliver. As a consequence, Easy goes directly to the offices of Todd Carter, and after verbally bulldozing his way through administrative assistants and lower managers, he is granted an interview with Carter. Easy learns that Carter and Daphne suffered a painful argument, after which Daphne absconded with thirty thousand dollars (in the battered suitcase) of Carter's considerable wealth. It seems that some of Carter's enemies had also threatened and blackmailed Daphne, and even though Carter had assured Daphne that she need not worry, she still fled. Carter begs Easy to find Daphne, a request that Easy agrees to honor once Carter supplies him with more funds, and only if Carter relinquishes DeWitt of his duties and ensures Easy's safety from DeWitt.

Realizing that he must enter the underground world of organized crime if he is to locate Frank, Easy goes to the one establishment that always has its metaphoric finger on the pulse of the community: the neighborhood barbershop. Not long after arriving there Easy meets up with Jackson Blue, resident bootlegger known to work for Frank Green. Using as an excuse a desire to find some cheap liquor, Easy inquires of Jackson how he might secure some. Soon learning that Jackson no longer works for Frank, Easy nevertheless pursues information from Jackson, in a nonchalant fashion, until he discovers where Frank makes his deliveries.

Easy returns home to figure out his next move. Moments after entering his house, Easy is knocked unconscious. Upon regaining his senses, Easy finds himself at the mercy of a very angry Frank Green (a.k.a. Knifehand), who, wielding a very sharp blade at Easy's neck, draws blood and threatens to kill Easy. Not knowing what to do, Easy thinks this is the end, when suddenly both men hear a third voice in the house. Raymond "Mouse" Alexander, Easy's longtime friend from Houston, has arrived just in the nick of time with gun in tow. Frank frees Easy and flees the scene. Surprised to see Mouse, Easy is nonetheless thankful for his timely arrival.

As Mouse and Easy prepare to leave the house in pursuit of further information, Easy is once again approached by officers Miller and Mason, who now want to question him about Richard McGee's murder. It seems that they found a note in McGee's house with "C. [Coretta] James" scribbled on it. And since they know that Easy had spent time with Coretta before her death, they believe there is a connection. They also want to ask him about Matthew Teran, who was recently found fatally shot. Because Howard Green (Teran's former chauffeur) and Coretta were both beaten to death in the same way, and because the police had informed Teran of the similarities (earlier on the night that Teran picked up Easy on the street), Miller and Mason think that Easy may be the culprit in all of these deaths. However, when they take Easy in to match his fingerprints with those found on the knife from McGee's body, they find no match and must release him.

Easy and Mouse then pay a visit to Junior Fornay. Easy knows that Junior killed McGee. When Daphne and Easy discovered McGee's body, Easy noticed on the floor a cigarette butt matching the brand that Junior smokes. Revealing this knowledge to Junior, Easy forces him to answer some questions. Junior had taken McGee home the night that Easy saw McGee at John's Place. McGee had agreed to pay Junior to take him home and to supply him with information concerning Daphne's whereabouts. Upon arriving at his home, McGee had refused to pay Junior unless Junior delivered a message to Frank Green (Junior had told McGee that Daphne was last seen with Frank) that he (McGee) and his acquaintance (Matthew Teran) had some damaging information on Daphne. When McGee went into the next room, Junior thought he might have been going to retrieve a gun, so he grabbed a knife and stabbed McGee.

Upon leaving Junior, Mouse and Easy split up, with Easy returning home. Soon, Easy receives another call from Daphne, who enlists his help again. This time Easy takes her to the secluded house of his old friend Primo. There, after making love with Daphne, Easy learns more about the murders of Howard Green and Coretta. Daphne had confided to Joppy a while back that Howard knew something about her and that he, along with his "friends" McGee and Teran, was blackmailing her. Daphne had dated McGee, and he was jealous now that she was seeing Carter. Though Daphne had asked that Joppy only scare Howard, matters intensified, and Joppy had beaten Howard to death. And when Joppy learned that Coretta had also harassed Daphne for money, he panicked and murdered her as well.

Later, Joppy and DeWitt find Daphne and Easy, and when Easy lets his guard down, Joppy knocks him out and the two men kidnap Daphne. Upon regaining consciousness, Easy decides to locate DeWitt's house, guessing that that is where the two have taken Daphne. Soon after arriving, Easy finds himself in the midst of gunshots and general confusion. During various scuffles, Mouse arrives on the scene, ultimately killing Joppy and shooting DeWitt, who later dies slowly while trying to escape.

Mouse confronts Daphne about the stolen money and insists that he wants a share, revealing as well that he knows her true identity. Daphne is really Ruby Hanks, a black woman, and she is Frank's half-sister. This was the secret with which McGee and Teran were threatening Daphne. McGee was angry that Daphne had ended their relationship in favor of Carter, and Teran was angry because Carter had used his political connections to thwart Teran's campaign for mayor. The conversation between Daphne (Ruby), Easy, and Mouse also reveals that Mouse killed Frank, supposedly to protect Easy, and that Daphne killed Teran to prevent further threats.

Daphne, Easy, and Mouse take ten thousand dollars each, and Daphne leaves town. Before departing, however, Daphne leaves Teran's child victim (sexual prey) in Easy's care, she having rescued the boy upon killing Teran. Easy places the frightened child in the care of Primo, who has a large, loving family. Easy then goes to Carter, explains to him that while Daphne did profess her love for Carter, she had to leave to prevent more pain in Carter's life. Soothing Carter's ego, Easy then convinces Carter to contact the police and, using his political and economic might, to present them with a tale that Easy concocts, one that exonerates Easy of any wrongdoing.

CHARACTER DEVELOPMENT

Without a doubt, protagonist Easy Rawlins emerges as a dynamic character, one who exhibits depth and presents measurable growth. A veteran of World War II, which has ended only three years prior to the story, Easy has witnessed the worst of human pain and violence. As a consequence, he has learned to survive. Tapping into these survival instincts, Easy has learned how to adopt practical strategies in order to surmount obstacles. He now uses this strength in his interactions with the ostensible opposition he faces periodically. When Easy first encounters DeWitt Albright, he almost succumbs to fear of the white man. But then he remembers all of the whites he had encountered during the war, particularly the ones he had killed, calming himself by recalling that they were all as afraid as he was to die. And this mutual fear, while humanizing, served also as a kind of racial equalizer.

Easy also shows himself to be a very responsible individual. He has completed his high school education by attending night school, and he plans to attend college. A new homeowner, Easy is proud of his modest abode, declaring that he will do whatever is necessary to meet his financial obligations and protect his investment. His willingness to accept DeWitt's job offer attests to this fact. According to Easy, "When I was a poor man, and landless, all I worried about was a place for the night and food to eat. . . . A friend would always stand me for a meal. . . . But when I got that mortgage I found that I needed more than just friendship. Mr. Albright wasn't a friend but he had what I needed" (21). Easy also takes pride in his ability to speak proper English (proof of his proven, and potential, intellectual skills), yet he admits preferring the poetry of dialect.

Easy's ability to "code switch" in language (to speak both proper English and dialect) underscores his ability to adjust his moral code to accommodate the need at hand. Easy has learned that questions of morality versus immorality are often blurred when one is trying to balance the various inequities in life. When he forces Carter (by threatening to reveal Carter's relationship with Daphne, a black woman) to corroborate his tall tale to the police concerning the murders, he is merely doing what is necessary to clear his name. He has committed no murder, yet he fears (because he has been threatened by officers Miller and Mason) that he will be accused of some of the crimes. In this way, Easy commits a wrong to ensure a right.

The one character who is guided by no moral code but his own is DeWitt Albright. A hired gun who performs any unsavory job for which the wealthy will pay, DeWitt has no qualms about theft or murder as long as he is paid. Always dressed in cream colors, DeWitt is described as serpentlike. A former attorney from Georgia, DeWitt understands the political, social, economic, and legal structures, fully appreciating the inequities built into these systems for the disenfranchised. As a consequence, he uses the hunger and economic desperation of people like Easy to impel them to do his bidding. Although he knows that the life designed for minorities in America is historically unfair, he still intends for himself, the white man dressed in white, consistent and frequent victory in all endeavors.

Similar to DeWitt is Easy's longtime friend Raymond "Mouse" Alexander. In fact, when Easy first meets DeWitt, he notices a resemblance, not in appearance but in attitude. Mouse firmly believes that the end justifies the means. And if the means is murder, so be it. Mouse appears suddenly, just like a cliché, when Easy finds himself in a precarious situation, at the mercy of gangster Frank Green. Threatening to kill Frank if he does not release Easy, stating that he will not count to warn him (he will simply shoot), a fearless Mouse confronts the most intimidating character in the novel. Even when Frank releases Easy, Mouse wants to kill him just for retribution. The latter response underscores Mouse's somewhat complex nature. While he is completely desensitized to death and violence (and would thus seem to be inhuman and robotic), Mouse is also a caring and loyal man. Completely devoted to Easy because of their long-term friendship, Mouse will strike down anyone who harms Easy.

When Mouse is introduced, he is confirmed as Easy's sidekick. He saves Easy not only from Frank, but also from DeWitt and Joppy. Like an almost supernatural figure, Mouse always arrives just when he is needed, and he insists on helping Easy until all mysteries are solved. When Easy initially rejects Mouse's gesture of assistance, Mouse insists, "But, Easy, you gotta have somebody at yo' back, man. That's just a lie them white men give 'bout makin' it on they own. They always got they backs covered" (153). Once again, Mouse presents his complexity. Not merely a one-dimensional, violent man, Mouse has an intellectual understanding of the world. He simply chooses very direct, unadorned "corrective" measures, because for Mouse, a poor man cannot live (survive) without some blood being shed (154).

Daphne Monet, another major character, finds herself caught in the web of circumstance. She suffers from victim blaming, that unfortunate situation whereby society prevents an individual from thriving and then criticizes the individual for not succeeding. In this case, Daphne is prevented from functioning fully because of her mixed race. Only twenty-two,

Daphne is forced to mature fast in a world that has exacted punishment on her for a factor that should be irrelevant and certainly one over which she has no control. To some degree, she is like DeWitt and Mouse in that she uses whatever is at her disposal to survive. When she initially asks Easy to help her by driving to McGee's, she presents herself as a helpless waif. But when they discover McGee's corpse, Daphne exposes her no-nonsense, take-charge persona. Quickly shedding her demure French accent, Daphne shifts to rapid-fire black dialect as she commands Easy to leave the premises immediately.

Joppy Shag serves not only as a major character but also as the catalyst for the major plot. Were it not for Joppy, Easy would not be involved in this entire situation. An ex–heavyweight boxer, Joppy is an intimidating figure. Yet he is also compassionate when he learns of the threats Daphne received. Though he murders Howard Green and Coretta, Joppy does so out of a feeling of protection. He even involves Easy in this entire situation in an effort to protect Daphne. Later, however, when DeWitt becomes incensed at the turn of events (and the possibility that Daphne may flee forever with that money), Joppy, finding himself at the mercy of a desperate DeWitt, ultimately betrays Easy, and Daphne, when he accompanies DeWitt in his effort to kidnap Daphne.

Frank Green (Knifehand) is also a complex major character, because he is both loyal and dangerous. To protect his sister Daphne's identity, Frank poses for the greater part of the novel as Daphne's boyfriend. Though Daphne risks betrayal by "associating" with blacks in this way, at the very least she diverts attention from her familial ties. A thief and purveyor of contraband liquor and cigarettes, Frank is firmly entrenched in the Los Angeles underworld. Until Mouse confronts him, Frank intimidates everyone with whom he comes in contact, as he is known for miles around for his ability, and willingness, to wield a knife with precision. And as a foil to Mouse (a foil is one who highlights traits in another character), Frank reveals the truth that intimidation comes only through bloated might.

Various minor characters people the novel. Odell Jones is Easy's most dependable, sensible, and steady friend. A religious man (though not a zealot), Odell still frequents John's Place for his periodic drink. When Easy finds himself in a precarious situation, Odell, always offering sound advice, suggests that he leave town. Coretta James and Dupree Bouchard are introduced early in the novel when they enter John's Place. From Coretta Easy gains his first lead on Daphne. And Dupree serves as Easy's link not only to Coretta, but also to his now-defunct job at Champion Aircraft.

Dupree urges Easy to seek reinstatement, insisting that their boss, Benito "Benny" Giacomo, will rehire Easy if he exhibits just a modicum of deference (see *Thematic Issues*). A good-natured man who gets along with everyone, Dupree will relinquish his last penny to aid someone else, a level of generosity that has resulted in his eviction and the necessity of his living first with Coretta and then with his sister Bula. Matthew Carter, Daphne's lover and also a catalyst for action, spares no expense in his search for Daphne. An extremely wealthy man who could ostensibly have anyone he wants, Carter finds that he, too, is a prisoner of racial prejudice. Were society different, he and Daphne could be together without issue. Yet Carter is powerless to overcome the social order that ironically affords him the wealth he enjoys while denying him the woman he loves. Maxim Baker is Carter's underling who tries to intimidate Easy and prevent him from gaining an audience with Carter. Soon, however, Baker finds himself no match for Easy's streetwise intellect, when Easy threatens to expose Carter's business. Maxim's presence in the novel serves to prove that when the most daunting types are challenged forcefully, even they succumb to pressure. Matthew Teran emerges as disease personified. In his only appearance in the novel, Teran is presented as a woefully disturbed man. Though well-heeled economically, Teran is spiritually, psychologically, and emotionally bankrupt. That he would molest a toddler is the height of sickness. With this character, Mosley exposes the depravity of the affluent (who are supposedly superior). Junior Fornay is a typical lowlife. A bouncer at John's Place, Junior is suspicious and uneasy in the presence of almost everyone. In addition, he is envious when others prosper. Easy interacts with him only long enough to gain information. Junior's volatility is evident when he murders McGee on the unfounded suspicion that McGee possesses a weapon. Like Junior, Jackson Blue is someone on whom Easy depends for information. Because Jackson is involved in various unorthodox and illegal activities, and because Jackson has conducted business with Frank Green in the past, Easy attempts to use Jackson, without Jackson's knowledge, to gain access to Frank. Hattie Parsons runs the convenience store that serves as a front for John's Place. Because John has had confrontations with the law earlier in his life, he cannot secure a license to serve alcohol. As a consequence, his club operates illegally. Hattie guards the premises and allows entrance only to regular customers. Officers Mason and Miller, whose presence in the novel sustains the tension, haul Easy to the precinct periodically to press him for information and to threaten him with incarceration if he does not cooperate. Appearing only in a phone conversation with Easy is Etta Mae

Harris (Alexander), Mouse's estranged wife. Described as a dependable, strong, and no-nonsense woman, Etta Mae, sensing that something is disturbing Easy, sends Mouse from Houston to Los Angeles to Easy's aid.

THEMATIC ISSUES

Each of the major themes, while highlighting an important topic in the novel, is also interdependent on all the other themes. The major themes are survival, financial independence, manhood, loyalty, and amorality. While the main plot concerns Easy's resolution of the murder cases, serving as a subtext is Easy's history and reputation as the consummate survivor. A veteran of World War II, Easy has witnessed the harsh reality of hand-to-hand combat, and he has killed in order to survive. Because of the skills he developed during the war, Easy knows how to strategize, how to maneuver and manipulate a situation to his advantage. He understands that the heat of war, a desperate circumstance, calls for desperate measures. Easy's motivation for survival comes to him when he is trapped in a barn outside Normandy. His two buddies are already dead, and a sniper has the barn under siege. Initially feeling defeated, Easy then hears an internal voice (alter ego) that commands him, in unapologetically vulgar language, to summon his courage and attack the sniper like a real warrior. Following the orders, Easy reigns victorious. Ever since that moment, whenever Easy feels cornered, the voice speaks to him and he obeys: "The voice has no lust. He never told me to rape or steal. He just tells me how it is if I want to survive" (99). And while the voice expects Easy to be courageous and face up to the opposition, it also expects him to use logic and not act precipitously. When Easy thinks about taking Odell's advice and just fleeing the situation with Daphne, especially after the police and DeWitt threaten him, the voice accuses him of cowardice, yet the voice also says, in what will become the recurring mantra: "Bide yo' time, Easy. Don't do nuthin' that you don't have to do. Just bide yo' time an' take advantage whenever you can" (97).

Easy's use of the voice as a means of survival also underscores Daphne's strategy for survival. When Easy engages in conversation with the voice, he emerges as two distinct personalities, both of which are needed in his struggle to achieve. Likewise, Daphne has created two personalities for herself: Daphne, the white woman who has attempted to remove race as an obstacle in her life, and Ruby Hanks, her given name, the mulatto woman who has been plagued by race and other impositions on her person. Described by Easy as being chameleon-like (evident in the changing color of her eyes, from blue to green and back again), Daphne has tried to negotiate around the arbitrary boundaries that society has established for her in an effort to circumscribe her life. Like the alter ego voice that Easy has invoked, Ruby Hanks has created Daphne, who challenges her opposition and thwarts its seemingly omnipresent power. And just as Easy was a literal prisoner when the voice initially called forth, Daphne is a figurative prisoner in a world that does not know how to define or accept her. Even hinting at this omnipotent white power that tries to rule the lives of "marginalized" people, Daphne states, "They don't have names. They're just the ones who won't let us be ourselves" (182). Daphne's dual personality is also the result of the sexual abuse she suffered as a child at the hand of her father. In shedding the Ruby Hanks persona, Daphne also tries to flee the experience of that young girl. Again, hers is an attempt to survive and retain sanity.

Financial independence also serves as a motivating factor in the lives of Easy and Daphne. The main reason that Easy accepts DeWitt's job is financial security. Because he has recently been fired and because he has the responsibility of a mortgage, Easy takes the job and later decides to milk as much money as he can from the affluent whites. Appreciating the fact that financial independence is the ultimate goal in a capitalistic society, Easy concludes that any legal means (though he manipulates the meaning of legal) of attaining money is defensible. When Daphne, Easy, and Mouse divide Carter's thirty thousand dollars among themselves, they have no qualms about this "theft." Deciding that economic and racial inequities justify their actions, they accept their newfound wealth with no guilt. To some degree, each of them feels as if he or she has earned a reward for enduring not only this most recent trouble, but also the continuous trials life has meted out.

For Easy, financial independence is inextricably linked to manhood. When DeWitt, once he has paid Easy, suggests that he now "owns" Easy, stating that any man is owned once he accepts money from another, Easy realizes that the only way for him to satisfy this debt is to secure his own money. Because Easy believes there is no established justice for the black man, he thinks that if the black man has some money, then he will have at least some justice. As he states, "Money isn't a sure bet but it's the closest to God that I've ever seen in this world" (121). For Easy, money becomes the means by which he is freed from slavery. When he states that he intends to buy his life back, he is, in fact, alluding to the actual slave condition of having to buy something (freedom) that should already be granted. So if he has to buy his life (freedom), and if it should already be his, then whatever means of attaining the freedom (and the money to secure it) is warranted.

This issue of manhood has plagued Easy ever since he was in the war. Finding himself in a war to ensure freedom abroad yet fighting in a military that still condoned segregated units, Easy felt the need to prove himself as a man. Because black soldiers were generally denied the privilege of combat and were then castigated by white soldiers for being cowards, Easy, who had previously thought volunteers were fools, volunteered for the invasion of Normandy and later signed on for the Battle of the Bulge in an attempt to prove himself worthy. Even if they would never like him, he wanted them to respect him. For the greater part of his life, then, he has tried to gain the respect of white men; he has tried to match their manhood with his own. In the war, it was combat; in the real world, it is financial security. Waging this war for his manhood and for respect has also affected Easy's attitude about his job. When his boss, Benny Giacomo, fires a hardworking and dedicated Easy because he supposedly is not "giving a little extra" by staying late on an already strenuous shift, Easy refuses to grovel in the way that Benny expects. And several days later, when Easy returns because Dupree has told him that Benny wants him back, Easy refuses to plead, insisting that he will not beg this "plantation boss" (66). Upon storming out of Benny's office, Easy thinks, "My bills were paid and it felt good to have stood up for myself. I had a notion of freedom when I walked out to my car" (67). Easy finally decides that he must make decisions that satisfy his own agenda for himself, rejecting any further attempts to secure another's validation.

Loyalty is presented as a very complex issue. Often loyalty exacts a price from those who try to preserve it. Frank Green, for all his unethical and illegal practices, exhibits an unfailing loyalty to Daphne. He threatens anyone who, he thinks, has designs on his sister. He has killed their father because of the man's most egregious display of disloyalty (child molestation) to a vulnerable and impressionable Daphne (Ruby). Mouse is loyal, to a fault, to his longtime friend Easy. When Mouse and Easy conduct their "interview" with Junior Fornay, to question Junior about his involvement in McGee's death, Mouse would have shot Junior if he had not answered all of Easy's questions satisfactorily. Given all his imperfections and his volatility, Mouse is still protective of Easy. In a very bizarre way, Daphne displays loyalty in her decision to leave Carter. Even though she absconds with his money, she also leaves him to protect him from public derision. Had others discovered that he was dating a black woman, his very livelihood, of which she took only a paltry share, would have been threatened and his reputation discredited. She leaves him to save him. Easy is also a very loyal person. Even though Mouse often unnerves him, Easy still acknowledges the redeeming qualities his friend offers. Generally a good person, Easy often finds himself in very bad circumstances, usually as a result of his attempt to honor a commitment or assist a helpless person. Each time he comes to Daphne's aid, he thinks she really needs his help. Because of the growing devotion he has for her, he does not return her to Carter, though he has been paid to do so. The novel also ends with Easy and Odell discussing this issue of loyalty. Easy is feeling somewhat guilty for turning over Junior to the police while allowing Mouse to go free. Without actually revealing to Odell the persons involved in this dilemma, Easy asks Odell a hypothetical question about loyalty and friends. Odell and Easy ultimately conclude that one owes loyalty only to those one considers his true friends (in this case, Mouse), regardless of the culpability of that friend.

This issue of amorality consumes much of the novel. Much of Easy's life is a struggle to be transformed from object to subject, or to be made an agent in his own life. Feeling, of course, that the political, social, and economic systems are established at variance with him, Easy finds that rules of right and wrong, what is moral and immoral, become confused. Though it may be wrong for him to milk Carter for as much money as he can while never honoring the contract (and returning Daphne to Carter), Easy discovers that for him to achieve freedom, or independence, he must use whatever methods present themselves. Or when Daphne leaves with her share of the thirty thousand dollars, one might argue that her decision is wrong. But the novel also suggests, via dialogue between Daphne and Easy, that it is wrong for the rich and powerful to exact punishment on others for characteristics that these less fortunate cannot control (e.g., race, social status). For both Easy and Daphne, their re-created selves (their subject selves, the voice and "Daphne") are right, and whatever means they had to adopt to transform to these new selves is to them justified.

It may be wrong for Daphne to kill Teran, but doing so saves the boy he has molested. Even Mouse's killing of Frank, Joppy, and DeWitt is done out of loyalty to Easy, to protect him and preserve him for the greater good. The entire novel is characterized by an amoral tone. When Easy notes that John's Place is an illegal establishment, he does so matter-of-factly. To Easy, John, who never actually appears in the novel, is just a struggling businessman who is trying to make a living.

HISTORICAL CONTEXT

Devil in a Blue Dress is set in the summer of 1948 in Los Angeles, the period immediately following World War II. While this era marked a time of change in America, with Jackie Robinson entering major league baseball in 1947, it also marked a time of uncertainty in regard to the pace of progress. This period ushered in the second Great Migration, that sociological phenomenon wherein scores of blacks moved from the rural South to northern urban centers in the hope of finding improved economic, social, and cultural opportunity. While many blacks in the southeastern states moved to New York, Philadelphia, Detroit, or Chicago, those, like Easy Rawlins and Mouse, from Texas sought their advancement in California. Hailing from Houston, Easy and several of the other characters in the novel have made their way to the West Coast hoping to leave behind forever the various restrictions imposed on them in an often hostile South.

However, just as southern blacks often found life in the northern cities less than favorable, those California migrants also discovered a life of struggle. According to Easy, "Life was still hard in L.A. and if you worked every day you still found yourself on the bottom" (27). In addition to the economic struggle, transplanted blacks also met with a more detached social interaction. Instead of friends and family taking leisurely strolls down a dusty road and greeting all whom they encountered, or hosting impromptu cookouts, black city dwellers found little time for recreational activities, choosing instead to work yet another job in the hope of saving more money. One Houston native, whom Easy mentions only in passing and who finds Los Angeles life unbearable, is Sophie Anderson. Deciding that she needs a slower and friendlier pace, Sophie chooses a reverse migration (a phenomenon that would actually emerge in the 1970s and 1980s, when northern blacks began to return to the South in search of fresh air, open spaces, and more reasonable real estate). When Sophie "looked out her window she wanted to see her friends and her family. And if she called out to one of them she wanted to know that they'd have the time to stop for a while and say hello" (49). Although many of the native Texans in the novel have formed mini-communities of social interaction (evident in the fact that several people from Houston frequent John's Place), clearly this era of migration was fraught with some anxiety and a struggle for adjustment and acclimation.

What often plagued black city dwellers was that certain negative elements of southern life dogged their efforts elsewhere. DeWitt Albright, the southern lawyer who initially seems progressive but later proves to be as bigoted as any stereotypical Southerner, even personifies these elements in the novel. Easy describes the working environment in the city (particularly the manufacturing plants) as modeling the slave plantation. The bosses assume the role of slaver, and the black employees are to accept their role as children who must endure whatever abuses, verbal or otherwise, that are visited upon them. Consequently, these blacks found life in the city harsher than they had expected, and largely for three reasons: (1) like Sophie Anderson, they did not have the emotional support of extended families that they did in the South; (2) they did not have the access to land upon which they could grow crops when they needed food; and (3) life could seem more difficult in the city because new arrivals did not necessarily expect such strident racial tensions, though they were always prepared for them in the South. Of course, those like Easy, quickly realizing these similar circumstances, simply tapped into that well of southern experience and surmounted odds at every turn. When Easy opts not to assume the role of sycophant for the pleasure of his boss, Benny, he rejects the slave mentality required to endure life on the plantation. Even Joppy Shag uses his southern experience to ensure his success as a business owner. Described as a superstitious man, Joppy, when deciding to open his bar in 1938, traveled all the way to Texas to retrieve a marble bar top from his uncle's former bar. Believing that if he had some token from his uncle's once-thriving business he would also succeed, Joppy in essence brings some of the South to California with him. Emblematic of southern strength, the marble top, over which Joppy spends countless hours hovering and buffing, represents the ancestral presence that should guide and protect.

Migration during this period was not restricted only to southern blacks. Many European Holocaust survivors also chose America as their land of opportunity. Often compared to American blacks, these Jewish champions of freedom and determination would rise above incredible odds to advance themselves in a foreign land. Mosley addresses the plight of the Jewish migrants when he introduces Abe and Johnny. Barbers from Poland, these two men had faced untold misery before coming to America (and opening a liquor store within two years). Married to Abe's sister, Johnny had suffered a mental breakdown when he and Abe were forced to cut their wives' hair before sending the two women to the gas chamber. As a result Johnny became so ill, physically and mentally, that Abe ultimately convinced the Nazi guards that Johnny had died and that the patrolmen had retrieved his body for cremation. Abe then hid Johnny in a hole in his cell, fed him, and cared for him for three months until the two were finally rescued by Russians. Their life story, while also an in-spiration and a testament to human endurance, sustains the anxiety and uncertainty that marks this period.

Still another way that Mosley historicizes this novel is by presenting the issue of the tragic mulatto. Largely a phenomenon of southern liter-ature from the nineteenth century, this character type was developed as a means for southern apologists (defenders of slavery) to condemn misce-genation (cross-racial breeding). Writers of such literature positioned the character against the impossible odds of social ostracism and even casti-gated her (it was usually a woman) for an inherent moral weakness. As a consequence, the character's only alternative was death, and hence the tragedy. In reality, this character suffered from victim blaming (the cir-cumstance whereby society creates a hostile environment for a person and then unabashedly blames that person for not thriving). By describing the character as a tragic mulatto, society places the burden on the victim, when in fact the real tragedy is society's hostile attitude.

The secret that is wreaking such havoc in the novel is, of course, the truth of Daphne's ethnicity. Hers is almost a story of the tragic mulatto. She cannot openly express her love for Carter, and she cannot openly declare her familial attachment to Frank. Her mulatto status seems to deny her an acknowledgment of the truth. That she must even reckon with such issues is unfair, especially given her lack of control over the situation. In fact, it is society's arbitrary rules and boundaries that even create the sit-uation. In developing a plot that turns on this very issue, Mosley is re-vealing the extent to which historical biases are visited on the present. Just as the southern problems often followed migrants to places north and west, historical influences plague the present. In short, the southern plan-tation is alive and well, still creating circumstances (e.g., a person of mixed ethnicity) that it would rather deny or even suppress (i.e., kill). However, when Daphne takes Carter's money, she rejects her tragic status, opting instead for control of her circumstances rather than being controlled by them. Because she did not create the societal bias against her, she accepts no responsibility for it. Yet, Mosley suggests, stories like hers will be re-peated again and again.

From a literary standpoint, Daphne's actions echo those of Huck Finn or Robin Hood, both of whom perform what society would deem an act that is wrong (from a broader, more enlightened perspective) but is per-formed for the right reason. When Huck decides that assisting in Jim's escape would be tantamount to going to hell, he struggles with the fact that the institution of slavery, which also defines the mores of his entire society, is inherently immoral (wrong). Thus, to perform a "wrong" act in this society is really to perform a right. Likewise, when Robin Hood steals from the rich to give to the poor, he is in fact paying the poor what should have been their rewards accruing from the earth's natural resources that all of the earth's inhabitants should enjoy (and would enjoy if the arbitrary class and social order were dismantled). To a great degree, Daphne's final act is her way of accepting the deferred salaries of her mothers, grandmothers, and great-grandmothers, who earned the money not only because of their hard work but also because of the physical intrusions on their persons that have resulted in the "mulattoes" of the world.

Also important is that the Los Angeles setting provides the appropriate context for presenting another post–World War II wonder: the advent of the big, superpowerful American automobile. Easy comments that all residents, regardless of financial circumstance, cherish their cars. From the 1940s on, Americans would become increasingly dependent on this machine as urban centers gave way to sprawling metropolises.

NARRATIVE STRUCTURE

Devil in a Blue Dress is narrated in the first-person by protagonist Easy Rawlins. From this vantage point, the reader gains insight into Easy's thoughts, feelings, anxieties, and triumphs. The first-person perspective provides an inherent narrative tension. The reader is consistently challenged with resolving (or at least better understanding) the conflict between the present-I and the past-I perspectives. The present-I is the Easy who is narrating the story, the one who has already experienced all of the events that he is now recalling and presenting to the reader. Ostensibly, this Easy is more mature, better informed, and more analytical. The past-I is the Easy in the story, the one whose progress the reader is charting through the various experiences. He is the uninformed one who will make various mistakes in terms of learning whom to trust and what clues to observe. For example, the past-I Easy makes the mistake of sleeping with Coretta while she is still ostensibly dating his friend and former coworker Dupree. The present-I Easy, regretting that decision, promises never to succumb to that temptation again (though he also admits that he will make that promise again and again). At the very least, however, he appreciates the fact this his behavior is misguided.

This conflict between the two Easys actually grounds the entire novel. Had not a somewhat naive Easy trusted Joppy (someone he considered a friend), he would not have suffered through the various trials and threats on his life. When one considers that the whole novel depends on this conflict, then one is reminded that the novel's structure is dependent on Easy's development from naiveté to maturity. While plot is obviously a dominant device in detective fiction (with the ever-important question, "What will happen next?"), character development—Easy's development—enjoys similar significance.

That Mosley is keenly aware of these two Easys is obvious given Easy's continuous observation "in those days in L.A." Mosley, via Easy, reminds us that Easy is in reflection mode, recalling experiences from his earlier days in Los Angeles. The reader might even assume that Easy is telling the story in the reader's present day. In this way, Easy's 1940s-something sociopolitical assessments are applied to (or at least considered significant to) today's issues. Easy's comments on race, male-female relationships, manhood, political corruption, and the like are, in fact, timeless.

In terms of pacing, Mosley cues the reader early in the novel when he reveals, of course via Easy, that the time frame is approximately one week: When Easy is debating with himself whether to accept DeWitt's job offer, he reveals that he has only seven days to earn this month's mortgage payment. And although the story line occurs over a week and a half, Mosley alerts the reader to the limited time.

As noted earlier, plot is of paramount importance in detective fiction. To this end, the various murders structure the narrative. Initially, of course, the two most important murders are those of Howard Green (who is killed before the novel begins) and Coretta James (who dies very soon after Easy approaches her for information about Daphne). And while these and all the other murders are connected to the Daphne Monet secret, the subsequent murders occur in a kind of snowball effect once Daphne's story begins to unfold (after all, Mouse kills three of the seven himself).

In terms of analyzing a tightly wrought narrative structure, with its attendant elements of foreshadowing, one must critique very closely the Howard and Coretta murders. The distinguishing factor with these killings is the brutal way in which the two are beaten—beyond recognition. Only when Daphne reveals that Joppy killed Howard and Coretta does the reader recall (unless she or he has been very shrewd) Easy's very early description of Joppy. Providing the reader with information about Joppy's background (consequently, the reader is focused on the past and not the present), Easy states, "He was ranked number seven in 1932 but his big draw was the violence he brought to the ring. Joppy would come out swinging wildly, taking everything any boxer could dish out" (7). The reader, and Easy, will later declare that only a boxer could have bludgeoned (with his bare fists) those two so violently. In addition, one must recall the location of Joppy's bar. It sits on the second floor of a butcher's warehouse, and the odor of rotten meat permeates every inch of the premises. Clearly, this initial setting serves also to foreshadow the fact that Joppy is linked to the foul odor of death.

The third murder serves an important narrative function. Naturally, the reader, in an urgent need to solve the crimes, wants to link it to the first two murders. Using expert narrative technique, Mosley uses this third murder (that of Richard McGee) as a relative distraction. Though McGee is involved in the attempted blackmail of Daphne, his murder actually has nothing to do with that issue. Junior Fornay simply acted irrationally and spontaneously murdered McGee. But because the reader, as noted previously, wants to link McGee's murder to Coretta's and Howard's, though the method of murder is different, the reader focuses desperately on McGee's murder and forgets all thoughts of Joppy Shag.

ALTERNATE READING: A HISTORICAL APPROACH

The purpose of historical criticism is to consider how military, social, political, cultural, scientific, or intellectual influences have helped to shape a particular literary work. Quite often this school of criticism allows the reader to understand more about the life of the author as well; however, this latter concern is important mainly when the author is writing in his or her contemporary moment. In Mosley's case, of course, *Devil in a Blue Dress* is set in a fixed historical moment, 1948, which predates the author's 1952 birth. Consequently, historical criticism is useful only in contextualizing the novel. More specifically, a sociopolitical analysis yields significant insight into the work.

Though *Devil in a Blue Dress* is mainly detective fiction, Mosley also uses the novel to articulate how key events have affected the lives of his characters. When Easy accepts DeWitt's job offer and when he is later forced to solve the crimes to exonerate himself, he is participating in a ritual that has harried him his entire adult life: the urgent need to prove himself worthy in a sociopolitical system that would rather he fail. World War II serves as the historical event that first introduced Easy to this dilemma. Upon joining the army Easy thought that he would be a full participant in the effort to bring democracy to the world. He soon discovers, however, a segregated military. Though trained as a foot soldier and a fighter, he spends the greater part of three years confined to office work. Only those black men who deliberately volunteered to fight were placed in action. Easy decided that he would not fight for a country that did not consider him equal to the task. But then his ego is challenged when many of the white soldiers begin to taunt the black soldiers and call them cowards. Immediately, Easy feels the need to defend his honor and his race. Easy fights, then, not just for America, but for his own dignity. World War II becomes emblematic of the war that Easy will wage forever against the inequities he must encounter as a black man in postwar America. The historical event sets the tone for the sociopolitical reality. When Easy says of his experience in World War II, "I never minded that those white boys hated me, but if they didn't respect me I was ready to fight" (98), he confirms the context for the rest of his life. To fight is not only to enter World War II combat but also to engage in a struggle for societal respect.

As noted in the *Thematic Issues* section, Easy's struggle is for manhood. This goal, for the African American man, has often involved the need to fight. One of the earliest examples of African American manhood asserting itself is presented in Frederick Douglass's 1845 *Narrative*, wherein Douglass describes a crucial moment in his life when he rejects the physical abuse of plantation overseer Mr. Covey and retaliates in kind. From that day forward, Douglass never considers himself anything other than a man. In the twentieth century, black men have also asserted their equality, even their dominance, in the realm of boxing. From Jack Johnson in 1908 to Joe Louis in the 1930s and 1940s, physical victory has emerged as one means to define manhood. Mosley uses this image of fighting in the crucial scene in the novel when Easy refuses to humble himself to his former boss, Benny Giacomo (see *Thematic Issues*). In two instances Benny is described as looking "like an advancing boxer" (65) and "the way a fighter does" (66). When Easy bests Benny in this battle, he is, to a degree, felling him as one boxer would another. This is especially significant given Benny's ethnicity, Italian, and given one of the most historic boxing matches ever witnessed. In 1935, on the eve of Italy's invasion of Ethiopia, Joe Louis defeated Primo Carnera, an Italian, in a match that would have far-reaching political symbolism. Easy's defiance of Benny (whom he describes as a plantation boss), then, situates him with black male antecedents from Douglass on who have willingly confronted adversity and bigotry to advance dignity and retain their self-respect.

Mosley also uses Easy's experiences in World War II to frame other observations in the novel. Reviling the abuse of the young boy in Teran's clutches, Easy remembers how one Jewish refugee child during the war is rescued, though he does not survive. Tree Rat, as Sergeant Vincent LeRoy has nicknamed the child, desperately clings to the sergeant and refuses to accept medical care, fearing abandonment from his new friend. Because the boy is hungry, the sergeant allows him to eat as much candy as he wants. Unfortunately, the child dies as a result of gorging on these sweets, and the sergeant, grieving and shaken, is racked with guilt for a long time afterward. Easy pointedly notes that in their brief interaction, the sergeant, a usually stolid man, treats Tree Rat with the compassion and sympathy denied the child whom Teran defiles. In making this comparison, Easy reminds the reader that the same mentality that abused and starved the Jewish child molests and harasses innocent children in America. The worldwide war fought to save, among others, Jewish children is waged on a smaller scale against the Terans of the country. Just as the maniacal Hitler attempts worldwide malevolence, corruption plagues the corridors of Los Angeles power. Teran, would-be mayor of Los Angeles, is linked to the affluent political power structure of the city. It is this structure against which Easy must fight for his own dignity. Therefore, when Easy pursues what might be perceived as a questionable (amoral) means, he reminds his reader that issues of morality must be suspended when one is fighting in a war.

As well as the actual war, the postwar period also situates the novel. The post–World War II era was a time of widespread prosperity for the country. Veterans returned home to take advantage of the GI Bill (pursuing education and purchasing homes), start families, and prepare for a promising future. The technological advances resulting from the war were translated to industrial jobs in America's cities. These booming times, to some degree, define the novel. Before being fired, Easy works at Champion Aircraft, a company that designs and constructs aircraft for both the air force and the airline industry. Given the skills he has learned in the army, Easy is well trained to work in this field. And with this job Easy has transformed himself into a responsible man who owns a house. Because he is man of property, as he proudly declares, he wants to lay the economic foundation for one day raising a family and pursuing other aspects of the American dream. Believing that he should benefit from the postwar prosperity, especially since he is a veteran, Easy works to realize his goals. He soon realizes, of course, that for black men this dream could very well be a nightmare.

With the narrative references to the plantation and with Easy's present-I

perspective on these 1948 events (the contemporary point of view in recollection mode; see *Narrative Structure*), Mosley invites his reader to consider the entire sociopolitical system as it relates to the black man's
struggle in America. The novel chronicles not only the black man's life in
white America, but also the black man's life in his own milieu.

4

Black Betty
(1994)

The fourth Easy Rawlins novel, *Black Betty,* takes place in 1961, with Easy attempting to balance his parental obligations and his work life. Responsible for both his adopted children, Feather and Jesus, Easy, now forty-one, rises to the challenge of single parenthood. Because of his involvement with and dedication to his children, Easy is more cautious about the risks he takes. Nevertheless, as always he finds himself in trouble with the justice system as he tries to unravel yet another mystery of violence, greed, and betrayal. His willingness to become involved is due in part to his financial circumstances. While he has enjoyed prosperity in the past, Easy, now living in a rented house, is almost bankrupt. This changed financial outlook piques the reader's attention, the result of which is a renewed interest in the possibilities for this seasoned protagonist. In *Black Betty* Mosley reveals his development as a writer in that the work is paced with greater regularity and the issues addressed are presented with narrative subtlety and complexity.

PLOT DEVELOPMENT

Saul Lynx, a white detective who has been hired by the Cains, a wealthy white family from Beverly Hills, wants Easy to find their maid, Elizabeth (Black Betty) Eady. Lynx has learned that Easy once knew Betty years ago when he was just a boy living in Houston, and he believes that Easy is the best person to locate the lost woman.

After agreeing to take the job (because he needs the money), Easy decides to visit Betty's cousin, Odell Jones, and his wife, Maude, believing that they have sent Lynx to him. Going to the Jones house is problematic because Odell and Easy, though formerly close friends, became estranged years before because Odell believed that Easy betrayed him. Arriving at the Joneses', Easy is greeted by only Maude, with Odell refusing to acknowledge Easy's presence. Easy does learn, however, that Odell and Maude did in fact send Lynx to him. Unfortunately, they know little else about why Betty has disappeared or why the Cains want so desperately to find her.

Easy's next move is to search for Betty's brother, Marlon, to whom Betty has always been very close. After pursuing a few dead-end possibilities, Easy learns that Marlon is living on the outskirts of Los Angeles in the desert. Driving in the general vicinity, Easy happens upon a dilapidated service station. While there, he has a conflict with the proprietor (who is known only by his nickname, Dickhead) when the white man rather unapologetically uses a racial slur. Physically subduing the man, Easy takes the gun that Dickhead brandishes, yanks the phone from the wall, goes outside and steals the battery from Dickhead's car, and then absconds with the items to prevent the man from pursuing him or soliciting help. Before leaving, however, Easy does manage to learn Marlon's exact address.

After arriving at Marlon's, Easy finds no one home. From the arrangement of the man's personal belongings, Easy knows that he left abruptly, and Easy suspects that Marlon is probably dead. He finds Marlon's wallet, a check made out to Marlon for five thousand dollars from Sarah Cain, and a more recent picture of Betty.

Easy decides to pay the Cains a visit in Beverly Hills. While there, Easy meets Sarah Cain Hawkes; her teenage son, Arthur; and the family attorney, Calvin Hodge, a brusque Texan who is offended at Easy's presumption. Easy learns that Hodge hired him through Lynx but that Hodge did not share this information with Sarah. In addition, Easy learns that the family patriarch, Albert Cain, has died two weeks earlier, just about the same time that Marlon received the check, which Sarah denies that she wrote. After a battle of wills with Hodge, Easy leaves, but only to be accosted by the police while driving away.

Captain Styles (known by everyone as Commander) takes Easy in for questioning, though he also brutalizes Easy when he thinks Easy is not forthcoming with the right answers. Easy learns that Styles is interested in Betty's possible whereabouts. After traumatizing Easy physically and emotionally, Styles locks him away. Fortunately, Easy is left in the care of a compassionate young officer, Connor, who allows him a phone call. Easy locates Mouse's former attorney, Faye Rabinowitz, who, along with Judge Mellon (a man sensitive to civil rights issues), discovers that the police have no basis for holding Easy, and he soon finds himself free. Deciding to contact Lynx and forcing him to reveal more answers, Easy pays Lynx a visit, only to have Lynx dismiss him from the case. Completely miffed, Easy knows that this case involves much more complexity than simply finding a maid for a rich family. Even before he begins to sort through the few clues he has, Easy receives a call from Gwendolyn Barnes, another woman who works for the Cains, who asks that Easy visit Sarah Cain again, this time at her private farmhouse.

During this second visit with the Cains, Easy discovers that Betty's departure came just after Albert Cain's death, which the police are still investigating. The death has left the will and the estate in limbo. Easy also learns that Sarah Cain is separated from her husband, Ron Hawkes, and has remained legally married only to satisfy their son, Arthur. Desperate to find Betty, Sarah offers Easy twenty thousand dollars if he will stay on the case and locate Betty, who he now knows sometimes spends time with her friend Felix Landry.

Easy decides to find Terry Tyler, Marlon's godson, a local boxer and illegal gambler, thinking that Terry might also provide some answers about Marlon, Betty, or both. After his old friend Jackson Blue gives him Terry's address, Easy decides to pay the athlete a visit, only to discover Terry's bloodstained body sprawled on the kitchen floor. While kneeling down to get a closer look, Easy is attacked from behind and knocked unconscious—but not before he reaches back and strikes his assailant in the face. Regaining consciousness, Easy finds that he was struck with a frying pan and impaled with an ice pick. Practically catatonic, he manages to pick up a photograph from among Terry's belongings and then drive himself home. Under the watchful eye and assistance of Jesus, Easy is nursed back to health.

After sending Jesus and Feather to visit his old friend Primo and his wife Flower, Easy finally pays a visit to his dying friend, Martin Smith, where he also finds Odell. Because Odell feels guilty about Easy's being attacked, he finally submits to talking to Easy again. Soon after, Easy contacts another old acquaintance, Alamo Weir, a longtime criminal, and asks

Alamo to help him burglarize Calvin Hodge's law office. From Hodge's files, Easy discovers that Captain Styles often performs private work for Hodge. Additionally, he learns that Marlon Eady had been arrested in 1939 on burglary charges at the Cain estate. The remainder of the Cain file had been transferred to a new attorney in 1959 at the request of Albert Cain.

Receiving a strange phone call from Odell, who once again insists that Easy stay away from his house, Easy ignores the demand and goes to the Joneses'. Forcing Odell to confess, Maude also reveals to Easy that Terry Tyler was, in fact, Betty's son and that Betty, who had been present when Easy went to Terry's, thought that Easy had murdered her son (and had telephoned Odell with this information, which was why Odell had demanded that Easy stay away). Betty was the person who had attacked and stabbed Easy. Easy also learns that Marlon's body is in the Joneses' basement. Marlon had been brutally beaten by the police but had managed to drive himself to Odell and Maude's, where he died soon thereafter. Not knowing what to do, Odell and Maude have been preserving the body with ice since just after Easy's first visit to their house. (A couple of days later, Easy will help them bury Marlon in their basement.)

Finally, Easy and Odell locate Betty at her friend Felix Landry's house, where they inform her about Marlon. Accompanying them back to Odell's, Betty participates in the brief funeral service for her brother. Now Easy gains the answers to most of the questions that have plagued him ever since Saul Lynx first sought his assistance. Soon after Betty was employed by the Cains in the late 1930s, Albert Cain began to sexually harass the young woman. Successfully avoiding contact with him for a while, Betty ultimately submits to his demands when he threatens to have Marlon arrested. This forced relationship with Cain produced a set of twins—Terry, who was sent to live with another family, the Tylers; and Gwendolyn, who is allowed to remain in the Cain household but does not know that Betty is her mother.

Confident that Betty did not kill Cain, and appreciating the fact that Betty did not want to return to the Cain house, Easy decides to free himself of the matter and forget about Sarah's reward—that is, until Saul Lynx visits him again. Though Easy is not happy to see Lynx, he does allow the man to explain himself. Lynx has learned that Cain left his entire fortune to Betty. Sarah has filed an injunction against the will, and Hodge, who was dismissed from Cain's employ two years earlier and is now missing out on hefty fees, is supporting Sarah in her actions.

Lynx and Easy decide to pay Sarah Cain another visit and challenge her on a number of issues. Accusing her of colluding in the murder of Terry and of wanting Betty dead, the two men prod and provoke until they get some answers. Sarah admits that somehow Hodge found out about the will and then contacted her about filing the injunction. She denies any wrongdoing other than keeping Gwen's true identity a secret. During this conversation Gwen is called away to answer the front door. After several minutes Lynx and Easy become suspicious, but when they look for Gwen, she is gone. Easy and Sarah search outside for her while Lynx looks in another direction. A few minutes later, Easy and Sarah find Gwen's body in a maze of shrubbery. Escorting Sarah back to the house, they find a dazed Lynx recovering from an attack by Arthur, who had fled the scene. Arthur will appear later at the Joneses' with his father, Ron.

Easy and Lynx take Sarah to the Joneses'. Easy learns from Lynx that on the night of Cain's death, Arthur, Terry, and Marlon had come to the house together. Apparently, Ron Hawkes (Sarah's estranged husband and Arthur's father; he had once been the Cains' gardener, and Albert Cain despised him) had convinced Arthur and Marlon (Ron and Marlon were old friends) that the only way for Betty, Arthur, Sarah, and the rest of the family to have peace was for Albert Cain to die. Later, Arthur confesses to his part in allowing Terry and Marlon access to the house on the night of Cain's death. Though Marlon is responsible for Cain's murder, Ron is responsible for Gwen's death, and Styles (also a friend of Ron's) is responsible for Terry's death. Together, they had beaten Marlon.

Ron had merely wanted access to Cain's money, and since he was still legally married to Sarah and he and Arthur still maintained a relationship, Ron had thought that he would finally become rich. And because Ron had promised Styles a sizable payment, the captain was more than willing to assist. But once everyone discovers that Betty and her children are the heirs apparent, Ron and Styles begin to murder everyone in Betty's family to prevent them from gaining their inheritance.

When his involvement in these matters is discovered, Ron Hawkes (in a crucial scene at the Joneses' when he tries to shoot Easy but injures Lynx instead) tries to flee, only to be gunned down by Styles. Just before Ron dies, Easy learns that Ron was Dickhead, the service station proprietor he had encountered in the desert while looking for Marlon. Arthur and Styles are indicted, but only Styles is found guilty. During the trial, Betty is made to look like a seductress, so the will is broken.

CHARACTER DEVELOPMENT

While Easy has most often functioned from a position of power in the past, racial challenges notwithstanding, in *Black Betty* his life is greatly affected by vulnerability. Because he is now solely responsible for the economic, moral, and intellectual well-being of his two adopted children and because he has recently suffered financial setbacks, Easy is forced to accept a crime-solving job that he would rather ignore. Given the dangers involved in his detective work, and knowing how sensitive his children are to fears of abandonment, Easy does not want to intensify their frustrations by endangering them or risking their security. His continued emotional development is dependent on his evolving relationship with them. When Easy hears Jesus speak for the first time (for all of these years, the boy has been mute), he admits, "It was the only time I ever cried from being happy" (58). Both Feather and Jesus provide Easy a means of exploring and nurturing his sensitive and compassionate nature.

Raymond "Mouse" Alexander returns to his former volatility. Released from prison after serving a five-year term for murdering Bruno Ingram, Mouse is extremely angry, and his sole purpose now is to exact revenge on the person or persons who he thinks betrayed him. Mouse firmly believes that he was justified in killing Bruno. To him, the homicide was an act of honor. Bruno and Mouse had made a twenty-five-cent bet on a baseball game, and when Bruno issued a disrespectful comment to Mouse and refused to pay, Mouse simply shot him. Because of Mouse's crazed behavior, Easy does not use him in any way to assist in solving the cases. For the first time in an Easy Rawlins mystery, Mouse's presence in the text is completely peripheral, until Easy decides to channel Mouse's anger into what Easy thinks is a constructive effort. Mouse serves here simply to remind Easy that he wishes to avoid all unnecessary violence in his life, especially given his role as a father.

William "Mofass" Wharton, as money-hungry as ever, finds himself once again at Easy's mercy. As in the past, Mofass has tried to make a quick profit without Easy's full knowledge, but when the deal goes sour, he finds that he needs Easy to bail him out. Instead of alerting Easy to the problems early on, Mofass does not consult Easy until he desperately needs help, even though Easy's finances are involved in the scheme. This time, however, Mofass's personal life is also embroiled in the difficulties. For the past few years, Mofass has been involved in a common-law marriage with Clovis MacDonald, a woman who once waited tables at a diner that Easy and Mofass frequented. Clovis, who quickly decides that Mofass will be her ticket out of blue-collar work, latches on to the otherwise un-desirable man. Possessed of a keen business mind, Clovis soon establishes Esquire Realty and, with Mofass's assistance and his contacts, transforms it into a booming venture. Mofass has learned that Clovis has been pil-fering from his personal funds, with the help of an estranged husband from Texas, and he now wants Easy's help in thwarting her efforts. In addition to these financial troubles, Mofass also suffers romantic troubles: he is in love with Clovis's sixteen-year-old niece, Jewelle, who is likewise devoted to him. Easy succeeds in protecting both of them from Clovis and her mean-spirited brothers until Jewelle becomes an adult, at which time she and Mofass are married. Now in his late fifties, Mofass, who suffers from emphysema, has finally found personal happiness.

The title character, Elizabeth Eady (a.k.a. Black Betty), serves not only as a major character, but also as a link to the past. Betty's entire life has been one of struggle and sacrifice. When she was a young woman sa-shaying down the street in Houston's Fifth Ward, Betty strove for accep-tance and requited love. Later, arriving in Los Angeles at the end of the 1930s, Betty sought simply to find a place where she could work hard and become a self-sufficient woman, with her only concern at that time pro-tecting and caring for her brother, Marlon. She no longer looked for her identity with anonymous men. Nevertheless, Betty is forced again to suc-cumb to the demands of an unyielding male dominance, this time in the person of Albert Cain, her white employer, who threatens trouble for Mar-lon if Betty refuses compliance. That she has survived, from her days in Houston and during the past twenty-five years in Los Angeles, is a tes-tament to Betty's resilience and resourcefulness.

Betty's cousin, Odell Jones, and his wife, Maudria (Maude), are also significant and strong characters. That Odell even directs Saul Lynx to Easy is a testament to this man's loyalty to family. Because Odell knows that if anyone can help find Betty, it is Easy, he relinquishes his pride, risking the possibility that he may have to confront Easy. Maude is also instrumental in this effort, in that she provides Easy with information about Betty and the circumstance even when Odell is still somewhat re-luctant to confront Easy directly. Maude and Odell embrace a practical religion, one that honors compassion and commitment to humanity in-stead of self-righteous judgment about the actions of others. When they willingly bury Marlon in their basement, regardless of his poor behavior in life, Odell and Maude present the best of human possibility.

Sarah Clarice Cain (Hawkes) is a tortured and misguided woman. Be-cause she was abused by her wealthy father, Albert Cain, and made to feel unworthy of his affection or his money, Sarah sought comfort in the only person on whom she could depend—Betty. After the death of Sarah's mother, Cassandra, Sarah looks to Betty to fulfill the role of mother. Never feeling completely whole, however, Sarah continues to seek affirmation from others. Later, it would be the Cain gardener, Ron Hawkes, whom her father despised and would ultimately force away. And then, upon the death of Albert Cain (some two weeks prior to the beginning of the novel), it would be Calvin Hodge, who insists that Sarah contest Cain's will. Sarah depends on men to direct her decisions; even her nineteen-year-old son, Arthur, controls her more than she controls herself. Because the elder Cain always used his money as a weapon to coerce others to do his bidding, Sarah believes that money controls everyone and every circumstance.

Ron Hawkes (a.k.a. Dickhead), scoundrel of the worst degree, marries Sarah Cain only for her money. Though he has been out of her life for more than ten years, he has maintained contact with Arthur for the sole purpose of gaining access to the Cain fortune. His overt racism, evident in the comments he makes to Easy early in the novel when Easy goes to the desert in search of Marlon, completes the villainous portrait. Though he has professed friendship to Marlon and Terry Tyler, Hawkes in no way sees them as equals. Every relationship he pursues is inspired not by a sense of humanity or devotion but by an egoistic need for self-aggrandizement. His cold-blooded murder of Gwendolyn attests to his vile nature.

Several minor characters populate the narrative, some of whom have appeared in previous novels. Jackson Blue, Easy's longtime friend, provides Easy with valuable information, as he always does after some prodding and intimidation. Though he is an extremely smart and gifted man, beneath the surface Jackson is a frightened little boy. Always giving Easy reading suggestions and always willing to engage in intellectual or philosophical conversations, Jackson nevertheless refuses to pursue a formal education. He is content engaging in the latest scam. Also reappearing from a previous novel is Alamo Weir, Easy's dependable white friend who assists him in securing access to Calvin Hodge's office. Somewhat akin to Mouse, Alamo is "the kind of crazy criminal who lied, cheated, and killed. You never knew what might be true about him" (196). He is also one who is not duped by the issue of race. Though he lives in a hotel for poor white transients, most of whom harbor racial prejudice, Alamo has risen above such ignorance. His animus is directed instead toward the wealthy. Easy's children, Jesus and Feather, also reappear. While Feather functions as a typical (though somewhat precocious) five-year-old, Jesus has developed markedly. Early in the novel, Easy discovers that Jesus can actually speak—both English and Spanish—but the boy will converse only with Feather. For a while, Easy is hurt that fifteen-year-old Jesus, now a star athlete at his school, will not speak to him. However, when Easy returns home after being attacked by Betty (though at the time he does not know by whom), Jesus expresses matter-of-factly, "Oh God, Daddy" (187), as though he had been speaking all along. He then prepares to nurse his father back to health. Mouse's ex-wife, Etta Mae, and son, LaMarque, make a brief appearance when Easy returns Mouse home following his release from jail. As well, Primo and Flower Garcias (though their last name is Pena in the previous novels), who helped to raise Jesus years before, once again assist Easy in taking care of the children as well as Mofass when he needs sanctuary.

Other minor characters include Saul Lynx, Calvin Hodge, Norman Styles, and Felix Landry. Saul Lynx, the white private detective who convinces Easy to accept the case, surprises Easy at the end of the novel when Easy learns that he has a black wife (Rita). Because their working relationship has been fraught with tension (even racial at times, Easy thinks), Easy never considered that Saul might be just a regular human being. Hodge is the Cains' embittered former attorney. Angry that Albert Cain fired him a while back, he is determined to access some of the Cain fortune, even if only in helping Sarah break the will. His is a fearless personality that will confront any obstacle before him. Detective Norman Styles has dishonored the badge he wears by engaging in intimidation, murder, and conspiracy. Promised a hefty reward by his friend Ron Hawkes, Styles is made more corrupt by the allure of money, which he thinks will protect him against any possible punishment. However, he, the working man, is left to shoulder all of the blame in the final analysis. Felix Landry is the one man who never wanted Betty for her body. A friend to her since their days in Texas, Felix simply provided a place for Betty to relax whenever she needed an escape from the Cain mansion. An honorable and religious man, Felix buys and refurbishes houses to shelter elderly black women.

Two minor characters who merit individual attention are Terry Tyler and Gwendolyn Barnes, Betty's fraternal twins fathered by Albert Cain. Raised apart because Cain could not allow both of them to remain in the house (he allowed Gwendolyn to stay for fear that Betty might otherwise leave), they become very different people. Terry, the streetwise boxer, is raised by a good family, yet upon reaching adulthood, he engages in illegal gambling and whatever else will yield a fast profit. Gwendolyn, on

the other hand, is raised to be graceful and polished. Though she ostensibly works in the Cain household, she never thinks of it as drudgery.
Unaware that she is Betty's daughter until just before she dies, Gwendolyn
does think of herself, recalling the historical stereotype, as being "a member of the (Cain) family." Both Terry and Gwendolyn, however, meet the
same fate.

THEMATIC ISSUES

Several related themes are presented in *Black Betty,* not the least of which
is the individual code of morality. Key characters are guided not by a
standard law, but rather by their own sense of right. What emerges as the
unifying thread with each character's perspective is the fact that a certain
(if somewhat warped) logic prevails. No matter the majority or societal
perspective, these characters never compromise their ethics. When Mouse
kills Bruno Ingram, he does so not out of simple malice, but because Bruno
has disregarded, or dishonored, a promise made to Mouse. The issue in
dispute, a mindless bet on a baseball game, is less significant, however,
than Bruno's betraying his word. That Mouse would murder someone
because of a twenty-five-cent bet seems quite ludicrous; however, to
Mouse the money issue is insignificant (highlighted by the fact that it is
an insignificant amount). Rather, Mouse thinks that there should be honor
even among thieves (Bruno, like Mouse, is an unsavory type). In essence,
when Bruno disrespects Mouse, he is attacking Mouse's sense of manhood
(the base of his code); therefore, Mouse feels the need to protect the self
that he has so sedulously maintained. In short, Mouse was righting a
wrong when he killed Bruno. And now, the very fact that he has lost five
years in a prison for simply correcting a mistake angers him intensely. As
a result, he must again right a wrong by killing the person, or persons,
who alerted the police to his guilt.

Like Mouse, Mouse's former attorney, Faye Rabinowitz, is also guided
by an individual code. Forever disputing societal mandates that restrict
civil liberties, Rabinowitz fights for those persons who she thinks have
been shafted by the system. When she assists Easy in his release from jail,
she does so not because she has any special regard for him, but because
she knows that he, as an individual citizen, deserves fair treatment by the
justice system. Her individual sense of right (as opposed to her responding to some general, ubiquitous code) is established clearly in a revealing
statement she made to Easy five years earlier when she defended Mouse
in court. She stated that she cares nothing about Mouse as a person, that

in fact he is no more than a thug, but she also thinks that the legal system should not be in the practice of murder (i.e., capital punishment), especially, she continues, when most of the influential persons in control of the system should die. Rabinowitz answers only to her conscience. Jackson Blue also lives by an individual code. Though he is the most intellectually talented of any of Easy's acquaintances, Jackson would rather use his streetwise sense to survive. And while Easy thinks that Jackson is wasting his talents and his life, Jackson argues that his life is his own to do with what he pleases. That he might one day suffer a tragic end is of little concern to Jackson. In a philosophical response to Easy, after one of Easy's warnings, Jackson states very simply and nonchalantly that there "[a]in't no such thing as a good end, brother" (179), a comment with which Easy ultimately agrees.

Still another important theme is the need to redeem the past. Once Easy learns about all that Betty has suffered in the Cain household, he redoubles his efforts to save her and to prove that she did not murder Albert Cain. Though as a young boy Easy did comfort Betty and offer her loyalty and friendship, he has always felt that he never did enough to ease Betty's emotional pain. Much of Easy's childhood has haunted him over the years, and his former interaction with Betty is just one aspect of that haunted past. As Easy states, "The desire to help her came back into me the way it had all those years before" (226). Having witnessed the abuse exacted on her by black men in the past, Easy is particularly perturbed to learn that the white and powerful Albert Cain caused even more pain. When Easy is finally afforded the opportunity in the present to offer solace to Betty, he takes his duty very seriously, caressing her and stroking her not as a lover but as a mother, "[a] mother whose child has come awake from a terrible nightmare" (285). Though Easy fulfills the role of mother, he, too, is the child (from that earlier time) who needs to be saved from the nightmare of the past. Reconciling himself to the past also entails his easing tensions with Odell. While his dispute with Odell is more recent than his boyhood days, making peace with the older man is relevant to Easy's childhood past. When Easy salvages his friendship with Odell, he also honors his friendship with the dying Martin, who, along with Odell, was responsible for raising him. Though Easy has never verbalized his thanks to the two men for all of their efforts, his reunion with Odell (and the happiness this newfound peace brings to Martin) will express his longtime appreciation. That Easy needs this reconciliation for his own emotional stability is evident in his description of Odell's touch when Odell cares for Easy's stab wound: "I hadn't had so much mothering since I was seven" (205). Yet again his relationship with these old men is inextricably linked to a past that is so much a part of Easy's present.

Perhaps the most compelling theme is oppression versus resistance, which is presented in two distinct examples in the novel. When Easy is driving along with Gwendolyn up the long country road leading to Sarah Cain's farmhouse (the only property directly bequeathed to Sarah), he notices all of the poor field hands (Mexicans, some blacks, and a few Japanese) slaving away, picking fruit. Easy comments that he feels as though he has been suddenly cast back to "the south . . . and all the way into hell" (155). He is especially angered to witness the powerless children who are forced to help their parents earn a meager wage. Gwendolyn rather stolidly responds by informing Easy that Albert Cain enjoyed (as one of his hobbies) owning a working farm, one that functioned as a result of human sweat and not machinery. For Easy, Cain's pleasure, or amusement, at the expense of human suffering is highly offensive, yet Cain's behavior is typical of the oppressor-oppressed paradigm. Often the oppressed suffer their condition simply to serve the whims of the wealthy. Trying to provoke even the slightest sympathetic response from Gwendolyn, Easy asks if she does not think that, at the very least, the children should be in school. Her brainwashed response is that they cannot even speak English, an ironic reply given the fact that their lack of access to the standard language (in 1961) is all the more reason for them to be enrolled in school. Though Easy makes no inroad into changing Gwendolyn's opinion, he does resist the oppression symbolized in the workers' plight when he confronts Sarah.

Soon after Easy arrives at the farmhouse, Sarah offers him twenty thousand dollars if he will agree to resume his search for Betty on Sarah's behalf (this after Hodge has ostensibly fired Easy). When Easy initially declines the offer, Sarah implies that he should not reject a request from a wealthy person, especially when that same person might be in a position to assist him if he were to find himself in trouble with the authorities. Easy quickly responds by informing Sarah when a white person hints to a black person about the white person's clout and influence, the white person is, in fact, threatening the black person, and the threat is tantamount to calling him a "nigger." Easy (in his ultimate moment of resistance) states to Sarah that such threats "might work wit' yo' people out there [in the fields]" (163), but they certainly do not frighten him.

The other example concerns Betty's rather surreptitious rebellion against Albert Cain's dominance. Though he professes an actual love for Betty, their relationship (such as it is) is still founded on the basis of their social inequality (he wields power over her). When Cain bestows upon Betty money and various gifts (believing that he is expressing his love and devotion), Betty exploits his efforts and converts the gifts into a sizable real estate portfolio for herself and Felix Landry. When the seemingly powerless circumvent obstacles in their enduring struggle for survival, their actions clearly articulate one of Easy's frequently repeated observations, that poor people must exploit the only luck they have–most often bad luck.

HISTORICAL CONTEXT

Both the literary and historical foundation for *Black Betty* is Harriet Jacobs's famous slave narrative, *Incidents in the Life of a Slave Girl* (1861). As is typical of this genre, the narrative charts the life of a former slave from her earliest memory up through escape. Jacobs's autobiographical account is particularly important because it renders a glimpse into the especial sexual and emotional traumas suffered by black women in slavery. That "peculiar institution," as slavery has been called, sanctioned the repeated physical violation of black women by their white owners, forcing them to submit lest they or other family members be further harmed. Quite often the slave woman found herself trapped between the vile overtures of an immoral owner (the master) and the jealous rage of his wife (the mistress). Because the white wife could not direct her frustrations toward her husband, she often abused the slave woman in retaliatory acts. More burdensome to the black woman was that her own husband or partner often blamed her for the forced sexual encounters (rapes). In short, she was doubly trapped. In the latter circumstance, she was compelled to negotiate a space between the owner's moral turpitude and her husband's (or the black community's) moral rectitude. If she submitted to the owner, she was perchance ridiculed by her community, yet if she tried to refuse the master, she possibly suffered untold abuse in addition to the rape.

Jacobs writes of these very issues in her narrative. Using the persona Linda Brent (in an effort to distance herself from the taboo sexual issues she would relate), Jacobs recounts for her reader the sufferings she endured while in the household of Dr. Flint. Though she is the victim in his repeated efforts to possess her physically, Flint's wife (upon learning of her husband's interest in the fifteen-year-old girl) blames Linda (Harriet) for enticing the predatory Flint. At the same time that Linda suffers constant verbal abuse from Mrs. Flint, she suffers the daily offense of Flint's vulgarities. Dr. Flint professes his love to Linda and promises her various gifts, including her own house, if she relents to his desires, forcing Linda to become even more adamant about protecting her virtue (from him) and agitating Mrs. Flint's mental instability. Finally, Linda, in a desperate attempt to save herself from Dr. Flint, knowingly begins a sexual liaison with another white man, Mr. Sands. Linda reasons that once Dr. Flint knows she is no longer chaste, he will curtail his advances. Her relationship with Sands produces two children, a girl and a boy. When her grandmother (who has served as her mentor after the death of her parents) learns of her first pregnancy, the old woman is angered and hurt, initially banning an apologetic Linda from her house. Later, however, the grandmother will reconcile with Linda, ultimately recognizing the fact that Linda was caught in an unfair circumstance.

Jacobs's story highlights the fact that black women have historically been objectified. While the southern white woman was put on a pedestal and defined by her sexual purity, the black woman was treated with contempt and defined by her sexual availability. The black woman was to have no sense of pride or nobility. When Jacobs writes, she directs her narrative to northern white women (those who might exhibit sympathy) in an effort to show them how their lives are markedly different from the life of a slave woman. While the white woman is considered noble and regal, the black woman is considered wanton and dishonorable. So since Linda, as a black woman, was to be defined anyway in unseemly terms, she decides to use her sexuality as a means of empowerment. And though she admits her logic may be faulty, she reminds the reader that the inherent immorality that grounds slavery results in a confusion of all moral principles; that is, whatever means she must undertake to survive in an innately evil world are to be judged fairly and ultimately excused.

Betty's story is similar to Linda Brent's (Harriet Jacobs's) in many ways. Like Linda, Betty is pursued by her employer. Upon Cain's initial advance toward her, Betty rebukes him and threatens to leave the house. Cain, much like Dr. Flint, accuses Betty of practically driving him mad with her beauty and sensuality. In short, according to Cain, Betty is to blame for his mental and sexual frustration. Deciding that he simply must have Betty, Cain threatens to have Marlon arrested (knowing that Marlon has recently been in trouble with authorities). Wanting to protect her only relative, Betty submits to Cain, and the result of her submission is the birth of twins Gwendolyn and Terry.

Though Betty always enjoyed working for Mrs. Cain (Cassandra), their relationship is strained as Cain and Betty continue their liaison. In this way, Cassandra assumes the role of the jealous plantation mistress. Because she cannot overrule her husband's authority and because she is unempowered economically, Cassandra has no recourse (in her opinion) but to hold Betty in contempt. Nevertheless, Betty remains devoted to her, the forced affair with Cain notwithstanding. Part of Betty's devotion involves her decision to stay in the Cain house even after Cassandra's death, which occurs only a few years after the birth of Betty's children. Even though Cain by this time has satisfied his lust for Betty (and no longer has an immediate use for her), Betty, who could have left with no serious repercussions, stays to comfort Sarah and her newborn (Arthur).

Like the black slave woman, Betty seems to be caught in a particular space or circumstance, and her survival depends on her wit and powers of negotiation. That Betty is caught between the same notions of rectitude and turpitude that trap Linda Brent is made painfully clear when Easy, in obvious victim-blaming mode, responds to Betty's recount of her past: "You didn't fight it?" (281). In simply posing this question Easy places the onus of responsibility on Betty's shoulders, as though she is to blame for being forced to engage in sexual relations with Cain. Just as Linda's grandmother holds Linda solely responsible for trying to fight against Flint's demands in the only way she knew how, Easy faults Betty for yielding to Cain. Yet Betty's retort to Easy's unfounded accusation silences the detective and reminds him of her precarious situation: "Fight him how? Hit him and then see Marlon put in jail? Kill him an' go to jail my own self?" (281). The only choice (i.e., chance at survival) Betty has is to engage in sexual acts with Cain. Easy will quickly come to understand Betty's predicament. Later, he will utter these words in another context, but they also apply to the Betty saga: "Truth and Freedom; two great things for a poor man, a son of slaves and ex-slaves" (296). To be sure, truth and freedom are important for the progeny of ex-slaves. The present generation, Easy's generation, must come to appreciate the sacrifices their ancestors made in the name of freedom, and a most significant component of such appreciation is accepting the painful truth of those sacrifices, including such truths relative to the sufferings of black women like Betty.

In addition to the historical past that influences *Black Betty*, it is important to assess the immediate historical moment of the novel—September 1961. President John F. Kennedy has been in office for eight months, and the Civil Rights movement is, in large measure, at its peak (the University of Georgia is integrated in September with the admission of Charlayne Hunter and Hamilton Holmes; the University of Mississippi will follow suit in 1962 when James Meredith gains admission). Americans, particularly black Americans, are hopeful about the future, in large part because of the apparent goodwill and progressive inclination of the Kennedy administration. Nevertheless, the period is also fraught with international tensions between the United States and the Soviet Union. Throughout the novel, Easy notes the daily fear that nuclear warfare will erupt between the two superpowers. This fall 1961 setting is positioned between two significant events: the Bay of Pigs invasion of April 17, 1961, and the Cuban missile crisis of October 1962. The former involved the unsuccessful invasion of Cuba by U.S.-supported Cuban exiles. These 1,500 people had been trained in Guatemala by the Central Intelligence Agency (CIA) and supplied with U.S. arms; their intention was to overthrow the Communist regime of Fidel Castro. When most of the would-be soldiers were either captured or killed, the U.S. government was highly criticized both domestically and internationally. Tensions between the United States and the Soviet Union also intensified, and one of the results was the Cuban missile crisis. Following the Bay of Pigs incident, the Soviet Union began constructing missile-launching sites in Cuba. Learning of this defensive posture, President Kennedy demanded on October 22, 1962, that the Soviets withdraw the missiles and imposed a naval blockade on Cuba. Six days later the Soviets finally agreed, and the crisis ended.

Tense Soviet-U.S. relations provide the ideal backdrop for this novel. Just as Easy is haunted by the possibility of international warfare, he is also haunted by the increasing possibility that Mouse will erupt and go on a shooting rampage to exact revenge. And just as these international tensions are presented subtly, Mouse's story (the murder of Bruno and its repercussions) serves as a passing but ever-present concern for Easy. The novel's preface is an italicized and abbreviated sketch of Bruno Ingram's murder, about which Easy is dreaming. Then, at the very beginning of chapter 1, Easy, upon awakening from the dream, tries to conjure up happier thoughts. But he quickly remembers that the world is being "rocked almost daily by underground nuclear explosions and the threat of war" (4). The juxtaposition of these two circumstances underscores how the international tensions reinforce the anxiety caused by Mouse's unpredictability.

NARRATIVE STRUCTURE

The dominant plot concern is, of course, Easy's locating Elizabeth (Betty) Eady. This focus also involves an analysis of the past-I versus present-I point of view. The adult Easy, the forty-one-year-old Easy (present-I), finds himself just as enamored of Betty as he was as a young boy back in Houston (past-I). Throughout the novel, Easy, in flashback, recounts for the reader a few past episodes with Betty. Such recollections not only provide a more comprehensive portrait of Easy but also highlight Betty's seductive control over most of the men with whom she comes in contact. Even when Easy becomes frustrated with the investigation and even after his life is threatened, some internal feeling (a sense of loyalty to Betty) compels him to fulfill his original intent to find her. Perhaps Easy's dedication to Betty is the result of her treating him like a young man, with respect and compassion, even though he was just a boy. In addition, Betty revealed to him her vulnerabilities and her pain even then. At the same time, therefore, that Easy idolizes Betty, he also witnesses her very human nature. The intermittent flashbacks provide a deeper assessment of Betty and Easy's emotional interaction.

Several other mini-plots undergird the main narrative, and they serve to sustain the reader's interest throughout the novel. The more dominant of these subplots concerns the whereabouts of Marlon Eady. After Easy searches for him in the desert, Easy suspects that Marlon is already dead. And though the reader, given a few clues, is encouraged to agree, he or she must still wait until Marlon's actual death is confirmed.

Another mini-plot involves Jesus. Early in the novel Easy learns that Jesus can actually speak. Shocked and pleased, Easy now begins to wonder first, why Jesus does not trust him enough to reveal his secret, and second, when he will unveil his ability to Easy. The reader also wonders when Jesus will finally speak to Easy. At one point, Easy even asks five-year-old Feather why Jesus will not speak to him, and the child says very simply that Jesus cannot do so just yet. In every ensuing scene that includes both Jesus and Easy, the reader wonders if this will be the moment when the boy speaks.

Yet another mini-plot concerns Mouse's pursuit of the traitor who alerted the police about Mouse's killing Bruno Ingram. After his release from jail, Mouse becomes obsessed with identifying the culprit. For the greater portion of the novel, the reader wonders whether Easy will prevent Mouse from killing another person, and whether the person's identity will be revealed.

A significant mini-plot focuses on Mofass and his financial and domestic problems, which also affect Easy's financial straits at least temporarily. When Easy has Mofass enlist the aid of Calvin Hodge to thwart Clovis's efforts to pilfer all of Mofass's assets, the reader is left to wonder if Hodge and Mofass will be successful. The question also remains as to whether Easy will exact revenge on Clovis and Mason LaMone, the white real estate agent who is involved in preventing him from developing prime land that he owns. By the novel's end all questions are answered, but in the meantime, the mysteries compel the reader to remain engaged with the novel.

A very minor mini-plot highlights Easy's relationships with both Martin and Odell. Near the beginning of the novel, Easy mentions that he really needs to visit the dying Martin, but because he does not relish the possibility of meeting up with Odell (from whom he has been estranged for several years), he has resisted making the visit. The reader is left, then, wondering if Easy will visit with Martin. However, Easy's fear of seeing Odell is soon made moot when Easy decides he must pay a visit to Odell. Ironically, only after Easy goes directly to Martin's house, where Odell is visiting, is Odell forced to communicate directly with Easy. While Easy searches for Betty, these other plot elements pique the reader's interest and help to sustain a sufficient level of suspense.

A FEMINIST READING

Feminist criticism has emerged out of a need to identify, expose, and then dismantle (or deconstruct) the various ways in which women are excluded, exploited, suppressed, and oppressed. Feminist critics examine images of women in literature created by both women and men in an effort to challenge the representations of women as "other," as less than or inferior to men. The critics, who themselves can be women or men, question literature's perpetuation of stereotypes about women. They ponder, for example, whether women and men are essentially different biologically or if they are socially constructed as different. For instance, the feminist critic, whose very political and social critique considers all fixed definitions of identity as tools of a dominant patriarchal structure, would be quick to point out that, even as society tries to define a man as strong, aggressive, and focused and a woman as passive, compassionate, and sensitive, examples abound that undermine this assessment: sensitive men and self-assured, demanding women. Feminist criticism asks, then, "What is a woman?" or "What is feminine?" and more importantly, "Who is crafting these definitions, and what is their sociopolitical purpose for doing so?"

Some feminist criticism may examine language and its collusion in the attempted dehumanization of women. Or it may assess the role of social institutions in the continued breach of individual women's rights. Feminist criticism may also investigate the function of race, class, and general social standing in one's exploited circumstance. In short, the feminist critic examines power relations in texts in order to expose such relations in life with the intent of razing patriarchal structures of inequality. For the feminist, reading (and critiquing) is always a political act.

Among the various issues presented in *Black Betty*, none is addressed more poignantly than the historical treatment of black and white women in regard to sexuality. Historians and literary critics alike have articulated how the oppression of both black women and white women has resulted in emotional tensions between the two groups, when in fact their circumstances are created by white patriarchy. John W. Blassingame, Minrose C. Gwin, and Katherine Fishburn, among others, have noted how the slave institution demanded certain codes of conduct from women: white women were expected to be virtuous (and were thus denied sexual identity) while black women were considered, by nature, to be hypersexual and available. Treating the white woman and the black woman differently yet expecting them to share the same domestic space, as noted earlier, created volatile psychological circumstances. Yet it was the black woman, the slave woman, who suffered especial trauma when she became the object of derision not only for the slave owner but also (and intensely so) for the mistress. The patriarchal institution encourages the black woman and the white woman to militate against each other rather than direct their frustrations at patriarchy. However, feminist criticism analyzes exactly how and why women must reassess their oppressive situation, exploring the same concern that a sociopolitical critique articulates on class issues: instead of pitting themselves against each other, the lower economic classes should direct their frustration at the cause of the problem— the ultra-affluent who control all resources. Likewise, feminist criticism stipulates that black women and white women should band together and rebuke their mutual oppressor, white patriarchy.

Black Betty explores these concerns comprehensively. Patriarch and tyrant Albert Cain not only forces Betty to engage in sexual acts but also abuses his wife, Cassandra. Refusing, however, to accept any responsibility for his actions, Cain declares that Betty's sensuality has practically driven him to madness. Then, physically attacking Cassandra and leaving her bruised and toothless, Cain venomously insists that since she is ugly inside, she might as well be ugly outside. As though he has performed some kind of corrective measure (by matching her physical condition to what he declares is her essence), he once again blames the victim for his actions. Cassandra's unfortunate response to his cruelty, however, is to hate an equally powerless Betty. Understanding more fully the evil of patriarchy (clarity resulting, in part, from her double minority status), Betty, rebuffing patriarchy, maintains compassion for Cassandra and remains loyal to her, the forced actions of Cain notwithstanding.

As a means of highlighting the precarious situation of women and of presenting how they are made the villains in their own victimization, Mosley encourages the reader to think, for the greater length of the novel, that Betty has murdered Cain. Because she is a black woman (given the various stereotypes of blacks and women), Betty is the likely candidate for this violent act. And with a male narrator (Easy), albeit a black one, patriarchal rule is strengthened. Of course, Mosley's ultimate goal is to undermine and expose the very patriarchy he has erected. When Betty finally reveals to Easy all that she endured those many years in the Cain household, blame quickly shifts to the rightful perpetrator, white patriarchy.

Still another way in which Mosley militates against the rigidity of patriarchy is to promote the concept of "mothering" as one of the few redeeming qualities in the novel. In so doing, Mosley celebrates a feminine sensitivity that is otherwise dismissed as weakness when positioned in the matriarchal-patriarchal paradigm. Several instances of character growth are presented in these "mothering" moments. After he is stabbed by Betty, Easy is comforted by Jesus, whose "gentle stroke" across Easy's face helps Easy to regain his composure. This gesture also indicates to Easy that his son is maturing by developing strength and compassion. In another instance Odell cares for the injured Easy and rubs salve on his wound. As the two men have been estranged for some time, this moment of tenderness and concern marks a crucial step forward in their friendship, a progressive move made possible only with a "feminine" response. Then, near the end of the novel, in a reversal of gender roles, Easy soothes Betty, who has just revealed to him her past with the Cain family. He embraces her with a "mother's stroke." Easy's mother role here not only highlights the importance of feminine sensitivity, but also rescues Betty from her villain status when Easy, as a man and as one who formerly doubted Betty's innocence, shows that he understands fully her plight.

A feminist reading helps to explore more fully the title of the novel. As this title indicates, with its focus on color and on a woman's name, both race and gender are important. As a black woman, Betty is burdened with particular traumas. Yet she understands that as a woman she is especially vulnerable in a patriarchal world. Much of her motivation results from her efforts to help the other women in her life (her concern for both Marlon and Terry a given): first, Cassandra Cain; then, Sarah and Gwendolyn. It is important to note that Betty is well aware that with regard to white patriarchy, gender *and* race function in tandem as oppositional forces. The feminist critique best articulates this truth.

5

RL's Dream
(1995)

Mosley's fifth novel introduces not only new characters and issues, but also a different setting. Unlike the Easy Rawlins mysteries that are set in Los Angeles during a period prior to the contemporary moment, *RL's Dream* is set in Manhattan in the latter 1980s. It charts the relationship of an aging and rapidly deteriorating former blues musician and his unlikely companion. Differing in race, gender, age, and general worldview, the two find commonality in their desire, their very need, for human contact. Suffering the ravages of an often indifferent environment, both Soupspoon Wise and Kiki Waters discover that one's life can change for better or for worse with the simplest of gestures from another human being. With this novel, Mosley explores how individuals can form bonds and cultivate interdependent friendships across the social chasms of hatred and distrust.

PLOT DEVELOPMENT

Aging musician Atwater "Soupspoon" Wise has escaped a local men's shelter and is determined to return to his former apartment. Though plagued by intense pain in his hip, Soupspoon reaches his destination, but not before soiling himself and suffering the stares of passersby. Soon after arriving home, the old man collapses on the floor.

In the following chapter Kiki Waters rides the subway home while observing the antics of various passengers and recalling some of the events from her life back in Arkansas. Having been stabbed in her side by young street punks a few days earlier, Kiki is returning to her apartment after spending some time in the hospital following surgery. Upon leaving the subway Kiki pays a visit to her on-again, off-again boyfriend, Randy, a street vendor and college student. Learning just now of Kiki's recent tragedy, Randy insists on escorting Kiki home. When the two approach the Beldin Arms apartment building, Kiki is alarmed at what she witnesses: her neighbor Soupspoon, with whom she has had only a passing acquaintance, huddled on the sidewalk while two moving men proceed to cast his belongings outside with him. Rushing to Soupspoon's aid, Kiki causes such a stir that a passing police car is alerted to the disturbance.

The moving men, Nate and Tony, inform the officers that they have been instructed by the landlord, Mr. Grumbacher, to remove Soupspoon from the premises because he owes several months' rent. They also allege that someone from social services will be along to retrieve the former blues musician. Kiki, however, berates the two for tossing Soupspoon outside in the cold weather so late in the day. Then, lying to the moving men and to the police, Kiki insists that Soupspoon (whom she calls Luther because she does not know his actual name) is her godfather from Arkansas and that she will take him in. The police, eager to resolve this matter, instruct Tony and Nate to move Soupspoon's belongings to Kiki's apartment. Thus begins the unlikely friendship between an almost seventy-year-old black man and a thirty-something, somewhat volatile white woman.

Severely weakened by pain in his hip and an unrelenting ache in his throat that has left him almost voiceless, Soupspoon cannot resist; instead he decides to let Kiki determine his fate. Taking the old man into her very small apartment, she cleans and feeds him, while telling him that he has nothing to fear any longer. Her recent brush with death has left Kiki with a renewed courage that she now wishes to instill in Soupspoon.

Returning to her job at an insurance company a couple of days after rescuing Soupspoon (never contacting her boss, she has been away for over a week), Kiki learns that she has been replaced. However, the firebrand redhead shames her boss, Sheldon Meyers, so mercilessly that he is forced to reinstate her. Though she needs her job for her own maintenance, Kiki also needs this gig to assist Soupspoon with his medical care. On her first day back on the job, Kiki wastes no time cozying up to the workers in computer operations, especially Fez, the oafish head of the division. After providing the computer workers with alcohol for their unauthorized departmental bar, Kiki then convinces Fez to let her enter into the computer database a new policy that she says she neglected to process earlier, insisting that her job will be in jeopardy if she is not allowed to correct this error. Kiki then writes up a policy for Soupspoon and his "wife," Tanya. From this moment on, whenever Kiki accompanies Soupspoon to his various medical appointments, she poses as Tanya.

After he has endured a battery of tests, Soupspoon discovers that he has cancer, both in his pelvis and in his lungs. Following the advice of his doctor, the old musician undergoes radiation treatment. Kiki informs Sheldon that she is required to attend follow-up appointments with her own doctor and uses the time to accompany Soupspoon whenever possible. In the ensuing days the two begin to depend on each other: the old man requires assistance when he feels debilitated, and Kiki simply comes to rely on Soupspoon's presence. As he nears the end of his treatment, however, Soupspoon begins to feel restless. He yearns as well for his former independence and sense of manhood (he does not wish to take advantage of a woman). Deciding that he must secure a job, Soupspoon seeks the aid of longtime friend Rudy Peckell. Proprietor of a rather run-down establishment that caters mainly to roughnecks and gamblers, Rudy (somewhat beholden to Soupspoon because of previous favors the old man did for him) is reluctant to hire the old man to play in his bar. He does finally agree to give Soupspoon a chance after the bluesman completes all of his treatments.

In the meantime, at Soupspoon's request, Kiki purchases a tape recorder so that the longtime bluesman can preserve his many anecdotes about his life as a traveling musician. Kiki even serves as a kind of sounding board for these effusions. From these stories, both Kiki and the reader get a real sense of Soupspoon's colorful life. As Kiki and Soupspoon solidify their friendship, Randy feels abandoned and consequently jealous of Soupspoon. However, when he witnesses Soupspoon's struggles with his cancer treatments, the young man warms to the old musician and begins to listen eagerly to his various musings.

Now feeling a sense of camaraderie with Soupspoon, Randy offers the bluesman an opportunity to showcase his talent. During an upcoming street bazaar Randy plans to peddle his T-shirts, and he invites Soupspoon to come along and entertain the crowd with his guitar. Eager to prove that he can still play (especially since he wants Rudy to hire him to play in his bar), Soupspoon accepts the offer. Immersing himself in his music again also gives Soupspoon a heightened and renewed sensitivity about his past life, a connection even more important now that he has chosen to record this history. When he visits a former friend and fellow musician in the hope of gaining some relevant information from him, Soupspoon finds that Alfred Metsgar has become a senile recluse. Upon leaving Alfred, Soupspoon feels an even greater urgency to complete his story.

As a consequence of this desire, Soupspoon decides to visit his former wife, Mavis. Though they have been apart for over twenty years (and Soupspoon has only recently learned of her return to the city), Soupspoon knows that his "history" project will benefit from her recollections and her perspective. Honoring his request, Mavis shares her point of view on their former life in the South and on the ensuing migration north.

While Soupspoon works to preserve the history of the blues, Kiki is presented with her own problems to solve. When Sheldon questions her about the falsified insurance policy, she feigns ignorance. Though Kiki feels a bit unsettled initially, she ultimately regains her composure and decides that she will survive the situation no matter what. Learning later that someone in computer operations has been blamed, Kiki is concerned that Fez will realize that she is the culprit. Her fear is realized when, at three o'clock in the morning, she receives a harassing call from the oaf, who has been fired. From that moment on, Kiki carries a gun with her everywhere. A few days later Kiki's job is terminated, and she is escorted from the premises. Kiki leaves, but with no regrets for what she has done.

Soupspoon is finally granted an opportunity to showcase his talent when he accompanies Randy to the bazaar. Though Randy sells fewer T-shirts than usual, Soupspoon is quite popular, amassing several dollars in the bowl that Randy provides for him. In addition to Kiki, many people come by to hear him play. In attendance are Rudy; Billy Slick (one of Rudy's employees/henchmen); and Rudy's barkeep, Sono, along with her two children and the teenager Chevette, whom Sono has taken in. Later, Sono's boyfriend, Gerald "Gerry" Pickford, joins the group. Eighteen-year-old Chevette is fascinated with Soupspoon, and when the group (except for Randy and an extremely intoxicated Kiki) decides to go out later to celebrate by treating the children to ice cream, Chevette becomes even more enamored of the old man. By the end of the night Chevette and Soupspoon make love and agree to spend some time together.

On the following day Soupspoon learns from Billy Slick, who has become interested in Kiki, that Rudy has decided to hire the old musician. Now preparing for his first official performance in quite some time, Soupspoon spends less time in the apartment with Kiki. An emotional wreck by now, Kiki spends the greater portion of her time drinking heavily and cultivating a new relationship with Billy, much to Randy's consternation. On the night of Soupspoon's debut, Kiki, completely out of control and forced to leave the club, is escorted home by both Randy and Billy.

Upon arriving at her apartment, the three are attacked suddenly by the vengeful Fez, who stabs Randy, strikes Billy, and attempts to stab Kiki. Kiki, however, manages to shoot him several times before she finally kills him. At that very crucial moment, Kiki rifles through his belongings, and after securing a stack of money, she flees. After spending three years in New Orleans, Kiki returns to her hometown in Arkansas, where she inherits the family photography business and other properties. She will later marry her childhood friend, give him four children, and live as normal a life as possible. Randy survives his wounds, and though Billy (William Hurdy) is initially held as a suspect in Fez's death, he is later released.

On the same night that Kiki departs, Soupspoon is left at Rudy's bar to finish his performance. On his way home, he collapses in the street, where he remains sprawled until the early morning when the police find him. Hospitalized, Soupspoon has suffered an apparent heart attack. In and out of consciousness, Soupspoon soon dies, as alone as he was when Kiki rescued him outside Beldin Arms. A few days earlier, however, Soupspoon had managed to give Gerry, a doctoral student in history, his tape recordings, along with precise instructions to transcribe the material and shepherd the project to publication.

CHARACTER DEVELOPMENT

The novel focuses primarily on Soupspoon and Kiki, who serve as the dual protagonists. Each of them is directly affected by earlier phases of life, especially childhood. That the novel opens with Soupspoon being cast from his apartment is significant, given that his boyhood in Mississippi is defined by his orphan status. At age five, upon the death of his parents and his brother as a result of a flu epidemic, Soupspoon (known then as Atty, for Atwater) is rescued by the only family he will ever really know, the lesbian couple Ruby and Inez. And though the two women make every effort to welcome him, Atty still yearns to find his own niche and to gain independence. His becoming a traveling musician is a testament to this yearning. Enamored of blues music ever since he first heard it at age eleven, a young Atty steals away at night after Ruby and Inez are asleep and makes his way to a local juke joint (a shabby nightclub). Skulking about outside, Atty listens to the musicians and the singers, becoming almost mesmerized by their rhythms and improvisational prowess. On occasion, a friendly adult ushers him in and even allows him to drink. From such experiences, Atty feels truly welcome in the smoky, almost surreal world of blues music. His big break comes one night when he is caught peering through a hole in the wall of the Milky Way, a local night-spot, and watching the performance of "Big Mouth" Willa Smith. After she spies him, Willa brings Atty inside and up on stage with her, fully appreciating that Atty is a true music lover. Because he cannot play an instrument, she teaches him how to play the spoons against his body and thus make music. Paying him ten percent of her earnings, Willa encourages Atty (now called Soupspoon) to hone his talent and learn the guitar. From his experience with Willa, Soupspoon is hooked on the music and on performance, and his "mothers" have given up on trying to keep him at home. Realizing that he can actually earn a living from his talent, Soupspoon considers himself, and prides himself on being, a free and independent man. Even in the present day, when he finds himself depending on Kiki's generosity, he is uneasy until he can at least try to earn a living (this time at Rudy's bar) and maintain himself.

As with Soupspoon, the initial presentation of Kiki is reflective of her childhood demons. Her recent attack by young ruffians is a recurrence of the almost daily violations she suffered as a young girl at the hands of her father, Keith Waters, back in Hogston, Arkansas. While Soupspoon was orphaned as a result of his family's demise, Kiki was "orphaned" as a result of betrayal and abandonment. When her father repeatedly raped her, Kiki's mother denied the abuse, though she heard the child's muted screams and appeals. From this experience, Kiki learns that she must always fend for herself and anyone else who seems powerless. Such an obligation is made evident when she rushes to Soupspoon's rescue at the beginning of the novel, though she has had only passing contact with him before. And even though she is a southern white woman whose upbringing would suggest that she stay clear of black men, Kiki knows that she has a human duty to protect anyone in need. In addition, she knows that the only people she needs to fear are those like her father. Kiki's friend-liness toward Soupspoon results also from her previous experience with black people. When, at age fourteen, a sick and recently raped Kiki finally flees her parents' house, she finds sanctuary with Hattie, a black woman who lives nearby. Hattie, along with her friend Hector, soothe the girl and nurse her back to health. Then, providing the girl with sufficient funds, Hattie sends Kiki to California. Kiki's very survival has resulted, then, from the sacrifice of practical strangers, each of whom risked the wrath of a powerful and influential Keith Waters to ensure Kiki's safety. The assistance Kiki offers Soupspoon is her way of honoring both Hattie and Hector. Even though Kiki has long closed that painful chapter of her life, she is still haunted by the memories. As a consequence, she drinks heavily and often hurls invectives at those closest to her. To some extent she has internalized the physical and emotional pain directed at her in the past.

Kiki's boyfriend, Randall "Randy" Chesterton, suffers from an identity crisis, also effected during his childhood. Randy's mother, Esther, told him that his father (who supposedly died before Randy was born) was a blue-eyed Arab of royal blood and that she was of South American lineage. Though Randy has decidedly black features, Esther always insisted that he was simply an exotic Caucasian. And she attributed her own tanned complexion to the influence of her Mayan ancestry. While Randy, now in his mid-twenties, remembers a visit at age fourteen from a black couple insisting that they were his father Jamal's cousins and that Jamal was alive and well in Atlanta, he has chosen denial. Randy would rather think of himself as exotic and special. His unwillingness to accept his true ethnicity perturbs Kiki. Because she knows that whiteness holds no special virtue (especially given the behavior of her father), she would rather Randy divest himself of such a myth and embrace his culture. Until Randy accepts the reality of his existence in America (and rejects the illusion in his own mind), according to Kiki, he will not fully thrive. Urging him to relent, Kiki states, "Don't you see how stupid this is, Randy? How somebody white has to tell you what you are?" (250).

Mavis Spivey, Soupspoon's ex-wife, figures prominently in the novel as well. Alerted by Rudy that her ex-husband has cancer, Mavis agrees to see Soupspoon again. Living in a one-room apartment and surviving by designing arrangements out of dried flowers, Mavis has created a pristine domestic space. All of her furnishings, her various decorations, are white or beige. Because she thinks the greater portion of her life has been dirty, Mavis now wants to be as clean as possible and to live with few intrusions. Before Mavis married Soupspoon, she lived with a man named Raphael in a common-law marriage and produced son, Cort. However, the boy perished in a storm drain during a flood back in Texas (where she would also later meet and ultimately marry Soupspoon). Mavis, forever haunted by the memory of Cort, believes that his death has served as her punishment for her unsavory life. Now that she has "cleansed" herself of that past (evident in her white surroundings), including her life with Soupspoon, Mavis would rather leave the past buried with her son.

The RL mentioned in the title is Robert Johnson (see *Historical Context*). On the literal level of the novel, RL serves as Soupspoon's mentor. Meeting him soon after he leaves home at fourteen, Soupspoon is practically mesmerized by RL's talent. Described as a skinny boy with one good eye and one dead eye and also as Satan's son, RL can play blues music like no

other, with a passion and uniqueness that drives listeners wild. As Soupspoon recalls, "I was moved by his wild voice and the way he th'owed
his head back like somethin' in 'im might break if he didn't holler it off
with a song" (131). When the two meet in Arcola, Mississippi, they join
forces and play their music on the street or in whatever shoddy nightclub
they can find. Because Soupspoon and RL are lazy, yet talented, they opt
to entertain the working people when they come in from the cotton fields.
RL also teaches Soupspoon how to survive. On one occasion when the
two are entertaining a crowd, the county sheriff, Heck Wrightson, approaches and demands that the group disband immediately. He then ar-
rests RL and Soupspoon. While incarcerated RL seems to enter into a
trance, swaying his body back and forth and screaming, "Oh, momma."
Oblivious to any of the sheriff's admonitions (even his physical attacks),
RL maintains this bizarre behavior until the frustrated sheriff releases
them.

Several weeks after that night, RL and Soupspoon play so vigorously
at the Panther Burn nightclub, causing the customers to dance so feverishly, that the place burns down. Mavis is one of those wild dancers
(though she and Soupspoon will not meet until much later) who must flee
when the club is left in nothing but smoldering embers. In all the confusion, Soupspoon loses RL. Weeks later, he learns that RL is dead. Ironically,
on that same night, as Soupspoon will learn years later, RL meets Mavis.
RL and Mavis enjoy a one-night affair and then part ways. Ultimately,
when Soupspoon meets Mavis, somewhere in Texas, and discovers that
she has been with RL, he finds that he desires her as well. And because
she is trying to recover from the death of her son, she agrees to marry
Soupspoon. RL, however, is the strange link that binds them.

On a more figurative level, RL seems to serve as Soupspoon's doppel-
ganger (an apparition that generally represents another aspect of a character's personality; it is a demonic counterpart, often anticipating death).
In the inscription that Mosley creates for RL's Dream, ostensibly from
Soupspoon's transcribed text, Soupspoon declares, "RL wasn't no real
man. . . . 'Cause Robert Johnson wasn't never born an' couldn't die." As
stated previously, RL represents the uninhibited personality, or alter ego,
that Soupspoon would like to unleash. The musical passion that RL showcases, as well as the sexual prowess that Soupspoon imagines RL has,
impels Soupspoon to emulate this otherwise lost little boy (in this way,
very similar to the younger Soupspoon). RL becomes the catalyst that
affects the rest of Soupspoon's life. After spending the one night with RL,

Mavis leaves for LaMarque, Texas, once she learns that three people have perished in the fire. Though she does not single-handedly cause the fire, she does not want to risk blame. In LaMarque, she loses her son in the flood (RL, as dopppelganger, presages death) and forever blames herself for taking Cort there. In some way, RL's (and Soupspoon's) music creates the atmosphere that causes the fire that forces Mavis to leave. Her leaving leads to her son's death, and her deep bereavement compels her later to accept Soupspoon's offer of marriage. It is also Soupspoon's determined attempt to be like RL that eventually contributes to the destruction of this marriage. As Mavis explains to Kiki, "That's why I had to leave Atwater. That's why he had to go. . . . Atwater married me, but it wasn't 'cause'a me. Even when he was lovin' me it was really Robert Johnson he was lovin'" (239).

Several minor characters flesh out the narrative. Rudy Peckell, owner of the bar where Soupspoon tries to reestablish himself, has not always been the hardened businessman he purports to be. Years earlier, when Rudy is six, Mavis and Soupspoon (after they are married and living in Harlem) spy him breaking bottles in the street. They discipline him and then take him home, where they discover unacceptable conditions. Rudy's mother, Jessie, is in bed with her most recent paramour while his siblings are left to their own devices. After condemning the mother for her negligence, Mavis later welcomes Rudy into their home from time to time for a hot meal and a good night's sleep. In this way, Mavis and Soupspoon become Rudy's surrogate parents.

In addition to RL, two other men influence Soupspoon during his youth—Bannon Tripps (for whom he would later name his guitar) and Uncle Fitzhew. Soupspoon meets Bannon, a sixty-year-old man, when he is ten. Bannon, described as a thief and a history teacher, serves as a surrogate father for Soupspoon. Giving the boy an Afrocentric worldview, Bannon teaches Soupspoon that Egypt was the cradle of modern civilization and that Europe simply stole all knowledge from Africa and then claimed it as a European creation. Because of this original theft (and many ensuing "robberies"), Bannon refuses to work in the white man's capitalist society. He argues that it is his duty to steal back from whites. According to Bannon, to work in the white man's world serves only to make the white man rich. Taking on Soupspoon as a kind of protégé, Bannon and the boy begin to steal from whites in the community. Though Soupspoon is still living with Ruby and Inez, he spends practically every waking hour with Bannon. On one occasion, when Soupspoon is to meet Bannon at his shack, he finds that the old man has been burned to death. Though Soupspoon will try to forget that horrid scene, he will always recall the wisdom imparted by the unique Bannon. Uncle Fitzhew, who is not a blood relative, gives Soupspoon his first guitar, and he visits Ruby and Inez on occasion and shares whatever folk wisdom he can with Soupspoon. Like Bannon, he is trying to instill in the boy racial pride and manly strength.

Though they appear only in flashback (as do all of the characters from Soupspoon's past), Ruby and Inez are significant in the musician's life. In much the same way that Soupspoon and Mavis would later care for Rudy, the lesbian couple (Ruby assuming the more sensitive role and Inez the role of disciplinarian) devote all of their energies to providing for and protecting the young Atty. And when they realize that he can no longer be kept from the transient life he wishes to lead, they relent, appreciating that they have fulfilled their responsibilities to him and must now allow him to lead his own life.

Kiki's boss, Sheldon Meyers, is presented as a weak-willed person. Though he is the superior, Kiki treats him more like an underling. The power shift occurred a few years earlier when Sheldon, who had flirted with Kiki daily, marries a Jewish woman instead, succumbing to family expectations. Kiki, who used to come to work early and buy Sheldon his favorite coffee, ceases doing both. And because Sheldon is too ashamed to tell Kiki himself about his marriage, he can never confront her about her tardiness. Until the day she is fired because of the insurance fraud, Kiki controls Sheldon mercilessly. While Kiki dominates Sheldon, she tries to avoid Fez whenever she can. Head of computer operations for the entire firm, Fez raped Kiki's best friend, Abigail "Abby" Greenspan, at the last holiday party. Because Kiki always sensed a crazed streak in Fez, she convinces her friend simply to leave town and start life anew. All of Fez's nonwhite coworkers disdain and distrust him. That Kiki would even seek his help is a testament to her desire (compulsion, even) to help Soupspoon. When Kiki is forced to kill him at the end of the novel, she is avenging the offense against Abby and the offense(s) she suffered at the hands of her Fez-like father during her childhood.

Hector and Hattie, Kiki's childhood saviors, are defiant in their efforts. When Kiki flees to Hattie's house, the old woman insists that Hector care for the traumatized girl. Though he is fearful because of his awareness of society's (in this case, Keith Waters's) potential reaction to a black man interacting in any way with a white female, Hattie, Kiki's former nursemaid, shames him by asking, "You more worried about some goddamn white man than you scared'a God?" (183). Hattie, and ultimately Hector, realizes that they have a greater responsibility to humanity (God) than they do to some arbitrary social order. When Kiki is finally well enough to leave the couple, Hattie gives to the girl the very handgun that she will use to kill Fez.

THEMATIC ISSUES

As the life of Soupspoon Wise provides the main focus for the text, the dominant theme is the impact of the blues not only on Soupspoon himself, but also on other major and minor characters. When assessing the blues tradition, particularly as it is applied in *RL's Dream*, one must distinguish between the actual condition and the music. The oppressive circumstances (social, economic, political, racial, etc.) define the blues condition. It entails the daily drudgery of existing and fighting against seemingly unassailable odds. Death and despair (with the ensuing raw and naked pain) become a way of life. As the narrator states frequently throughout the novel, "People died in the Delta; they died all the time" (74). In fact, "Young people died from hard blows, disease, and from taking their own lives. If you cried for every one of them you would have died from grief" (91). This is the kind of life that Soupspoon witnesses as he travels throughout the South, especially in Mississippi, Louisiana, and Texas. The most troubling aspect of these circumstances is the sometimes arbitrary, and always senseless, nature of all the pain and anguish. While some people seem to suffer for no reason, others suffer simply as a result of the whims of the oppressors. In one instance, Soupspoon recalls the indefensible death of his friend Jolly Horner. Known for his unmatched strength, Jolly is forced to carry a pig to the upper loft of a barn, simply to entertain a group of white men. Upon reaching the top, Jolly falls through the unstable floor into the mare's stall, whereupon the frightened horse rears back and crushes Jolly's face. This kind of tragedy, occurring day in and day out throughout the South, is the blues itself, and it causes blues feelings in those who witness the horror.

While the blues condition is clearly one of toil and frustration, the blues music, though reflective of this despair, is a vehicle for confronting, enduring, and surviving the pain. As Soupspoon attempts to explain to Kiki, "We were the lowest kinda godless riffraff. Migrants and roustabouts, we was bad from the day we was born. Blues is the devil's music an' we his chirren. RL was Satan's favorite son. He made us all abandoned, and you know that was the only way we could bear the weight of those days" (140). RL, with his wild blues music, offers an opportunity for the downtrodden to release their pain. Though described as Satan's son, he is also compared to a Baptist preacher who somehow inspires his followers. The blues tradition entails, then, not just toil and suffering but also inspiration, creation, and triumph. The title of the novel underscores this fact. The only "dream" that RL has occurs when he and Soupspoon are temporarily incarcerated. RL falls into a trance and disturbs their jailers so much that the two are ultimately released. About the incident, Soupspoon states, "I don't even think it was real for him. It was more like we had passed through a dream and now we was back to where we was" (138). RL's dream, then, offers an opportunity for survival. This bluesman, while re-creating in his music the blues experience of the forlorn throughout the South, also creates the music (and in the case of the trance, a different circumstance) that defies the oppressive condition.

Another significant theme, also linked to survival, is validation of self. After Soupspoon regains his health, he decides to record his life story, along with some of his music, for posterity's sake. Now that he has gained some distance from many of the painful experiences in his past, the blues-man is prepared to confront the memories. When he asks Kiki to secure him a tape recorder, Soupspoon assumes control of his own story. While many people, including ex-wife Mavis, have considered the lives of blues musicians a waste and often a disgrace, Soupspoon will offer an insider's perspective. When Kiki responds by suggesting that he simply contact the man who had wanted to interview him twenty years earlier, Soupspoon insists that he wants to tell the story his way, without unnecessary ques-tions and interruptions from an intrusive interviewer: "I don't wanna call'im, goddammit! I wanna tell it an' play it right here. I wanna tell it my own way wit'out all kindsa questions an' shit. I just wan' it, wan' it the way I wan' it" (100). Soupspoon also states that he wants the same freedom that Bannon enjoyed to relate his stories. Just as Bannon shared his views from an Afrocentric perspective, Soupspoon demands the op-portunity to tell the story of a black bluesman from a black bluesman's perspective. In this way, Soupspoon validates not only himself, but also the oral tradition (he will, of course, speak into the tape recorder) and the improvisational spirit of blues music.

The interconnectedness of human experience is still another significant theme. That Kiki and Soupspoon have endured past traumas that, in many ways, have brought them together is a testament to such linkage. The molestation and the attacks she survives not only strengthen her resolve to live and inspire her to rescue Soupspoon, but also compel her to seek compassion in a male figure, lest she think ultimately that all males are violent and abusive like her father. Other character links are made in the novel as well. When Kiki begins to care for the sick Soupspoon, she is reminded of her sick aunt, Katherine Loll, who lived with Kiki's family as she slowly perished from throat cancer. Kiki reminds Soupspoon of Ruby and Inez. Just as the couple rescued him from homelessness—or worse, an orphanage—Kiki prevents Soupspoon from being cast away in a men's shelter or simply left on the street. In addition, Kiki reminds Soupspoon of RL. Soon after Kiki welcomes the musician into her home, Soupspoon thinks how strange life can be—when a virtual stranger (Kiki) suddenly becomes closer than a family member. He recalls having the same feeling years before when he met RL. In terms of saviors, then, Ruby and Inez are linked to Kiki, and they are also linked to Hector and Hattie, who saved Kiki from abuse years earlier. Fez, Kiki's crazed coworker, is equated to her father, Keith. The same weapon Hattie gives her, ostensibly to be used in defense against Keith, is used instead to kill Fez. And Kiki almost uses it to kill the young boy who attacked her. Her young attacker(s) are likened, then, to Keith and Fez. When they rescue Rudy, Mavis and Soupspoon are linked to Ruby and Inez, to Hector and Hattie, and to Kiki; and Rudy, of course, is linked to any of those who have ever been rescued by other caring characters. Soupspoon also draws a connection between Jolly Horner and Bobby Grand (the gay white AIDS victim whom Soupspoon meets during his chemotherapy). Upon the death of both men, scores of friends come out to honor them. Soupspoon simply recalls the many (and diverse) well-liked people he has met throughout his life. The purpose of this theme is to awaken in the reader the realization that human beings are perhaps more alike than they are different. Had Kiki not been willing (and Hector and Hattie before her) to defy the socially imposed boundaries of age, race, and gender, Soupspoon (an important human life) would simply have perished. Yet because of her effort (despite her decidedly racist upbringing), Soupspoon is afforded several more weeks of life and contribution. Interestingly enough, music also provides another means of connection. While Kiki is bathing (translate: renewing, inspiriting, nurturing) Soupspoon soon after his arrival, she hums a tune, one that the old man does not recognize. However, he "heard the long-drawn country notes in it" (35). Kiki's Arkansas-inspired country music "speaks to" Soupspoon's blues roots, as each musical form echoes human despair and struggle. The blues music presented throughout the novel, then, connects all of the characters as it affirms their humanity and absorbs their pain.

HISTORICAL CONTEXT

In *RL's Dream* Mosley celebrates the blues music tradition. The novel, set roughly between 1926 (when Soupspoon is five) and 1987 (the date given for the fake insurance policy that Kiki drafts), explores the influence of blues not only on the lives of key characters, but also on popular culture. With its emphasis on suffering, survival, and social communication, the blues serves as the ideal musical genre for assessing this period of African American life. Because blues music is embedded in the oral tradition, locating its origins has remained an elusive task. However, most maintain that it first appeared in the 1890s when performed by self-taught musicians in ramshackle clubs and on street corners. Because the music, as indicated earlier, focuses on survival and self-determination despite the oppressive environmental circumstances, it perhaps gained increasing currency in this decade as a result of the paradoxical condition of African Americans. The generation that produced the blues had been born in the postslavery era (and thus had aspirations of attaining the kinds of rights and privileges denied their ancestors), yet this same generation would witness the systematic removal of certain rights gained during Reconstruction, with the final death knell echoing with the 1896 *Plessy v. Ferguson* Supreme Court decision (legalizing the doctrine of separate but equal).

W. C. Handy (1873–1958), known as the "Father of the Blues," performed the earliest published blues music. Hearing blues performed in black communities and working camps in Mississippi at the turn of the century, Handy attempted to elevate and polish the genre to access a popular audience. By 1920, and with the influence of the Great Migration (rural southern blacks moving in droves to northern cities), black music enjoyed a growing market. In that same year, Mamie Smith made the first recording of sung blues and prepared the way for other black artists. The 1920s also witnessed the emergence of "race records," established specifically for the black listening public and ushering in a pronounced blues music craze. Bessie Smith, "Empress of the Blues," made several of her best recordings in this decade. Because of the unexpected popularity of the music, recording companies focused on less polished, and more "authentic," forms of blues. In 1924, famed poet Langston Hughes published his volume of poetry, *The Weary Blues*, in homage to this distinctly black American musical form.

Mosley's way of honoring this distinct tradition is to fictionalize in *RL's Dream* the already sketchy details of the life of famed guitarist Robert

Johnson (1911–1938). Though he lived only twenty-seven years and re-corded only twenty-nine songs in his brief career, Johnson is considered today to be the most influential blues musician of all time. He is respon-sible for both the modern blues tradition and early rock and roll. Traveling throughout the Delta in the early 1930s, Johnson lived a colorful life. Ac-cording to legend, he sold his soul to the Devil to acquire his unmatched talent. By 1930 he had married and lost his wife, who died in childbirth. Johnson's own life ended abruptly when he was poisoned by a man with whose wife Johnson reportedly had had an affair.

While the blues tradition still thrived in southern nightspots and juke joints during the 1920s and 1930s, urban influences would increasingly define the genre. Famed mid-century musician Muddy Waters (1915–1983), who was directly influenced by Johnson, represents this phenom-enon. First recorded on a Mississippi plantation in 1941, Waters later moved to Chicago, where he added to his musical style a hard, impas-sioned, urban-inspired flair. He and others would later influence the rock tradition of the 1950s and rhythm and blues.

Via Soupspoon's life, the novel indirectly charts the development of the blues. The old musician first hears the blues in 1932 outside a barn party when he is eleven. The music speaks to him in such a deep way that he is almost unprepared for the wrenching effect. A week earlier, Soup-spoon's friend Bannon had been killed, but the boy had not grieved the death. Unaware that he even had the blues, Soupspoon discovers that "[t]hat music had changed him" because it "made him want to move, and the words, the words were like the talk people talked every day, but he listened closer and he heard things that he never heard before" (74). From that moment on, until he leaves home for the road in 1935 and beyond RL's death in 1937, Soupspoon will devote his life to honing his skills as a blues musician. The most influential period is Soupspoon's time with RL (the fictionalized Robert Johnson), who teaches him about the culture of the traveling musician. From RL, Soupspoon learned how to work both sides of the street. RL would set up on one side, while Soupspoon per-formed on the other. In this way, they drew a more substantial crowd. In addition, one was available to defend the other, if a jealous field hand decided to exact revenge on one of them for appealing too deeply (via the music) to a softhearted woman.

Though the two work to protect and reinforce each other, they also differ in their respective opinions about what should be the future of blues music. Soupspoon wants to travel north, make a race record, and earn some money, while RL, who has been to Chicago and New York, argues that the blacks there have forgotten who they are, that they simply do not function in a real world. RL believes that authentic people and authentic music are found only in the South, particularly in the Mississippi Delta. Soupspoon, however, feeling the effects of the Depression on an already oppressed people, believes that his future lies in the migration northward.

After marrying Mavis, Soupspoon finally decides to leave the South. Spending days, even weeks, on the road, he leads the life of a true bluesman. This particular life, however, is not one that Mavis can abide. Realizing that a blues musician needs a gritty life, one reeking of "foul-smellin' bars . . . [or] whores an' gunfights and blood" (240), Mavis will ultimately discover that she can no longer live with Soupspoon. And even though Kiki, in the present moment, sees good in Soupspoon, Mavis still cautions the young woman that even angels "draw up to all the evil and all the hurt in the world. . . . They take all the pain and shout it out. Angels livin' with evil and with death" (238). Mavis underscores the fact that no matter where Soupspoon finds himself, in the North or the South or in Kiki's apartment, he is still the consummate bluesman whose very way of life was long ago determined. No one or no circumstance, in Mavis's opinion, will change that condition.

Clearly, Mosley honors the great blues musicians, not only Robert Johnson but also Muddy Waters. That the author would give Kiki the surname Waters and Soupspoon the first name Atwater is a testament to such deference and honor. Mosley also links both characters to the depths of human pain, as well as the heights of potential human triumph. Because bluesmen, according to Soupspoon, are black men "goin' nowhere and findin' hard fists and bone-breakin' rock in their path" yet who also "demand freedom in the blues" (202), they could very well be the world's saviors. Having suffered the world's pains, the bluesmen know how to survive them. Although Soupspoon, in despair, retires his guitar for thirty years after he and Mavis part and lives in practical isolation, he still endures, becoming his own salvation. Working as a janitor for three decades, he is self-sufficient until he is "retired" and left without a livelihood. Kiki, then, who has also been affected not only by a "blues-inspired" life back in Arkansas but also by black men who have lived the blues, assumes the role of savior. Important to note is that Kiki is saved twice by black (blues) men. Hector is responsible for saving Kiki from her abusive father, while Randy (a black bluesman, though he cannot yet claim the title) takes the bullet meant for Kiki when Fez tries to kill her. Both Kiki and Soupspoon serve to validate and preserve the legacy of the blues tradition.

NARRATIVE STRUCTURE

The improvisational nature of blues music influences the narrative structure that Mosley employs in *RL's Dream*. Resisting a traditional linear format, Mosley instead opts for a cyclical design. While the main story line is set in 1987 and concerns the developing friendship between Kiki and Soupspoon, the novel also explores both characters' earlier lives. Charting Soupspoon's life from one of his earliest memories in the mid-1920s up through the 1940s and highlighting moments from Kiki's childhood in the late 1950s and 1960s, *RL's Dream* engages the intermittent flashback in order to interrupt the chronological flow. Though he uses the third-person perspective throughout, Mosley limits this perspective from either Kiki's or Soupspoon's point of view, depending on whose present life or former life is being presented.

Mosley also uses the genres of autobiography and the confessional as models for this novel. When Soupspoon decides to record his life story, along with some of the music he has performed over the years, he assumes the role of autobiographer, insisting that he relate the story in his own unique way. In addition, in revealing previously untold details from his life, Soupspoon uses the autobiography to confess or to purge himself of all the emotional baggage that has burdened him over the years. Just as bluesmen historically used their music to express the frustrations that they could not voice in any other public forum, Soupspoon uses his tape recording to speak truth. Soupspoon's story also reinforces the cyclical nature of the novel. Though he will die by the end, he leaves his history to be transcribed by Gerry, who will then present it to the world and to the future. Mosley even creates the transcribed text, a book entitled *Back Road to the Blues*, and uses a quotation from Soupspoon to serve as the inscription for *RL's Dream*. In this way, Soupspoon's story exists, quite literally, outside the text of the novel.

That the novel resists being confined to a fixed structure (with a beginning, a middle, and an end) is evident also in other narrative manipulations, one of which is the treatment of Kiki. Though her story (her life with Soupspoon) ends when she flees, the narrator provides some insight into her future. After returning to Arkansas, she marries her childhood sweetheart and ultimately gives him four children. Kiki's saga, then, continues beyond the novel's last page. The novel's opening (the first chapter presented to the reader) also defies traditional structure. Instead of incorporating a prologue, Mosley opts to label the first section "Zero." In this section, a tired and rapidly deteriorating Soupspoon, who has just fled from the men's shelter, is introduced before he collapses on the floor of his apartment. The official first chapter then introduces Kiki, who is returning from her stay in the hospital. By labeling the first section "Zero," Mosley indicates that it is an integral part of the novel, and since it also serves as the reader's introduction to Soupspoon, the old man is positioned as an integral part of the novel. Had Mosley labeled the section as the prologue, it would be structurally detached from the rest of the novel. Regardless of any author's intent, most readers consider the actual beginning of a novel to be the first chapter. As a consequence, they consider the prologue an extraneous component. Why, then, does Mosley not simply introduce Soupspoon in the first chapter and Kiki in the second? By using the "Zero" designation, Mosley suggests that this story has already begun before words were actually printed on the page. In short, the story began before the beginning. Clearly, then, there is no fixed beginning, just as there is no fixed ending.

Mosley's narrative strategy is influenced by modernism. Given that this movement emerged after World War I not only as an artistic phenomenon but also as a general cultural phenomenon, it is logical that Mosley would adapt modernist techniques in a novel partially set during the actual period. Modernism, while purporting to question and challenge the norm, initiated stylistic innovations, disrupting form; blurring the boundaries among genres; and, in the case of the written word, experimenting with syntax, unity, and coherence. In general cultural matters, modernism interrogated notions of normalcy and tradition. In addition, modernism addressed the plight of the disintegrated human personality, dehumanized by an increasingly insensitive, mechanized environment. Quite simply, modernism attempted to derive a new sense of order out of a rapidly changing society.

When Mosley disrupts the fixed status of *RL's Dream* by incorporating autobiography and the confessional, and when he presents Soupspoon's completed book in the inscription for *RL's Dream*, he engages in an intertextual strategem that was often the hallmark of modernist literature. Also, Mosley, via the limited omniscient point of view from both Kiki's and Soupspoon's perspectives, has each character reveal throughout the novel isolated details from their lives. As they continue, they repeat certain details while adding a few more observations so that the reader very slowly and methodically begins to piece together a whole portrait. In this way, the story (or stories) are repeated again and again, just as the modernist writer would present them. The modernist argues that the actual story is never finished; it is simply retold. Because the modernist questions all notions of order and stability, he or she cannot accept the idea of a stable (i.e., complete and uniform) story. Therefore, the story is always in flux, just like the real world.

This focus on instability and the unknown facilitates not only the time period that consumes part of *RL's Dream*, but also the blues context. Oppressed, disrupted, unstable lives define the blues condition, while the blues music recaptures the instability in its improvisational, ever-changing technique. In short, the blues is modern, and the modern is blues. Such a claim is verified in one of the most important scenes in the novel. When Soupspoon performs (and for the first time in over thirty years) at the street bazaar alongside Randy's vending concern, he is struck with the significance of the moment: that he is reclaiming himself and his past. As Soupspoon begins to feel the music, he thinks about his departure at fourteen from Ruby and Inez; about JoDaddy Parker, who taught him to play the guitar; about Bannon, who taught him certain truths about life; and about meeting Mavis. "He remembered decades between notes. He had everything right there in his heart" (210). Just as the blues music must be played again and again, so, too, must the stories be told, then summarized, then told again. In this way, the narrative structure (the summarized stories), influenced by modernist tendencies, reinforces the content (blues music).

A DECONSTRUCTIONIST READING

Deconstruction strives mainly to uncover the ambiguities, contradictions, and ironies in a given text. This school of thought emerges out of the belief that language itself is inherently imperfect; consequently, meaning is arbitrary. Deconstruction analyzes the language to find the meaning below the surface. According to renowned theorist Ferdinand de Saussure, there can be no fixed, known, or stable relationship between a word (symbol, or signifier) and the object (or signified) to which the word supposedly refers. For Saussure, the relationship is purely arbitrary, as imperfect human beings have assigned meanings to words as a means of trying to communicate, but there is no natural or inherent connection. For example, *cat* has no real connection to the feline creature it conjures up in our minds. And to be sure, in another language a different symbol would attempt to call up the same object or image. If language is imperfect in this way, says the deconstructionist, then whole texts comprised of this flawed language are also subject to faults. It is the task of the deconstructionist to expose these various gaps, paradoxes, ambiguities, and ironies. Because *RL's Dream* draws heavily from modernism (as noted earlier, a genre that questions and challenges), it lends itself quite naturally to a deconstructionist reading.

One of the more compelling ideas presented in the novel is the resistance to labels. In almost every aesthetic aspect (character development, setting, structure, etc.) the novel rejects fixed definitions, arguing instead that much of what exists as real in life is, in fact, arbitrary, titular, or both. The two main characters are prime examples. Kiki is a thirty-something southern alcoholic white woman, while Soupspoon is a rapidly deteriorating, poverty-stricken sixty-something former traveling musician. The social order would dictate that these two have nothing in common and that they should never share the same domestic space. This is especially true given Kiki's deep-rooted prejudice (evident is her frequent use of the epithet "nigger"). However, Mosley compels his characters to spurn not only their imposed identities but also their preconceived notions of others' identities. In the chapter that introduces the reader to Kiki, the young woman, while riding the subway home, makes mental assessments about the other riders, among whom are three black teenage girls. When Kiki considers the girls, she reveals her deep-seated biases about blacks. Nonetheless, when Kiki is confronted with the inhumane spectacle of Soupspoon's eviction, she rises above such feelings and disregards the imposed boundary meant to separate her from the likes of a Soupspoon. The old musician seems to understand the importance of eradicating such unnecessary boundaries because of his former friendship with Bannon. Commenting to Kiki about this man, Soupspoon tells her that when he was only ten and Bannon was over sixty, the two of them were still the best of friends, because "back then, in the country way'a life, you could have friends all kindsa ages an' there wasn't nuthin' weird about it" (96). Soupspoon's most meaningful relationships have been with people whom, according to certain societal rules, he should have avoided. The novel presents other character associations that defy the social order.

In regard to setting, the atmosphere created in the novel is hazy and surreal, reinforcing the dream mentioned in the title. The reader is thus forced to question what is real and what is imaginary. Because much of the novel occurs in flashback, this hazy aspect is sustained when the past continually collapses into the present. Kiki's actual nightmares about her father affect her behavior. On a couple of occasions, Kiki (with no apparent provocation) attacks Soupspoon. However, she is responding to what she perceives is Soupspoon's nonchalance about all that she has done for him.

This perceived indifference reminds her of her father's behavior; she consequently lashes out at Soupspoon. Kiki's outbursts also invite the reader to question the distinction between sanity and insanity (these two concepts collapse into one). While Kiki seems a bit crazed at times, Soupspoon reconciles his initial concern about her behavior by remembering that this same "craziness" compelled her to rescue him. Instead of Kiki being "crazy" or "not crazy" (absolute and fixed concepts), her craziness is made "normal" because it is functional. Just as Kiki's past affects the present, Soupspoon's recollections about RL and the early days of the transient blues life seem to influence his present life more than the immediate forces do. Though Soupspoon has spent the greater part of thirty years serving as a janitor, as he now approaches the end of his life he wants to recapture (in part for his book project) the old blues life. By the time he dies at the end of the novel (not before a final visit from RL), Atty, Atwater, and Soupspoon (all of his past selves) have become one. This fluctuation from past to present forces a disruption in the temporal (or chronological) structure in favor of an aesthetic order (serving the integrity of the text). The purpose of this strategy (in true modernist style) is to shock and destabilize the reader in order to challenge his or her preconceived notions of value and order (the deconstructionist argues that value and order are arbitrary anyway). The surreal setting created is consistent, then, with deconstructionist belief that no vision can be clear, vivid, or "real."

Mosley also adopts another modernist device, one that affects narrative structure: intertextuality. He, like modernist writers long before him, uses it to dismantle the notion of a fixed and stable text. However, Mosley also challenges the very nature of his own work. *RL's Dream* is juxtaposed with the book and accompanying recordings that Soupspoon hopes to complete. In this way, Soupspoon's stories become an integral part of *RL's Dream*, and vice versa. One text depends on the other, in a kind of intertextual dance. By providing an inscription from Soupspoon for *RL's Dream*, Mosley even suggests that Soupspoon is a real person. But the most compelling example of poetic license is Mosley's dating Soupspoon's inscription 1986, a year earlier than the supposed time setting for *RL's Dream* (the reader is led to believe that the setting is 1987 when Kiki drafts the fake insurance policy). If as part of the plot for *RL's Dream* Soupspoon is *preparing* his story, how can he *present* the story a year earlier? Once again manipulating time, Mosley suggests that the very text of *RL's Dream*—a tangible work that the reader, in the real world, can hold—is just that, a dream. Or at the very least, it defies being fixed in only the present moment.

From the ongoing analysis of deconstruction, one might assume that its ultimate goal is to destroy a text in its apparent implication that attempting to critique a literary work is a futile pursuit. However, the theoretical framework strives instead to highlight multiple meanings rather than suggesting no meaning at all. Deconstruction resists all either/or declarations, inviting instead a both/and perspective. In this way, possibility, not limitation, becomes the governing force. Kiki can be both a bigot and a savior; the story of RL can exist both in the past and in the present; and the text proper can be both real and ephemeral, existing simultaneously in Soupspoon's imagination and in Mosley's. Only the reader can "fix" the final (or infinite) truth.

6

A Little Yellow Dog
(1996)

With the novel *A Little Yellow Dog*, set in 1963, Mosley returns to famed protagonist Ezekiel "Easy" Porterhouse Rawlins. Though Easy is once again trying to lead a normal, upstanding life, this time as a custodial supervisor for the local school district, Easy finds himself connected to three murders. And as is always the case, if he does not help to solve the crimes, he may be accused of them himself. With a zealous detective dogging his every move, Easy is immersed in one of the most complex cases of his life. Caught among police, gamblers, gangsters, drug traffickers, and thieves, Easy must continually negotiate and strategize to save himself as well as other innocent victims. Along with his present responsibilities as a single parent, Easy must also reckon with a past that always seems to impact his present life at the most inopportune moments.

PLOT DEVELOPMENT

Easy reports to his job as senior custodian at Sojourner Truth Junior High School. Because it is quite early in the morning, he is surprised to find one of the teachers there already. Upon entering her classroom, Easy finds a visibly shaken Idabell Turner and her pet dog, Pharaoh. Knowing that pets are not allowed on school grounds, Idabell begs Easy to keep the dog for her until day's end because she fears that her husband intends to kill Pharaoh. He relents, but not until after he and Idabell enjoy a quick and spontaneous tryst.

After greeting his employees (who include his old friend EttaMae) and assigning them chores, Easy is called to Principal Hiram T. Newgate's office, where he is informed that he has been accused of stealing school property. Easy dismisses the accusations and disregards the principal's veiled threats. He then leaves the school to retrieve a stranded Mouse (Raymond Alexander), who works the later shift at the school. When the two return, they find the school abuzz with police and later learn that a body has been found in the school's garden. Easy is questioned briefly by Sergeant Sanchez, who is suspicious of the senior custodian. Because Easy gained his employment two years earlier via unorthodox means, and because he has hired Mouse (with his notorious past), Easy knows that he must be careful in Sanchez's presence.

Easy was hired by area supervisor Bertrand Stowe when Easy agreed to help him and his girlfriend, Grace Phillips (also a former friend of Easy's longtime friend John), out of a delicate situation. Bert met Grace two years earlier when he accompanied Bill Bartlett (who formerly held Easy's position) to a party hosted by gangster Sallie Monroe. Even though Grace is an occasional prostitute, Bert (a married man) falls in love with her. When Sallie learns of their ensuing affair, he threatens to expose the two unless Bert agrees to allow Sallie access to various schools. Sallie wants to steal valuable properties and then profit from the resale. Easy, after subtly threatening Sallie, pays off the gangster and buys Bert and Grace's "freedom." Forever grateful, Bert, after firing Bartlett, hires Easy for the supervisory position.

Later, Easy describes the corpse found in the garden to EttaMae, who suggests that the body is probably that of Idabell's husband. Now concerned about his own involvement in the situation (Idabell's nervousness, the romantic interlude, his acceptance of Pharaoh), Easy looks for Idabell, only to discover that she has suddenly left the school, informing officials that her dog was hit by a car. Knowing that Idabell has lied, Easy now reasons that he must resume his role as a street detective. Perusing Idabell's personnel file (after office hours), Easy finds the fugitive teacher's address as well as the name of a friend.

Taking Pharaoh home to his children, Feather and Jesus, Easy decides to go to Idabell's house. When no one answers the door, Easy steals his way in, only to find the second corpse of the day. Sitting in a chair is the body of a man who looks exactly like the one found earlier at the school; even the clothing is the same. After riffling through the man's wallet, Easy leaves and goes to the apartment of Bonnie Shay, the friend whose name he found in Idabell's file. Though she is leery of Easy (or acts as though she is), Bonnie refuses to share any useful information but agrees that if she should hear from Idabell, she will give her Easy's phone number.

The contents of the wallet reveal that the corpse found in the house is that of Idabell's husband, Holland Gasteau. Later, Easy finds out that the corpse at the school is Holland's twin brother, Roman. Using an alias and depending on his streetwise instincts, Easy visits Roman's apartment complex and surreptitiously interviews the neighbors about Roman, soon learning that the dead man was a fast-talking hustler and gambler who would do almost anything for quick money.

After receiving a call from Idabell (whom Easy suspects of killing Holland, Roman, or both, though he does not know exactly why), Easy agrees to meet her and to return Pharaoh. Idabell assures Easy that she had nothing to do with the murders. While it is true that Holland threatened to kill Pharaoh if Idabell refused him a particular favor, Idabell insists that her only intention was to leave Holland and to leave town with her dog. After they engage in one more tryst, Idabell asks Easy to take her and Pharaoh to Bonnie Shay's and then to the bus station. Arriving at Bonnie's, Easy, leaving Idabell in the car, agrees to deliver a note to the friend, but then decides to keep the note for himself. Upon returning to his car, he finds a dead Idabell; she has been shot in the head through the car window. Not wanting to be linked to any of the murders, Easy leaves Idabell's body on a park bench after removing all identifying information. The note that Easy was supposed to deliver expressed Idabell's regret for having sabotaged her friendship with Bonnie.

Thinking that he needs to pursue the gambling angle of Roman's life, Easy seeks the help of his longtime friend Jackson Blue, resident gambler and general con artist. Having learned from Idabell that Roman liked to frequent the Chantilly Club, Easy asks Jackson about the establishment. Because Jackson has recently found himself in trouble with local gangster Philly Stetz, who runs the Chantilly, he provides a wealth of information. Knowing that Jackson needs his help as much as he needs Jackson's, Easy agrees to hide Jackson until he can assist the foolhardy man with his troubles.

Finding his way to the Chantilly, Easy befriends waitress Hannah Torres, who confirms that Roman did frequent the club as well as an after-hours bar called the Hangar. Thinking Easy attractive, Hannah decides she will accompany Easy to the Hangar later. While waiting for her to finish her shift, Easy strikes up a conversation with his old friend, blues musician Lips McGee. From the old man Easy discovers that Roman trafficked in drugs, particularly heroin. Lips also reveals that while Roman was the more likable of the twin brothers, Holland (possessed of a mean streak) was extremely envious of his brother. After listening to Lips perform a few songs, Easy steps outside to wait for Hannah, where he is knocked unconscious.

Easy awakens to find himself in a toolshed facing Joey Beam (who immediately questions Easy about his interest in the Chantilly and the Gasteaus) and Beam's two henchmen, Rupert Dodds (former wrestler and now doorman/bouncer at the Chantilly) and L'il Joe. Creating an alias for himself, Easy answers a few questions, but then he suddenly strikes out at all three men, ultimately fighting his way out of the situation. He runs for several blocks and then phones John (the former speakeasy owner from the earlier novels), who retrieves him.

Deciding that he needs answers, Easy returns to Bonnie's. While the two are talking (with Bonnie gradually beginning to trust Easy), henchman Rupert pays Bonnie a visit (banging on her door and threatening her). Only when Bonnie's neighbor, Mr. Gillian, threatens Rupert with his gun does the aggressor leave. Now realizing that she has only Easy to trust, Bonnie shares more information after he convinces her that she will be safer staying with him and the children. Bonnie tells Easy that she met Roman through Idabell and began dating him, even moving to Los Angeles from Paris (her home base as a flight attendant), though she continues her international flights. Roman convinces her to import for him what she thinks are French toys, but she later discovers that she has been smuggling drugs. When she refuses to continue, Roman abruptly ends their relationship, whereupon Holland coerces Idabell to transport one last package during a trip that she and Bonnie make together (unbeknown to Bonnie). When Bonnie later learns that Idabell hid the drugs with Bonnie's belongings, she simply tosses them in the trash. Easy, however, realizing that Idabell was killed because of the drugs, locates the lost drugs and will use them as leverage.

Soon Easy discovers exactly why Roman was at the school. Bertrand Stowe had given Roman (under the alias Landis Defarge) a job as night building consultant. Bert hired him only to keep him away from Grace, whom Roman has transformed into a junkie and with whom Roman has fathered a child. Easy now knows that Roman was stealing from the school, and he will soon know that Roman was working in conjunction with Joey Beam in drug trafficking. And Beam, looking to find that last drug package and thinking that Idabell has it, kills her while trying to retrieve it.

Because Jackson is in trouble with Philly Stetz and because Joey Beam (using Rupert) has targeted Bonnie for vengeance, Easy attempts to satisfy both men by using the recently reclaimed drugs. Setting up a meeting with Stetz, Easy informs him that if he will agree to leave Jackson alone, Jackson will deliver to Stetz all of Jackson's illegal gambling supplies, from which Stetz will make even more money. In return, Easy wants Stetz to contact Beam and tell him that his drugs have been found and that he need not threaten Bonnie any longer.

Easy, taking Mouse along for added protection, is to make his deliveries to one of Stetz's warehouses. However, both men are ambushed by Beam and Sallie Monroe (Easy's former nemesis). In the scuffle, Mouse is shot, and both Beam and Monroe are killed. After driving a rapidly deteriorating Mouse back to EttaMae (who directs her shock and anger at Easy), Easy returns home with the gambling supplies and the drugs, confused about what to do next. Soon, Rupert arrives, bringing Easy over six thousand dollars (the equivalent of one year's salary), explaining that Stetz has sent it in payment for the supplies and as recompense for Beam's betrayal. Rupert has worked mainly for Stetz, though he has been involved in Beam's drug trade and in Roman and Beam's theft ring.

Unfortunately, after spending some time in the hospital, Mouse dies. Because EttaMae is still angry at Easy, Easy never has a chance to see his friend again. When he goes to her house, Easy finds that she and son LaMarque have abandoned the place without a trace. Bonnie Shay decides to return to Paris, but not before admitting to Easy that she killed Holland. On the night that Easy discovered Holland's body, Holland had called Bonnie to the house by threatening to reveal her involvement in the drug-smuggling operation. After she arrives, Holland rapes her and then admits that he killed Roman. When he insists that Bonnie now become his wife (since Idabell has left), she believes her only alternative is to kill him.

Easy is left once again to fend for himself and his children. Though Bonnie has become fond of Feather and Jesus, she cannot stay in Los Angeles. However, Easy will be forever connected to these recent events because he still has his love-hate relationship with Pharaoh, the little yellow dog who is now a permanent resident.

CHARACTER DEVELOPMENT

Now forty-three years old, protagonist Easy Rawlins has matured in an effort to achieve a more orderly life. Having accepted long ago his role as a single parent, Easy desires only balance and consistency. Admitting that he no longer yearns for quick-money schemes, Easy is happy with his stable job and steady income. As head custodian and supervisor, Easy is responsible for managing several other workers, all of whom have come to respect him. Though he could have accepted a job as a regular janitor or a dishwasher, his sense of pride demands that he accept only a position with a modicum of status. And although the white principal, Hiram T. Newgate, resents having a black man (especially one who did not come up in the ranks) in a supervisory position, Easy is prepared for the job because of his life experience and his real-estate ventures.

Easy's most compelling motivation in life is the care of his children. Though he can be tough on the street, he is sensitive and compassionate in the presence of Jesus and Feather. He reveals more of the sensitive side of his personality in regard to the title character, the little yellow dog, Pharaoh. Even though Pharaoh despises Easy and snarls at him consistently, Easy finds that he can neither harm nor abandon the orphaned dog. And especially after Feather takes an immediate liking to Pharaoh, Easy cannot hurt his daughter by removing the canine. Because Easy understands that somehow Pharaoh contributes to the harmony that he tries to sustain in his family, he would rather endure the love-hate relationship with the dog than disrupt the relative bliss.

Recurring major character Raymond "Mouse" Alexander, Easy's long-time sidekick, has outpaced all other characters in regard to growth and development. Always the unapologetic gangster, Mouse has now achieved a composure that had always eluded him. Easy explains that two years earlier Mouse killed Sweet William Dokes, an older musician from Texas rumored to be Mouse's real father. William had recently moved to Los Angeles, and he and Mouse began socializing together. However, in a dispute over a woman, Mouse fatally shoots William. Racked with guilt, Mouse decides that he needs to forgo his wild life on the street and assume a more responsible, steadier pace. For the past two years, Mouse has been working diligently for Easy on the custodial staff, along with wife EttaMae. Recently, however, Mouse has begun to feel somewhat remorseful about other incidents from his past. His main concern is that he never felt anything before; he would simply act out of instinct. Now, his guilt about not feeling guilty has even compelled him to seek the advice of EttaMae's minister, no insignificant action for Mouse. The minister tells Mouse to seek forgiveness from God, after which time God will give him a sign that he has been forgiven. Ironically, it is Mouse's desire to gain forgiveness that compels him to become involved in Easy's situation, a decision that will result in his untimely death.

Serving as a major character because she is the catalyst that sets in motion Easy's involvement in the murders is Idabell Turner, schoolteacher and native of French Guiana. In addition, the thirty-two-year-old Idabell is the link among various other characters in the novel. In the recent past, Idabell has hosted several tea parties in her home, inviting a few of her colleagues. When her brother-in-law, Roman Gasteau, comes to town, he charms many in the group and begins to have his own parties at various venues in the city. And because her husband, Holland, is envious of Roman's affability and magnetism, he will add stress and turmoil to Idabell's life. On the one hand, Idabell wants to remain loyal to her husband and stroke his fragile ego; on the other, she is leery of the illegal activities that Holland and Roman are engaged in and that they want her to support. Because Idabell feels trapped, she thinks her only alternative is to flee. She is presented as a complex character because she is at once a victim and also a culprit.

Bonnie Shay, Idabell's best friend, is perhaps the most sympathetic character in the novel because she is exploited by almost everyone. An international flight attendant, Bonnie has been unwittingly used by Roman (and later Holland via Idabell) to transport illegal drugs from France. Also a native of French Guiana, Bonnie has taken pride not only in her professional achievement but also in her personal commitment and loyalty to friends like Idabell. She is especially miffed when she discovers that she has been betrayed. That Bonnie is a sincere person is evident in her interactions with Jesus and Feather, both of whom are immediately drawn to her. Assuming the role of surrogate mother and participating in all domestic activities while in the Rawlins household, Bonnie is the first woman whom Easy has taken seriously in some time.

Although both are dead from the beginning, Holland and Roman Gasteau figure prominently in the novel. Like Idabell and Bonnie, the twin brothers are also from French Guiana. These cultural ties draw both women to the men. Unfortunately, Holland and Roman are more concerned about their own agendas than they are about Idabell and Bonnie. Whereas greed defined Roman, envy identified Holland. When Roman arrives in town, Holland becomes obsessed with emulating his brother. Desiring the fast-paced life, the flashy clothes, and the admiration that Roman seemed to spark in others, Holland quickly loses his contentment with his more staid existence. Managing newspaper routes no longer seems sufficient. Though Roman humors his brother, he never accepts Holland as his equal, often ridiculing and mocking him. Even though Roman uses Holland's newspaper shed as a temporary warehouse for stolen property and even though Holland is always eager to accommodate his brother, Roman still denies the fawning Holland full acceptance. Roman's detachment causes Holland's increased resentment, which erupts initially in the abuse of Idabell, then finally in the murder of Roman and the attack on Bonnie.

Like Mouse, another recurring major character is Jackson Blue. Described in earlier novels as both a brilliant and a stupid man, Jackson Blue is the most well read of Easy's acquaintances and the most disappointing. Instead of using his intellect in some constructive pursuit, Jackson would rather be a criminal. Two years earlier Jackson and his "business" partner Ortiz, eager to encroach upon the business of established white gangsters, devised a telephone-answering system that allowed them to tap into phone lines and record incoming gambling requests without actually operating a centralized office. Now, two years later, Ortiz has been arrested, and Philly Stetz (one of the white gangsters) has announced that he wants Jackson dead. Once again, Easy must come to Jackson's rescue and hide Jackson away until he can figure out what to do. After sequestering Jackson in two different places (one of which is Mofass's house), Easy secures Jackson's freedom. However, Jackson repays Easy by absconding with all of Jesus's savings. In typical Jackson Blue fashion, he betrays everyone for self-aggrandizement.

Easy describes Philly Stetz, the leading gangster in the novel, as a "good-looking white man" who is "tall and comfortable with the elevation" (279). Rather than being the stereotypical menace to society, Stetz is polished and sophisticated. Not intimidated by anyone or any circumstance, Stetz is a strong man who appreciates courage and strength in others. Though he is initially unfazed by Easy's suggestion that Jackson relinquish his answering devices in exchange for his life, Stetz will ultimately accept the offer because of Easy's determination, directness, and apparent bravery. And while Stetz does offend Easy with his use of "nigger," Easy still acknowledges shared qualities with the man. When Stetz rather casually dismisses one of his underlings, treating the man as no more than a slight nuisance, Easy is reminded of how he interacts with the cleaning staff at the school by assuming a posture of gracious condescension. In comparing himself to Stetz, Easy achieves and maintains an equal footing with white men in general.

Less sophisticated than Stetz, Joey Beam, the other white gangster, is perhaps the most ruthless of all the characters in the novel. He kills Idabell without remorse, and he (along with Sallie Monroe) attempts to kill Easy. Though he and Stetz have collaborated on some jobs, Beam is considered to be more villainous. As noted earlier, Stetz honors his agreement with Easy, while Beam (in the attempt to kill Easy) betrays a trust. And because Beam is involved with illegal drug distribution (which even Stetz finds abhorrent), he is presented as the true menace.

Rounding out the list of major characters are Sergeant Sanchez, Bertrand Stowe, and Grace Phillips. As the lead investigator in the Gasteau murders, Sanchez serves as Easy's nemesis. Because he knows that Easy has suffered run-ins with the police in the past, he is suspicious of Easy's involvement in these cases. Sanchez's commitment to solving the murders (and if need be, implicating Easy) stems in part from his obsession about proving himself as a Mexican American. Because Latinos and blacks are stereotypically considered to be lazy and immoral, Sanchez has attempted to distance himself from his own community in an effort to be accepted by the majority. During one of his interrogations, he informs Easy that he disdains blacks and Mexicanos, people like Easy who live "like dogs instead of standing up and taking advantage of what's right in front of them" (223). Though Sanchez is dedicated to his job, his obsession skews his objectivity and potentially jeopardizes Easy's life.

Bert and Grace are significant because they are the link between Easy and Sallie Monroe (a minor character), between Easy and Bill Bartlett (a minor character), and between Easy and the Gasteau murders. Because of Easy's involvement in relinquishing Grace and Bert from Sallie's clutches (as noted in *Plot Development*), he is awarded employment at the school. However, because Sallie is angry at Easy for forcing him to retreat and because Bartlett is fired as custodial supervisor (when Easy assumes the position), both men have reason to seek revenge against Easy (though Bartlett does not discover exactly who Easy is until much later). Nevertheless, Easy's association with Bert and Grace place him in a potentially dangerous situation. When Bert, once again trying to save Grace, gives Roman Gasteau a night job at the school, he inadvertently links Easy to Roman. When Roman's body is found on school grounds, Easy becomes an easy target for Sanchez, of course (Easy's liaison with Idabell notwithstanding).

Several minor characters populate the text. Rupert Dodds, bouncer at the Chantilly Club, is a self-serving character who feigns loyalty for the greatest reward. Having worked for both Stetz and Beam, Rupert will ultimately align himself to Stetz because of Stetz's financial and streetwise power. Knowing that only the strongest endure in a competitive urban environment, Rupert undertakes whatever is necessary to survive. Though Rupert may appear to be a dumb ex-wrestler (as Easy observes), he is, in fact, a shrewd strategist. Easy's various employees (in addition to Mouse and EttaMae) present a microcosm of multicultural Los Angeles. Garland Burns, the daytime senior custodian, is a "hale vegetarian from Georgia" (11) and the only black Christian Scientist whom Easy has ever known. Helen Plates is "an obese blond Negro from Iowa who claimed her good health was due to the fact that she ate a whole pie every day of her life" (11). Jorge Pena, a chubby and good-natured worker, is possessed of "dark eyes that laughed silently and often" (11). Archie "Ace" Muldoon is the first and only white man Easy has hired. Easy is suspicious of Ace, because he thinks the man resents working for a black man, especially since Principal Newgate has prodded Easy to grant Ace more responsibility. However, Easy will later learn that Ace is a loyal employee who highly respects him. Only Newgate has a problem with Easy's managerial position. Simona Eng, an Italian-Chinese woman, is working her way through night school. Simona, however, is slightly involved in the murder cases. When Idabell hosted her tea parties, she invited Simona to attend, having befriended the young woman who was trying to better her life. After a while, Simona and Roman began dating, but after she witnessed Roman's attempts to control her life and rebuked the efforts, the relationship ended. Nevertheless, she is afraid that the police will try to implicate her in Roman's murder, especially since she did periodically attend some of his marijuana parties.

A few recurring characters take on minor roles in *A Little Yellow Dog*. Easy's children, Jesus and Feather, have grown and assumed more trustworthy functions in the household. Though she is only seven, Feather accepts full responsibility for the orphaned Pharaoh. On one occasion, when she suspects that the dog is ill, Feather decides for herself to stay home from school to care for the animal. Even though Easy is miffed by her decision, he fully appreciates the fact that he is "seeing the woman in the child just beginning to flex her muscles"; consequently, he is forced "[to] smile at the beauty of Feather and her power to love" (138). Jesus, now a junior in high school and a track star, continues to care for Feather in Easy's absence. Early in the novel, Easy learns that Jesus has been caching money in his room. When he interrogates the boy about the four hundred eighty-nine dollars, he learns that Jesus has skimmed funds from the grocery money. Fearing that Easy might one day be unemployed (given his father's erratic work history), Jesus, bravely entering manhood, decides to save for less-prosperous times. EttaMae Harris, Mouse's on-again, off-again wife, provides her usual stability in the novel. Always a hardworking woman, EttaMae has proved to be an asset to the school's custodial staff. Her longtime consistency has finally influenced Mouse. The anger that she will ultimately direct at Easy upon Mouse's fatal wounding is a testament to the love and dedication she has always felt for the volatile (and often misunderstood) Mouse. Etta's loyalty has been revealed in her continued efforts to protect both Easy and Mouse from themselves. When she flees at the end of the novel, her departure will result in a void that Easy will not handily fill.

Other recurring minor characters include William "Mofass" Wharton, manager of Easy's various properties, and his young girlfriend and caretaker, Jewelle. Though his relationship with Mofass has been erratic over the years, Easy has come to depend on Mofass's loyalty and discretion. When Easy needs to hide Jackson for a few days, he calls on Mofass and Jewelle, who happily oblige. In addition, when Easy needs a safe haven for Jesus, Feather, and Bonnie, he calls upon his old friends Primo and Flower, who have always helped Easy since the time in 1948 when they welcomed Jesus into their home. Throughout the years, they have remained loyal and dependable.

THEMATIC ISSUES

Several themes are presented in the novel. One of the more striking issues relates to egotism and power, the extent to which a position of authority compels a person to exhibit egomaniacal behaviors. Principal Newgate, as he prefers to be addressed, is a prime example of such a person. Because he has been newly installed as the head administrator at Sojourner Truth Junior High School, his authority is still a novelty to him. As a consequence, he expects all who report to him to be particularly obsequious. And according to Easy, Newgate, a white man, wants such behavior from black workers especially: "Haughty and disdainful, the principal hated me because I wouldn't bow down to his position" (15). Newgate also believes that a black man like Easy should not have a supervisory position, evident in the fact that he constantly prods Easy to give the only white worker in Easy's employ, "Ace" Muldoon, more responsibility. Easy interprets this request to mean that Muldoon should really have Easy's job. Easy's refusal to assume the sycophantic role expected of him perturbs Newgate, especially since Easy insists on dressing like the supervisor he is instead of like a typical blue-collar worker. To show his disdain for Easy's style of dress, Newgate always makes a special point to identify the brand of one of Easy's clothing items. However, because Easy reports to area supervisor Bertrand Stowe and not to Newgate, the principal can make no real demands of Easy. Nevertheless, when Newgate receives a phone tip accusing Easy of stealing from the school system, Newgate thinks he has finally found a way to terminate Easy.

The relationship between egotism and power is also relevant to another theme: domestic abuse. Because both Holland and Roman Gasteau are so determined to achieve a certain economic and social status (with the attendant power and prestige) by any means necessary, they exact emotional and physical abuse on the women they supposedly love. When Idabell is reluctant to assist Holland in his competition with Roman by trafficking in illegal drugs, Holland threatens to harm Pharaoh. However, he insists that he wishes to do only what is best for both him and Idabell. In reality, Holland is concerned only for himself, evident when he states in a letter to Idabell that he is meant to live a more prosperous life and not the life of a newspaper deliveryman. Even though he insists that he is concerned as much for Idabell's welfare as for his own, Holland's sublimated egotism is quite apparent. He goes almost mad when he thinks that Idabell doubts his devotion to her (even though he is, in fact, devoted only to himself). He threatens to kill her if she does not oblige his every demand, attempting to make her a complete prisoner in her own home. Fearing that she is devoted more to Pharaoh or to Bonnie, Holland, ultimately achieving complete paranoia, practically screams the following in another note written to Idabell: "I am a man Idabell. Not a henpecked thing for you and your friends to mock. It's me who you have to support and stand behind. Not your girlfriends and not that damn dog" (234). And then, refusing to take any responsibility for any past or future actions, Holland states that if Idabell makes him angry enough, he may be "forced" to take drastic measures. This compulsion for power completely unhinges Holland, and the result is untold spousal abuse.

Like Holland, Roman also exhibits this volatility. Though he is usually an easygoing man, when he feels that his power is threatened, he goes berserk. Once, when Bonnie leaves a package at the airport (she still thinks she is only transporting French toys), Roman abruptly transforms into an abusive tyrant when Bonnie suggests that she wait until the next day to retrieve the item. Roman strikes her, knocks her down, pulls her by the hair, and threatens to kill her until she agrees to return to the airport at three o'clock in the morning and recover his property. Even though they are not married, Roman still treats Bonnie as though she is somehow tethered to him, as though she owes him something. He acts out the words that Holland articulates. But because she is not legally bound to him, Bonnie severs all ties to a man she once thought she could love. His love of money and lust for power ultimately dehumanize Roman and undermine their budding relationship.

Still another important theme, one prevalent in other Mosley works, is loyalty. This theme is presented twofold: family loyalty and friendship. In addition to Easy's loyalty to his children (evident in this and earlier texts), the reader finds yet another unique example of family commitment. Two years earlier, Mouse killed his good friend and mentor, Sweet William Dokes. Though Mouse has killed many people throughout the years, he is quite unsettled about this murder. For one reason, the police who arrested him have no real concern about the lost life; they in fact soon release Mouse without even pursuing the case. Their lack of concern is especially troublesome for Mouse because he fears he has killed his father. While Easy knows that William was Mouse's father, Mouse has only a suspicion. Nevertheless, Mouse is horrified that he has killed his kin. Mouse's loyalty is shown in his remorse and in the fact that he is forever changed as a result of this incident. Another example of family loyalty is presented in the dedication shown by Simona Eng to her father, Conrad Eng. When she tells Easy of her past relationship with Roman, she reveals that at one time Roman wanted her to move to Paris with him and study at the Sorbonne. But because of her devotion to her slightly senile father, Simona sacrificed the opportunity. Acting instead in the best interest of her father, she remained in Los Angeles and kept her minimum-wage job. While Mouse's form of loyalty to his father emerges after the fact, Simona's dedication has potentially prevented a tragedy in her life (to have been dependent on Roman in Paris more than likely would have resulted in a tragic end).

In regard to friendship, the relationships between both Idabell and Bonnie and Mouse and Easy endure even though each is tested and threatened. Idabell and Bonnie's friendship is jeopardized by the men in their lives, Holland and Roman. Because Idabell introduced Bonnie to the soon-to-be abusive Roman, she assumes some responsibility for the infraction. However, in an ironic way, when Idabell deceives Bonnie by harboring illegal drugs during their recent trip together from Paris, she is really acting in an effort to protect Bonnie. Because Holland has already threatened Idabell (and hinted at threatening her friends) and because the same drug dealers who beat Roman might also attack Bonnie if that last shipment of heroin is not transported from France (Bonnie has refused to deliver even one more package after Roman assaults her), Idabell feels compelled to make the delivery herself, in part to protect her friend. Idabell's remorse concerning all that has transpired (in a brief note she leaves for Bonnie) reveals her feelings of loyalty and devotion. And Idabell makes the ultimate sacrifice: her life. Like Idabell, Mouse also makes this sacrifice. Though he has been transformed for the better part of two years (since the death of Sweet William Dokes) and has resisted all street violence during that period, Mouse willingly comes to Easy's aid when his longtime friend needs him for backup. Mouse warns Easy, however, that he is not equipped with a gun (the lack of a gun is Mouse's concession to his new role as diplomat and his challenge to Easy that, while not fully committed to this engagement, he is acting only out of loyalty); nevertheless, he agrees to accompany Easy. Because their relationship has survived so many obstacles and perils over the years, it has been so strengthened that Mouse willingly sacrifices once again for his friend. Important to note as well is the fact that Mouse thinks his assistance to Easy will help to redeem him for William's death.

Perhaps the most unusual of friendships presented in the novel is the one between dog and humans. Idabell, in risking her life for Pharaoh, shows the potential depth of human compassion. When Bonnie learns that Idabell has entrusted the dog's care to Easy, she begins to trust Easy also. That Feather becomes enamored of the dog speaks to the innocence that love and compassion reinstate to the human condition. Hers is an unconditional and reciprocal love; she adores Pharaoh simply because he exists, and he returns equal feeling. Even Easy, who harbors ill will for the dog because of the various trials Pharaoh has brought to his life, cannot neglect or abandon the creature. Because Easy "had lived a dog's life and knew what it was to have the big world turn against [him]" (38), he must remain faithful to Pharaoh, even though the canine houseguest often snarls and growls at him. Pharaoh's presence in the novel underscores the complexity of the human-to-human interactions noted previously.

In addition to the aforementioned themes, the complexity of race emerges as a dominant issue. While race always plays at least a minor role in all of Mosley's fiction, in *A Little Yellow Dog*, Mosley addresses some of the racial paradoxes assessed in *Devil in a Blue Dress*. In addition, race is used, in part, as a metaphor for exploring the notion of difference in general. Mosley acknowledges the typical racial tensions (between blacks and whites) while also observing how society, as a whole, increasingly defies racial boundaries. In describing the corpse of Roman Gasteau, Easy notes that while the body did not seem to be that of a white man, it did not appear to be that of a black man, either. Instead, "his racial roots could have been from at least four continents, or a thousand islands around the world" (29). This description underscores the strange contradiction of society, on the one hand being so beholden to racial demarcations, yet on the other engaging in acts of miscegenation, both historically and in the present. Simona Eng, for example, is both Italian and Chinese. She, like the Gasteau brothers, confirms America's paradoxical treatment of race. Such cross-racial interaction is presented again in two other relationships. Idabell Turner and colleague Bill Preston establish a romantic friendship when Idabell confides in him about her domestic troubles. Preston admits to Easy that they have fallen in love with each other. While the Turner-Preston relationship might seem odd, the Grace Phillips–Bertrand Stowe pairing is all the more bizarre, not only because of race, but also because of a difference in social status. Ultimately, however, their class difference has no more importance to them than their racial difference. They are simply two human beings who have found each other. In this way, difference (race, social status, etc.) becomes an arbitrary notion that real human beings disregard in the better interest of compassion and commitment. Nevertheless, Mosley acknowledges that race (arbitrary though it may be) is a factor that people must confront. Easy, commenting on Bonnie's naiveté about the impartiality of the justice system, notes, "I knew right then she wasn't a fully American Negro. A black man or woman in America, with American parents, knew that innocence was a term for white people. We were born in sin" (201). Even though Bonnie thinks that justice is color-blind, Easy knows that such a belief is unfounded. Mosley, then, addresses the reality of race in America while also exposing America's inconsistencies. He even ridicules the demarcation of race along ethnic lines when he has Easy mock the very idea of race: "Cops is a race all its own" (142). Here Easy suggests that regardless of their ethnic background, all members of law enforcement are a breed unto themselves, a group that one would do well to avoid. Race, then, is used as an expedient way to separate people once they accept the racial division as a natural (and thus real) construct instead of as a social (and thus contrived) construct.

HISTORICAL CONTEXT

A Little Yellow Dog is set in November 1963, during the week leading up to the assassination of President Kennedy. Like all of the Easy Rawlins novels, this one is not set in the turbulent South; however, the civil rights tensions of the period do frame the text. For example, when Easy is brought into the police precinct for questioning, he states that he feels as though he is "back, suddenly, in the deep south. . . . Back to a time when the rear door was the only door. . . . " (154). Easy's connection to his Southern youth reminds the reader of the events that took place earlier in 1963.

During the spring of the year Dr. Martin Luther King Jr., while incarcerated in Birmingham, Alabama, drafted his famous "Letter from Birmingham Jail." In what would become an important historical document, King bemoaned the resistance (from white ministers) to his nonviolent campaign for civic equality. Echoing the words of Thurgood Marshall that "justice delayed is justice denied," King urged the citizens of Birmingham to rally around the efforts for social equality. The sentiments expressed in that work would prepare King for his most famous speech (later known as the "I Have a Dream" speech), which he delivered on the grounds of the Lincoln Memorial at the March on Washington in August 1963. Then, less than a month later, in mid-September, one of the most horrific occurrences of the Civil Rights Movement would shock America: the bombing of Birmingham's Sixteenth Street Baptist Church, which resulted in the tragic deaths of teenagers Denise McNair, Carole Robertson, Addie Mae Collins, and Cynthia Wesley (to be known across America as those "four little girls"). At the same time that Bonnie Shay, of French Guianan descent, thinks that justice is meted out fairly in America, the contemporary historical moment would suggest otherwise. Still, America was changing rapidly, and no one was fully prepared for all that would occur. Even Easy notes, "I could feel the world turning under my feet. At any minute I could have gone spinning off into space. . . . The headlines spoke of every kind of tragedy" (286).

In addition to his reference to the Kennedy death (on November 22), Easy also notes the passing on November 21 (one day before the president's assassination) of Robert Stroud (1890–1963), the infamous Birdman of Alcatraz. Stroud was imprisoned in 1911 for murdering a man in Juneau, Alaska, in 1909. Always defiant and contemptuous of authority, Stroud murdered a prison guard at Leavenworth in 1916 and was sentenced to die. However, President Woodrow Wilson commuted the sentence to life imprisonment. To pass the time, Stroud became interested in the study of birds (ornithology) and fancied himself an authority on the subject, though his expertise was always in dispute. Nevertheless, he maintained an aviary first at Leavenworth and later at Alcatraz. To many, Stroud was an unstable psychopath; to others, a legend. He was immortalized in the 1962 film *The Birdman of Alcatraz*, starring Burt Lancaster in the title role. As Easy states, Stroud was a hero among black people because of his defiance and because he understood the odds that blacks faced.

Mouse's death occurs within hours of Kennedy's assassination and, of course, within a day of Stroud's. In many ways Mouse is presented as a combination of the two men, both saint (Kennedy) and killer (Stroud). After Easy leaves an injured Mouse with an angry EttaMae, he drives home while noticing that people along the sidewalks and on the streets seem to be in suspension, moving about in a kind of surreal haze. Because he has not yet learned of the president's death, Easy thinks that perhaps they are already mourning Mouse's imminent death. To think that an entire population would react to Mouse's death is tantamount to exalting Mouse. And because Mouse's longstanding brutality has been tempered with his recent transformation (he even tries to confess to EttaMae's minister), the reader more readily accepts such a presentation of Mouse. On the other hand, Mouse is also similar to Stroud. During a conversation with Easy about the rationale for having to kill someone, Mouse ultimately concludes that killing is all right because one must do so in order to survive. In fact, continues Mouse, the police and the government kill all the time, and no authority holds them accountable. Like Mouse, Stroud attempted to justify the two murders for which he had been convicted: the first he committed supposedly to avenge the beating of a woman, while the second murder (of the prison guard) he committed because he feared the guard was going to draft a disciplinary report that might have resulted in Stroud's being denied an impending family visit. For Stroud, the end clearly justified the means. By juxtaposing the death of Mouse (a most important character in the whole Rawlins series—Easy's sidekick and best friend) with the deaths of Kennedy and Stroud, Mosley forces the reader to reassess Mouse's status and to resist an extreme characterization.

Important to note as well is Mosley's ending the novel with the Kennedy assassination. With Mouse's death, with EttaMae's abrupt departure, and with Jackson Blue's sudden flight, Easy's world will never be the same. Likewise, the president's murder changed America forever. While the Kennedy reign was described as a time of hope, innocence, and romance (with its Camelot identity), its unexpected end left an irreplaceable void. Though the Civil Rights Bill of 1964 and the Voting Rights Act of 1965 will follow, the remainder of the decade will witness major unrest. Easy's Watts neighborhood will erupt into a veritable inferno by mid-decade, and the life that he once knew will no longer exist. The drugs that

Roman Gasteau was instrumental in importing to the area (and other drugs that will follow) will have a devastating impact on the community. By ending the novel with President Kennedy's assassination, Mosley confirms the end of one era and the beginning of another, wherein the Easy Rawlinses of the world will not as easily negotiate urban perils.

In regard to a literary framework for this novel, Mosley borrows in part from the tradition of naturalism. Easy refers at one point to the famed French writer Emile Zola (1840–1902), often touted as the originator of naturalism in western literature. Naturalism, of course, applies to literature the principles of scientific determinism. It states that human beings are impacted by both biological determinism (controlled by certain innate urges) and socioeconomic determinism (affected by the environment). The usual setting for a naturalistic work is the city, presented metaphorically as a jungle or zoo. Humans are depicted as animals who act typically on instinct rather than with logic, in an effort to survive in an indifferent, if not hostile, world. While all of the Rawlins mysteries exploit this genre to some degree, *A Little Yellow Dog* is especially naturalistic. The very fact that an animal is the title character supports this observation. Also, Easy's carnal interaction with Idabell at the beginning of the novel obligates him to care for Pharaoh, a circumstance that involves him in the ensuing murder investigations.

Throughout the novel, Easy compares himself to Pharaoh, allowing that maybe he and the dog hate each other so much because they are so much alike. In one scene, Easy "bared [his] teeth and snarled" (123), forcing Pharaoh to retreat. Prowling around the streets of the Watts "jungle," Easy, in some ways, becomes the animal who acts more on instinct than logic. In making the comparison, Easy anticipates and highlights the naturalistic allusions in *A Little Yellow Dog*. Early in the novel, when describing Idabell's beauty, Easy states that all men, "from Cro-Magnon to Jim Crow" (2), would find her attractive. In mentioning Cro-Magnon man, Easy alludes to the theory of evolution, a significant component in naturalism (the notion that only the strongest evolve and hence survive). At the same time, however, in mentioning Jim Crow (the term used to refer to legalized segregation), Easy suggests that mankind really has not progressed very far—that is, one who harbors Jim Crow tendencies is just as animalistic as an actual Cro-Magnon man.

Easy makes other animal references throughout the novel. He and Idabell "wrestled across the floor more like snakes than humans" (126), and in a dream, Easy "wanted to grow fur and scurry off between the thick branches that bristled at the road," that is, "to become a beast and run" (126). And later, when Easy is trying to negotiate with Stetz, he finds that Stetz is "a cat in the window, frozen before his leap" while Easy is "a bird on the ledge, praying for glass" (282). Mouse also contributes to the dialogue on naturalism when he posits that life in general is concerned with killing, arguing that animals, bugs, and even plants kill in order to survive. For Mouse, then, such naturalistic tendencies are simply "natural." While the environment may *encourage* the behavior, it is not responsible *for* the inclination. This novel, like the others, forces the reader to confront these truths.

NARRATIVE STRUCTURE

Like all of the Easy Rawlins books, *A Little Yellow Dog* is narrated in the first person by Easy himself. Though Easy has ostensibly experienced all of the events presented in the novel, he still maintains the mystery by either deceiving the reader or delaying information. Such a ploy requires extreme attention to detail, especially in a novel that is paced within only a five-day frame. The novel begins on Monday morning, November 18, 1963 (the reader calculates the date later), when Easy goes to work to discover that Idabell Turner has already arrived. From that moment on, until Friday, November 22 (the reader, aware of history, knows it must be Friday because President Kennedy is shot), the tightly wrought plot moves along smoothly, with every detail contributing to the overall aesthetic experience. With an almost minute-by-minute accounting of events, Easy manipulates every detail during this five-day period to keep the reader on edge and heighten the suspense.

The first few chapters provide key examples of this structure. When Idabell asks Easy to keep Pharaoh temporarily, the plot (the mystery) is set in motion. Later, after Easy agrees, a body is discovered. EttaMae suggests that the corpse might be that of Idabell's husband. Then Easy learns that Idabell has rushed from the school after informing the officials there that her dog has been injured. Even though Easy, at this point, is willing to protect Idabell and her alibi, he (and the reader) suspect that she has had something to do with the murder. Then later, when Easy steals his way into Idabell's house, only to discover yet another corpse (which looks exactly like the first one), he (and the reader again) are especially suspicious of Idabell (it is evident that she is hiding something). But when

Idabell is also murdered, the questions really mount, and the plot moves swiftly as Easy works tirelessly to unravel the mystery by investigating Idabell's relationships with various other people at the school.

In addition to the questions about the murders, other questions about Easy's personal and professional life help to structure the novel and compel the reader to proceed. Early in the novel, Easy discovers that Jesus has been hiding away what Easy thinks is stolen money. But because he is so involved in these cases, the answers to his questions about Jesus are not given until much later. However, the reader suspects all along that the revelation of the answers will mark a turning point in Jesus and Easy's relationship; and an interest in this development propels the reader (and the novel). The reader also wonders if Principal Newgate will be successful in implicating Easy in the school robberies, or if he will succeed in forcing Easy to promote Archie Muldoon.

Perhaps the most compelling narrative element to prod the reader, though, is Mouse's amazing transformation. That Mouse would begin to feel remorse about any past action (and that he would seek the counsel of a minister) is almost incomprehensible. The reader expects that at any minute Mouse will resume his former behaviors and exact violence on anyone who tramples on his territory. Even when the novel progresses and Mouse becomes more diplomatic, the reader is poised for Mouse's relapse. Clearly, though, Mouse's newfound moderation alters what has been a stock structure in all the other Rawlins mysteries—that is, Mouse's recurrent personality has become a vital narrative element. Usually, Mouse rises to Easy's defense (sometimes, quite unexpectedly) and succeeds. This time, however, Mouse (for the first time not equipped with a gun) is left defenseless, and the typical narrative structure collapses and is changed forever.

In the previous novels, Easy often makes at least one reference to the future (sometimes even to a specific number of years into the future); in this novel, however, he makes only one passing reference to the future. When Bonnie Shay explains to him her resistance to Roman Gasteau's demands, stating that she refused to act as his whore, Easy notes that he would remember that phrase again and again over the next several weeks and years. In only this instance, and once again when Easy recalls Mouse's beginning transformation two years earlier, does the novel veer from this one-week period in November 1963. At the very end of the novel, Easy projects the story forward by one week, but only to note that America spent the week mourning the death of its president. As noted previously, the bulk of the novel consumes only five days.

A READER-RESPONSE ANALYSIS

Reader-response criticism developed in the 1970s, largely in the work of renowned scholar Stanley Fish, particularly in *Is There a Text in This Class? The Authority of Interpretive Communities* (1980). However, traces of it were evident as early as 1938 when Louise Rosenblatt, in *Literature as Exploration,* called for interpretations that allowed for "an unself-conscious, spontaneous, and honest reaction" (67). Not until she published *The Reader, the Text, the Poem* in 1978 did the rest of the academy catch up with her. By then, Fish, David Bleich—in *Readers and Feelings* (1975) and *Subjective Criticism* (1978)—and others would champion the cause of reader response.

This brand of criticism celebrates different readers bringing to the intellectual discussion varying interpretations. While accepting as fact that every reader is engaged in an act to better understand himself or herself, it acknowledges also that a given reader's personal involvements (i.e., his or her cultural, social, ethnic, economic, and gender-driven experiences in life) will shape the literary critique. Instead of fearing the possibility that such latitude will compromise legitimate "authority," these critics maintain that such diverse views will ultimately enhance the reading and intellectual exchange. Noting the reality that one reader will have different responses to a given text over the course of a lifetime (as the person changes, develops, and experiences more) and will benefit from revisiting the text through these various experiential lenses, the reader-response critic believes that different readers at one time, bringing different views, can effect the same dynamic interchange. Every act of response, whether it is with one reader over time or with a host of readers within a restricted time, is desirable and valuable.

To allay the fears of those who foresee a "collapse" of the text, reader-response critics argue that all individual readers will find themselves as part of interpretive communities (Fish) wherein their interpretations are to be challenged and questioned, the result of which is ultimately a richer understanding of the text. Such analytical sparring, or "negotiation" (Bleich), will enhance the reading experience and encourage individual readers either to solidify their beliefs or to embrace other possibilities. In addition, Rosenblatt calls for a "transaction" between the reader and the text. Whatever the individual reader's interpretation, it must be supported by textual evidence. In other words, the reader cannot simply respond emotionally (i.e., cannot respond with just "feelings"); rather, the reader must interpret intelligently and systematically. The ultimate interpretation, then, is made by the reader *and* the text.

What a reader-response critique offers is a challenge to absolute truth. It rejects a too-narrowly focused point of view and instead compels broader receptivity. One example of such criticism that benefits the intellectual experience is the assessment of a particular character. Because a reader's response to a given character is so instrumental in his or her assessment of the larger narrative (other character interactions, plot, theme, etc.), the reaction to a signal character can dramatically affect the overall interpretation. This observation is particularly important in *A Little Yellow Dog*. Of significance to this discussion is the relevance of the first-person perspective in all of the Easy Rawlins mysteries. This point of view invites the reader along with Easy as he conducts his various investigations, making Easy and the reader co-investigators. In these mysteries, then, the reader's response is inextricably bound to Easy's response. This is not to suggest that the reader's response mirrors Easy's. As the protagonist responds, so does the reader (either to confirm Easy's response or to question it). Easy, along with the reader, is challenged either to be suspicious of characters or to trust them. An error in judgment could cost him his life.

Mosley seems to toy with this notion of response to character in his presentation of the twins. On the one hand, Holland and Roman are identical. When Easy first spies Holland's corpse, he notes how Holland has chosen even to dress like Roman. However, the two brothers are quite different. Holland is violent and crazed, while Roman, though capable of abuse, is mainly easygoing and accommodating. When compared to each other, Holland emerges as the evil brother and Roman as the kinder one. Mosley could easily have presented two brothers with opposing personalities without their being identical twins. However, the deliberate inclusion of twins forces Easy and the reader to consider quite carefully how they are to judge the men, a task made slightly more difficult because both men are the victims of murder. An initial response might not be accurate. Even when one considers Roman singly, one discovers a complex character. In the same scene when Bonnie reveals Roman's physical abuse to Easy, she also tells of his kindness to his elderly neighbors, for whom he often bought groceries and paid the rent. At the same time that he is involved in theft and drug smuggling, he is sensitive enough to exhibit compassion for the aged. One reader might perceive Roman as an absolute scoundrel and take comfort in his demise, whereas another might assess only his positive characteristics. A conversation between the two readers could result in the former coming to terms with human complexity and addressing the varied motives that trigger human actions, while the latter might acknowledge the possibility that Roman contributed to his ultimate downfall. The interpretive community that reader-response criticism supports encourages such exchange to mitigate oversimplified responses and interpretations.

The question of trust in responding to characters is addressed quite poignantly in a crucial scene with Easy and Bonnie Shay. Just moments into their first in-depth conversation, Easy reveals to her aspects of his life that he has deliberately concealed in the past. The reader is forced to question Easy's judgment, and because even Easy comments on the fool-hardiness of his slip—after all, "survival depended on keeping the people around you in the dark" (200)—the reader is presented very openly with the questions of discernment and of whose powers of discernment are more dependable. This scene marks one of those moments when the reader chooses to separate from Easy in an attempt to gain objective distance. The reader thinks that if Easy can so easily suffer a lapse in judgment (even though Bonnie will later prove herself trustworthy), then perhaps the reader must rely only on his or her own perceptiveness and discretion in gauging future encounters.

The complexity involved in judging characters is actually highlighted before one reads even the first word of text. When the reader peruses the title and considers a little yellow dog, he or she thinks of an innocent and vulnerable pet, and this response is validated, to some degree, in the first few chapters. Because Idabell is so devoted to Pharaoh, and sacrifices her own life for him, the reader is led to believe that he, too, is a devoted companion. Pharaoh's relative innocence is verified also in the fact that he has attracted to his care two females (first Idabell, then Feather). However, Pharoah despises Easy, evident in his assumption of the attack posture whenever he encounters Easy or in his leaving for Easy little "gifts" on the bed or in Easy's slippers. The most obvious example of Pharaoh's disdain for Easy is his deliberate assault of Easy when Easy is attempting to defend himself against Sallie Monroe. Instead of attacking the actual villain, Pharaoh tries to bite a plug from Easy's ear. And even at the end of the novel, Easy comments that Pharaoh, having tasted Easy's blood and now hungering for more, would continue to be a dangerous part of his life that always threatened. Pharaoh will remind Easy not only of the less-exemplary aspects of his life but also of the divergent perspectives that consume our lives. Pharaoh adores certain people in his life, and he despises others (Easy most of all). The reader, who has now journeyed at length with Easy, thinks that Pharaoh is perhaps precipitous in his reaction; that is, he has exhibited poor judgment. However, Pharaoh's error, in reminding the reader of the possibility of error, challenges the reader to reconsider his or her assessment not only of Pharaoh (an innocent pet, or a ruthless animal) but also of other characters and circumstances. While the individual reader's response must be respected, it must also be considered in conjunction with other viable responses.

7

Always Outnumbered, Always Outgunned
(1998)

In his eighth novel, *Always Outnumbered, Always Outgunned*, Mosley creates a new protagonist, Socrates Fortlow. Having spent twenty-seven years in an Indiana prison, Socrates has now been released for eight years. In a series of single-chapter vignettes set in the mid-1990s, the novel charts several months in his life as he continues to adjust to living as a free man in the Watts section of Los Angeles. Though he wants desperately to lead a productive life devoid of the violence and poor judgment that resulted in his incarceration, Socrates finds himself confronted with social ills and injustices that test his mettle and potentially threaten his freedom. Along the way, however, he encounters people who do not judge him unfairly, and they help to restore and preserve the humanity that he strives to maintain. Still, Socrates understands that the rules of the street sometimes require him to pursue unorthodox methods not only for his own survival, but also for the survival of those about whom he has come to care.

PLOT DEVELOPMENT

In the chapter entitled "Crimson Shadow" the novel opens at six o'clock A.M., when Socrates spies a boy moving about stealthily in the alley adjacent to his rented house. Suspicious, Socrates confronts the child, Darryl, and finds that he has just killed the neighbor's rooster. Forcing the eleven-year-old into his house, Socrates interrogates the boy about his actions and then instructs him to pluck the bird. Afterward, Socrates cooks the rooster and prepares other foods while continuing to question Darryl about his indifferent behavior. Socrates learns that Darryl lacks a male presence in his home and that for the most part he is left to his own devices. Deciding to take the young man under his wing, Socrates hopes to usher the boy into manhood by protecting him, if possible, from the lure of street life.

"Midnight Meeting" witnesses Socrates, along with four of his friends, trying to decide what course of action to take regarding neighborhood drug addict, thief, and murderer Petis. Markham Peal, Right Burke, Stony Wile, and Howard Shakur have convened in Socrates' small living room to discuss Petis's recent offenses. Ultimately, they agree that they will confront Petis and force him to leave the neighborhood. Socrates, as spokesman, "speaks" to Petis in the only language he understands (physical force). Felling Petis and divesting him of his weapon, Socrates informs him that he must flee, lest Socrates and his men be forced to kill him in the interest of the neighborhood.

In "The Thief" Socrates patronizes the diner owned by Iula LaPort. On this particular day, after Socrates finishes his meal, he still feels quite hungry, but because he has only limited funds, he cannot purchase more food. In walks a twenty-something young man, Wilfred, who initially seems personable and respectful. Ordering himself a sizable meal, Wilfred offers to replenish Socrates's plate. While the two men eat, Wilfred engages Socrates in conversation, and the young man ultimately reveals that he is a professional thief. Taking exception to his career choice, Socrates bemoans the fact that this well-spoken and obviously talented man would prey upon society. Wilfred then reveals a sudden temper when Socrates challenges his lifestyle, and for several seconds the two men almost come to blows. Socrates, however, wins out by staring Wilfred down. After this encounter, Socrates decides that he needs to find gainful employment.

"Double Standard" presents yet another confrontation between Socrates and a young man. Socrates has observed a man and a woman engaged in an amorous embrace. Reminiscing about youthful passion and appreciating the couple's intensity, Socrates does not begrudge their apparent devotion. However, when the two approach and the woman calls out the man's name, Socrates recognizes Ralphie McPhee from his own neighborhood. What causes him great concern, though, is that Ralphie ignores Socrates as though he is a bum. Though Ralphie is not acquainted with the older man, Socrates still thinks that Ralphie, as a fellow human being, should acknowledge his presence. Angry at Ralphie's insensitivity, Socrates confronts the man about his infidelity, urging him to think about the potential repercussions of his affair. Reminding Ralphie that his wife, Angel, and their son could easily discover his adultery if he chooses such a public spectacle, Socrates strives to instill a sense of guilt in the young man.

Socrates challenges other offenses directed at him in "Equal Opportunity" when he seeks employment. Arriving at the Bounty Supermarket, he is treated with disrespect by both the manager, Halley Grimes, and her assistant manager, Alton Crier. Initially refusing even to give him an application, they must relent when Socrates reminds them of his legal rights. Socrates returns to the store every day for several days to inquire whether the central office has acted on his application. Ms. Grimes, who feigns fear about Socrates' persistence, calls in security guards from Bounty's corporate offices when Socrates comes back for the fifth time. Parker and Weems, the guards, question Socrates about his alleged intimidation tactics. Denying the accusation, Socrates simply expresses that he only wants a job. The hired policemen, not completely indifferent to Socrates's plight, decide to find him work at another store in the Bounty chain where he will be more readily accepted.

Darryl returns to the story in "Marvane Street." Knowing that growing boys are always hungry, Socrates feeds Darryl a hearty meal and then asks about how his life is progressing. Sensing that the boy is troubled, Socrates prods Darryl to confide in him. After voicing his fears to Socrates, Darryl finds that he can rest only in the presence of the ex-con. For a week following, Socrates returns home to find an exhausted Darryl sleeping there.

In "Man Gone" Corina Shakur, wife of Socrates's friend Howard, pays a visit to Socrates while also searching for Howard. She explains to Socrates that Howard left suddenly the day before following a heated argument between husband and wife. The older man admits to Corina that if he had a good wife like her, he would never abandon her and their children, not even for one day. He also states that if Howard refuses to regain his senses and return, Socrates, himself, will take the liberty to start calling on Corina. When she leaves, Howard himself emerges from Socrates's other room. Angered that Socrates would flirt so openly with his wife, Howard positions himself for a fight. In no way intimidated, Socrates chides Howard for his lack of integrity and shames the young husband into returning home.

Though Socrates has lived in Los Angeles for eight years, he has never seen the Pacific Ocean. In "The Wanderer" he decides to pay a visit to the coast, recapturing along the way the same burst of freedom he felt upon his release from prison. Upon his arrival at the beach, Socrates proceeds to walk about while reminiscing about the past, both the favored memories and the painful ones. Along the way, he encounters a couple, Gordo, a Vietnam veteran, and Delia, his young girlfriend.

"Lessons" finds a rapidly growing Darryl now living with Socrates. Unfortunately, Darryl, now plagued by the menace of gang warfare, has already been threatened by three young ruffians. In this chapter, Socrates forces Darryl to defend himself against the ringleader, Philip. Though he is frightened, Darryl makes a courageous effort to fight. Soon finding the boy outnumbered by Philip and his juvenile henchmen, Socrates must intervene. Nevertheless, Socrates is proud of Darryl for defending himself, regardless of the outcome.

"Letter to Theresa" presents a confused Socrates attempting reconciliation with his past. Socrates is so haunted by memories of his ex-girlfriend that he cannot sleep at night. In an effort to rest these demons, Socrates decides to send her a letter. After a grueling month's wait, Socrates finally receives a reply from Theresa's mother, who informs him that Theresa is dead. Feeling cheated, Socrates pays a visit to Theresa's grave in the hope of bringing closure to this memory.

In "History" Socrates is faced with a moral dilemma. Watts has been thrust into civil unrest, and the result has been widespread looting and destruction of property. To protect himself, Socrates stays in his house for three days, choosing to witness the spectacle only on his television. On the third day, however, while Socrates continues to watch the footage, he notices a billboard that reminds him of his life when he first arrived in Los Angeles eight years earlier. During that time Socrates frequented the small but popular Capricorn Bookshop. Now, returning to see what destruction has been visited upon the establishment, Socrates finds a burned-out shell of a space. Rifling through the remains is his old nemesis Roland, who has also come to bemoan the fate of the store. After discovering that Roland is plagued with cancer, Socrates cares for the man in his remaining days.

Fire and arson link "History" with the next chapter, "Firebug," in which some unknown arsonist has destroyed abandoned buildings and houses in a dozen fires. The most recent fire has killed a homeless squatter and his girlfriend. On the night of this fatal fire, Socrates discovers who the culprit is. Initially unsure of what to do, Socrates decides to contact, through his friend Stony Wile, a police officer he thinks he can trust to ensure that the suspect, Ponzelle Richmond, is treated fairly. Unfortunately, when the police go to arrest Ponzelle, the guilty man shoots himself. Though Socrates feels remorseful about his indirect involvement in the man's death, he still accepts the fifteen-thousand-dollar reward.

After leading a model life for eight years, Socrates almost returns to prison in "Black Dog." Late one afternoon as Socrates prepares to leave work, he observes a speeding car strike a dog. Rushing to give aid to the injured creature, Socrates is approached by the car's driver, Benheim Lunge, who is fearful of the consequences of his actions and tries to force Socrates to hand over the dog. Suspecting that Benheim intends to kill the dog and suppress the evidence of the accident, Socrates strikes Benheim, who is wielding a dumbbell. Arrested and arraigned for assault, Socrates is lucky to receive a suspended sentence.

The final chapter, "Last Rites," focuses on the last days of Socrates's best friend, Right Burke. Completely consumed with pain and bedridden from the cancer that has overtaken his body, Right begs Socrates to give him a gun so that he can kill himself. Unable to bring himself to honor this wish, Socrates chooses instead to purchase Right a supply of painkillers from a neighborhood gangster. After taking some of the medication, Right begins to feel better, strong enough to enjoy one last night on the town with Socrates. The two old friends patronize a local bar and drink as much as Right can stomach, while also flirting shamelessly with the waitress. Socrates is pleased to see his friend happy once again. Later, while waiting at a bus stop to escort Right home, Socrates is faced with a dilemma when Right commands Socrates to leave him there on the bench. After much coaxing, Socrates decides to withdraw. The novel ends with Socrates boarding the approaching bus, and though he still questions his decision, he reconciles his doubt by remembering that Right should have the right to chart his own fate.

CHARACTER DEVELOPMENT

Eight years free from a twenty-seven-year prison term, Socrates Fortlow, now age fifty-eight, continues to acclimate himself to the outside world. Convicted of both rape and murder, he has had much time to reassess his life while also engaging in deep introspection. His sole motivation now is to maintain control of his life by keeping his emotions and internal drives in check. As a young man, lulled into a drunken stupor while out carousing with his friend Shep and Shep's girlfriend, Muriel, Socrates loses his grip on reality. As a consequence, when Shep falls asleep completely inebriated, Socrates takes advantage of Muriel. Upon awaking, Shep intercepts, only to have Socrates attack him with a fatal blow. Later Socrates strikes Muriel and continues to rape her. The next day, Socrates awakes to find both people dead. Socrates will forever suffer pangs of guilt about this tragic event.

Socrates's most commendable efforts are evidenced in his interaction with eleven-year-old Darryl. Realizing that the boy needs a strong and stable male presence in his life, Socrates willingly fulfills this role. Darryl functions as a major character mainly because he draws forth Socrates's more human attributes. With Darryl, Socrates is both stern and sensitive, and Darryl, by modeling Socrates, learns how to be both tough and compassionate. Because his own father was in jail before he died, Darryl is responsive to Socrates as a father figure. He is also respectful of Socrates's plight, both past and present. Finally, Darryl finds someone with whom he can share his innermost thoughts and fears. When Socrates insists that Darryl protect himself against one neighborhood bully, the boy, though gripped with fear, heeds Socrates' admonition. Darryl's survival and longevity give Socrates hope for the future.

Socrates's closest friend is Right Burke, the oldest of the group of men who pay an occasional visit to Socrates's modest rental unit. A veteran of World War II, Right has been partially paralyzed for over a decade, and he also suffers from cancer. As the eldest of the group Right has the freedom to voice his opinion with impunity. Socrates has come to appreciate, and to depend on, Right's abiding honesty.

While Right is the oldest of Socrates's friends, Howard Shakur is the youngest and the heaviest. Presented initially as a man very protective of his family, Howard will soon expose a more selfish side to his personality. When Howard discovers that his very young daughter, Winnie, has witnessed Petis killing someone, he refuses to subject the girl to police interrogation, clearly assuming the posture of a caring father. Later, however, when Howard's wife Corina visits Socrates, the story reveals a more self-consumed Howard. In recent weeks, after losing his job, Howard seems satisfied at having Corina work outside the home, and he assumes responsibility for the house and the children. He refuses even to accept a minimum-wage job. Ultimately, though, Howard is frightened out of his complacence when Socrates threatens to court Howard's family. He emerges as a man when he begins working at a fast-food restaurant while waiting for advancement.

Stony Wile, a former welder and shipbuilder who now works on a fishing boat, functions as Socrates's other confidant in addition to Right Burke. When Socrates is struggling to secure a job at the supermarket,

Stony offers advice and support while at the same time cautioning Socrates not to jeopardize his freedom by intimidating the store management. Generally preferring a conservative approach over direct confrontation, Stony does not want to risk, nor does he wish his friends to risk, the modest gains achieved in life. Unlike Socrates, Stony feels powerful only in the company of others.

Other major characters who serve as allies to Socrates include Iula LaPort, Dolly Straight, Winifred and Oscar Minette, and Corina Shakur. Iula is described as an industrious and dedicated woman. With feverish intent, she has kept one of the neighborhood's few businesses thriving. Her commitment to her community extends to her concern for Socrates. Iula's function in the novel is to challenge Socrates's feelings about his past. Though he appreciates her loyalty, Socrates, still harboring guilt about the rape and murders, does not think himself worthy of a woman's love. Still, Iula, at the very least, forces him to question the validity of those current feelings.

Dolly Straight is one of the more distinctive persons whom Socrates encounters. A bohemian veterinarian and daughter of a now-deceased radical activist from the 1960s, Dolly is sensitive to the injustice visited upon Socrates when he tries to save the injured dog. When she welcomes him into her home, Socrates is surprised that a white woman, after hearing about his record during the court proceedings, would take such a risk, especially with a black man. Dolly respects anyone who would risk his own life in the interest of a weak and powerless creature. Dolly is someone, then, who responds only to action, not to empty, meaningless words.

Owners of the Capricorn Bookstore, which Socrates frequents in his early days in Los Angeles, Oscar and Winifred Minette welcome Socrates into their establishment. Because they have created a haven where black people can engage in intellectual discussions about culture, history, and politics, Socrates considers them revolutionaries. Though they are elderly, the couple are quite active in the social and political life of the neighborhood.

In addition to being a loyal wife and mother, Corina emerges as a devoted friend to Socrates. She awakens in him feelings that have long been dormant. An attractive and sincere twenty-three-year-old woman, Corina helps to restore in Socrates part of his lost humanity. Even Socrates is amazed when Corina stirs his sexual passion. Appreciative of Socrates's efforts to restore her marriage, Corina will always extend a welcome to the older man.

Several major characters—Luvia Prine, Ralphie McPhee, Halley Grimes and Anton Crier, Kenneth Shreve, Roland Winters, and Wilfred—function as Socrates's nemeses. They attempt to belittle or demean him, either intentionally or unintentionally. Presented as both a self-righteous yet generous and charitable woman, Luvia Prine has chosen as her life's work the protection and salvation of the downtrodden and poor. As Right Burke's landlady, she operates a boardinghouse for the retired and infirm. Though she is willing to assist anyone in need, Luvia has little regard for Socrates. Aware of his questionable past, Luvia thinks that he is a negative influence on Right.

Though an unwitting nemesis, Ralphie McPhee still makes the mistake of demeaning Socrates. Ironically, though, his actions force Socrates to grow and mature and to exhibit a level of integrity that surprises even Socrates himself. Ralphie forces him to acknowledge his own insecurities about aging and virility. Ralphie's presence in the novel reveals how even a relatively despicable person can enlighten another and help the latter to evolve.

Halley Grimes and Anton Crier, supermarket manager and assistant manager, respectively, attempt every strategy at their disposal to discourage Socrates from securing a job. Unsure whether race or age is the factor, Socrates decides that he will not be intimidated by either one. By societal standards, the older white woman and the younger white man are supposed to instill fear in Socrates. However, with both patience and persistence, Socrates remains undaunted. Grimes and Crier represent the kind of people who see themselves as the ultimate source of power, and whose authority is to be accepted without challenge.

Kenneth Shreve, the police sergeant whose advice Socrates seeks regarding the recent arson attacks, proves to be the stereotypical policeman. Seeming to lack any discernible humanity, Shreve is concerned only about capturing the criminal. While Socrates is worried whether the suspected arsonist will be treated fairly by police and then the justice system, Shreve can promise only that "he'll get as fair a deal as I can give" (179). Even though Socrates has been assured that Shreve, a black man himself, treats all prisoners fairly, the sergeant's aforementioned comment would seem to belie this reputation. And given that the arsonist dies in his encounter with police (though the arsonist kills himself), Socrates regrets trusting Shreve.

One of the people Socrates meets when he first patronizes the bookstore is Roland Winters. Immediately, the two men are pitted against each other by their philosophical differences. Roland, of a more conservative inclination, dismisses all of Socrates's comments on the black man's plight.

Thinking Socrates to be a proponent of violence, Roland argues that black people need to assume responsibility for their own circumstances. Though the two men engage in many heated discussions that take place eight years earlier, they reconcile their differences in the present.

Wilfred, the other customer in the diner, threatens Socrates's character when he chooses to dress like a poor person to commit robberies. As a result, argues Socrates, Wilfred validates white society's belief that poor black men are menaces to society. Wilfred is presented as an aberrant individual whose illogical reasoning potentially undermines not only Socrates but the very milieu that now nurtures him.

Several minor characters also populate Socrates's world. And like the major characters, some of them contribute to his well-being, whereas others work to undermine him. Positive characters include Marjorie Galesky, Sol Epstein, Delia and Gordo, and Brenda Marsh. Mrs. Galesky testifies on Socrates's behalf when he is accused of assault. She, along with Dolly Straight, restores Socrates's faith in humanity regardless of race. Both of these white women defend Socrates against the false accusations of Benheim Lunge. That seventy-nine-year-old Mrs. Galesky refuses to align herself with Lunge simply because he is white is a testament to her integrity and character. Sol Epstein, the assistant manager at the supermarket where Socrates is ultimately hired, treats Socrates with dignity and respect, evident in Sol's sincere concern about Socrates during his three-day illness. When Socrates resumes work, Sol is very happy on his return. Delia and Gordo offer Socrates food, drink, and companionship when he is introduced to them at the beach. Because Gordo is a Vietnam veteran who has seen warfare and death, he is unconcerned about Socrates's past. Quite aware of the pain that life can bring, Gordo and Delia focus solely on the pleasure of the moment. Socrates's defense attorney, Brenda Marsh, redeems herself when she convinces the judge to suspend Socrates's sentence, this after she is consumed with guilt for losing the case. Compromising her own dignity, she pleads with the judge until she finally relents.

The negative minor characters who potentially sabotage Socrates's new life include Benheim Lunge and Conrad McAlister. By bringing assault charges against Socrates, Lunge attempts to divert attention from his own aggressive actions: brutally striking down the helpless dog with his car and then threatening Socrates with a dumbbell. Accustomed to a certain degree of privilege and power, Lunge refuses to admit his errors. Instead, in an effort to retain his primacy (and thus the moral high ground), he positions himself as the victim. His arrogance and fragile ego almost cost Socrates his freedom. Along with Lunge, Conrad McAlister, the prosecuting attorney, works to damage Socrates's reputation. Described as a "pudgy café-au-lait" man, McAlister is presented as a black man who has become a pawn of the unjust justice system.

THEMATIC ISSUES

The novel's title highlights the major theme. If one is "always outnumbered" and "always outgunned," then one confronts a life fraught with unfairness, injustice, and general confusion. In short, the novel presents as its overarching theme the extraordinary difficulty of ordinary life. This paradoxical reality is reinforced by the fact that everyone must, however, strive to endure. Even when faced with social, political, or economic oppression, one must militate against all obstacles to sustain a life that, by its very inception, is meant to thrive. Nonetheless, forces exist solely for the purpose of undermining this attempt. In one of the lessons he teaches Darryl, Socrates exposes society's determined effort to subvert human dignity, promote human failure, and sustain social conflict. Still, it is incumbent on the individual human being first to think critically and shun the indoctrination, and second to challenge the societal agenda.

Socrates takes Darryl to Right Burke's place on Marvane Street and reveals to him several social contradictions. The neighborhood house occupied by the group Young Africans is under surveillance, simply because these young black people take pride in their ethnicity and culture. They are considered to be potentially un-American because they challenge white superiority. Socrates finds the authorities' treatment of this group offensive, especially when there are actual drug houses in the neighborhood that the police could raid. Additionally, Socrates suggests to Darryl, money spent on maintaining hours and days of surveillance could be used to care for the elderly, like Right Burke, who can hardly pay for their own food. And Socrates is bothered that black policemen are charged with spying on these black college youth. Socrates points out to Darryl that society's seemingly illogical actions have a specific purpose: to keep the downtrodden in their lowly position. However, even though they are outnumbered (in terms of their apparent powerlessness), people must still pierce through society's illogic (thinking critically and then challenging the status quo) and strive for a better existence.

Life as paradox is also explored in other subthemes, one of which is the challenge of redemption. Doing good in a world so consumed with evil has been a lifelong struggle for Socrates: "He swore to try and do good if the chance came before him. That way he could ease the evil deeds that he had perpetrated in the long evil life that he'd lived" (60). And when he tries to repay his debt to society in order to redeem himself, he is faced with even more challenges, not just within himself, but also in his interaction with others. After struggling internally, he must struggle externally. While one might think that Socrates would be encouraged in his transformation by the one self-proclaimed Christian in the novel, he is, in fact, practically condemned. Luvia Prine, though she happily accepts her Christian duty to help others in need, demeans Socrates. With such treatment, then, Socrates is forced to seek redemption under more difficult and trying circumstances. Exposing the religious injustice of his treatment, Socrates states to Darryl: "Christians believe in redemption, that's true. But usually you have to die in order t'get it. I guess Luvia would say a few nice words if I died. But it would take somethin' like that" (90). That Socrates would have to die in order for Luvia to voice kind words reveals two contradictions: one, Christians, though they profess the power of Christianity to improve humanity, do not really believe; and two, Luvia expressing kind thoughts about someone she has despised after his death bespeaks the greatest hypocrisy. With such religious confusion and contradiction, the possible redemption of a Socrates Fortlow seems all but impossible. However, Socrates will come to realize that only he, returning to and then reconciling that internal struggle, is responsible for his redemption.

Still another important subtheme that functions in tandem with redemption is the acceptance of appropriate retribution. Socrates's achieving redemption is contingent not only on his bearing punishment (a condition satisfied with his long-term imprisonment), but also on his fully appreciating the concept of punishment. When Socrates expresses guilt upon the suicide of Ponzelle Richmond, the arsonist whom he exposed to the police, he reveals that he understands the importance of retribution. Because Socrates thinks that he and Stony are partially responsible for Ponzelle's death (Stony helped Socrates locate Sergeant Shreve), he thinks that someone should be punished or, at the very least, be made to feel as guilty as he feels. Even though Ponzelle is responsible for countless burnings and two deaths, Socrates still thinks the man deserved a fair judicial proceeding. Now recognizing clear-cut degrees of right and wrong, Socrates has become a vigorous advocate for honoring virtue and penalizing villainy. When he gives to Stony a small share of the reward money (for capturing the arsonist) and says, "That's your share for helpin' t'kill Ponzelle" (181), Socrates is ridiculing Stony and exposing the irony of receiving such a reward. To receive money for involving oneself in the death of another person strikes Socrates as being both inappropriate and offensive. And while he does not relinquish his own reward, at the very least he feels chagrined by the ordeal.

Yet another significant subtheme, and one also related to redemption, is reconciliation with the past. When Socrates writes the letter to his former girlfriend Theresa, he once again accepts the responsibility of his past mistakes, appreciating the fact that had he made different decisions, he would have had a different (and perhaps better) life. Socrates's greatest regret is not just that he killed in the past, but that he killed a woman. In writing to Theresa he apologizes not only for causing her heartache, but also indirectly for causing the death of another woman. That he constantly thinks about his mother, Irene Fortlow, and occasionally about his aunt, also underscores his regret for killing a defenseless woman. In thinking about these women who were so important to him, he further appreciates the depth of his crime against all women.

This hope for the future introduces yet another important subtheme: the importance of accepting one's civic and social responsibility, with all its attendant frustrations and confrontations. When Socrates willingly assumes the role of mentor for Darryl, he contributes positively to society by preparing the young man to become a productive citizen in the future. Because Socrates understands that life will not be easy for the boy, he employs tough love in his interactions with Darryl. In thinking about his duty to Darryl, Socrates bemoans that he did not have a male mentor in his past to prod and admonish him. In his desire to "pick Darryl up by those bony shoulders and slam him up against the wall," Socrates wishes that "some man had had that kind of love for him before he'd gone wrong" (80). Though the process is not an easy one, the particular tactic he takes with Darryl now will shape his future. In addition to disciplining and protecting Darryl, Socrates (along with friends) takes the initiative to rid the neighborhood of detritus like Petis, whose only role in life is to terrorize and destroy. If the neighborhood is to have any promise for the future, it must be cleansed of parasites like Petis. Still, the effort is not made without some doubt (which, in this case, is indicative of the paradoxical nature of this civic obligation). When Stony suggests to Socrates that they should coerce other evil elements to leave the neighborhood, Socrates demurs because he does not want them to become a gang of vigilantes. While he appreciates the importance of his obligation, he must always assess the methods.

A final subtheme, one that recurs in Mosley's fiction, is the defense and maintenance of black manhood. While Socrates is, of course, sensitive to the plight of black men (evident in his acknowledgment of their being "outnumbered" and "outgunned"), he still expects black men to embody strength and determination. When they succeed despite the odds (and success is often just surviving long enough to battle yet another day), they, according to Socrates, engage in the most forceful kind of revolution. According to Socrates, "[A]ny black man that ever did a thing for hisself broke the rules—he had to because the rules say that a black man cain't have nuthin'" (163). Socrates believes that black men must confront the reality of their circumstance and work tirelessly to improve upon those conditions. They must, however, envision themselves beyond the circumscribed space originally allowed them. The ever-improving life he now leads is a testament to the possibility for realizing such a vision.

HISTORICAL CONTEXT

Always Outnumbered, Always Outgunned is set in the mid-1990s, yet it also focuses indirectly on the thirty-plus years prior to this period. Signal historical events are highlighted to underscore the recurring motif of life as a war. During his encounter with Delia and Gordo, Socrates, of course, learns that Gordo is a Vietnam veteran. Still affected by his wartime experiences and plagued by the killings he discharged, Gordo has set out on his annual trek to the beach to celebrate one of the twenty-six men he executed. For each of the last twenty-six years since he last killed a Vietnamese soldier, in 1969, Gordo has conducted this tribute. The reflection on Gordo's actual experience in war reinforces Socrates's embattled life. Socrates and Gordo share "war" stories about various killings, with Socrates admitting not only the murders that landed him in prison, but also the murders he committed while in prison. Socrates explains that in prison, one either commits a crime or suffers a crime every day: "Once you go to prison you belong there" (122). Actual war, or the war in prison, commands its own rules. While these rules might seem inhumane from a more objective perspective, the wartime culture demands that real fighters, survivors, and ultimately victors must act (kill) instead of waiting to be acted upon (killed).

Another historical event employed to contextualize the novel is the 1992 Los Angeles response to the infamous Rodney King trial. When the four white police officers accused of beating motorist Rodney King in 1991 were acquitted of criminal charges, the Watts region of the city erupted in civil unrest. This actual event is used to frame the "History" chapter of this novel, evidenced when Socrates ensconces himself in his house to watch the television coverage of the unrest and witnesses the "continual video replay of some white man being dragged from a truck and beaten by raging black men" (153). This fictionalized account refers, of course, to the now-famous white truck driver, Reginald Denney, who is forced from his vehicle and brutally beaten during the rioting. Socrates understands the frustration felt by the black community. And though he does not condone the citizens' destructive behavior, especially within their own community, he recalls the rage and frustration he felt while incarcerated and is somewhat tempted to join the crowd. In other words, Socrates almost allows the same suspension of civil rules that he and Gordy acknowledge in their previous wartime and jail-time experience. He is reminded once again that life in the real world is war, and in a war notions of right and wrong are quickly muddled. However, Socrates is ultimately horrified by the ensuing events, especially when he discovers the complete destruction of the Minettes' bookstore. Knowing now that his freedom is always tenuous, Socrates does not wish to jeopardize his liberties voluntarily.

In addition to the Rodney King trial, another Los Angeles–centered yet nationally renowned event to be referenced (and one that also reinforces Socrates's appreciation for freedom) is the O. J. Simpson trial. When Socrates is awarded a suspended sentence in his assault case, Right Burke tells him how lucky he is simply to be free, reminding him that "after that big trial they just had the court wanna put ev'ry black man they can in the can" (196). The feelings of betrayal that many felt subsequent to the Simpson trial could have resulted, suggests Right, in the unfair treatment of Socrates. As in war, one casualty deserves another. And since a significant portion of both the Los Angeles and American populations believed the Simpson verdict yielded a miscarriage of justice, then a Socrates incarceration would have been a just exchange. Nonetheless, just as Socrates has survived all previous "wars" in his life, he emerges as victor in this latest brush with the law.

While references to the aforementioned historical events add texture to the novel, the name of the protagonist is also significant in establishing context. No doubt, Socrates is named for the ancient philosopher. Though the Athenian Socrates (469–399 B.C.) left no actual writings, his methods for pursuing knowledge and his guiding philosophy are revealed in the works of his most famous pupil, Plato. Reputed as being neglectful of his own affairs, Socrates instead devoted his energies to discussing virtue, piety, and justice with his fellow citizens wherever they congregated. Devising the method now known as Socratic dialogue, or dialectic, Socrates extracted knowledge from his students by posing questions and examining the implications of their answers. This method registered with his philosophy that all knowledge rests in the self and that true knowledge (which Socrates equated to virtue) results from a keen self-awareness. For him, the soul serves as the repository of moral character. Highly misunderstood and drawing many enemies as a result of his criticism of political and religious institutions, Socrates was ultimately tried, convicted, and executed for corrupting the minds of Athenian youth. In short, he was viewed both positively and negatively.

Like the philosopher, protagonist Socrates is also a teacher who demands that his students participate in the learning process. On at least three occasions in the novel, this role is manifested. Early in the novel, when Socrates and his friends are debating what to do about Petis, instead of declaring a plan (as his friends would prefer that he do), Socrates simply allows the conversation to proceed. Finally, when Howard reveals the suitable answer, Socrates, the reader is told, "smiled like a teacher approving of his student's lesson" (32). Later, when Socrates is discussing the Young Africans and other Marvane Street occurrences with Darryl, he is said to be interacting with his pupil, whom he will, of course, directly instruct in the chapter "Lessons." And finally, at the end of the novel, before Right Burke and Socrates depart, Right shares heartfelt sentiments with his friend. He reveals that he has always believed Socrates to be the teacher in the group of men, that in fact Socrates, who seemed already to know everything, was, by all indications, just testing them. And in true philosopher fashion, Socrates encourages his audience to think even more intently about issues; he keeps the "answers" ever elusive by seeming to contradict his own views.

NARRATIVE STRUCTURE

Unlike the Easy Rawlins mysteries, which are told from the first-person perspective of the protagonist, *Always Outnumbered, Always Outgunned* is presented from the third-person point of view. While the first-person perspective establishes intimate contact between the narrator and the reader, with the reader given access to all of the narrator's thoughts, the third person creates a certain detachment between the reader and the characters, even though a third-person narrator can ostensibly be omniscient. In this novel, the third-person narrator does occasionally present the story from the limited omniscient perspective, a circumstance whereby the detached narrator delivers the story from the vantage point of a particular character. From time to time throughout the narrative, the reader gains insight into the thoughts and feelings of this character. In *Always Outnumbered, Always Outgunned*, the character from whose perspective the third-person narrator presents is, of course, protagonist Socrates Fortlow. Even though the reader gains access to this signal character, Socrates is still portrayed as an enigma, a very complex man who is acquainted with the reader only as his daily experiences unfold. With each dream, with each recollection, with each new encounter of the protagonist, the limited omniscient perspective discloses a few more details about the main character. The noted detachment of the third-person point of view, albeit with limited omniscient intrusions, maintains the mystery that is so vital to the depiction of the often puzzling Socrates.

The novel is made up of fourteen separate stories, nine of which were published separately before the novel's release. As noted in the *Historical Context* section, it is set in the mid-1990s, notably 1995. Three details from the novel indicate that the primary year is 1995. When Socrates is freed of assault charges, Right Burke makes a reference to the 1995 O. J. Simpson trial. In addition, while Socrates is socializing with Delia and Gordo, the Vietnam veteran indicates that this is the last year for his annual tribute to each of the twenty-six men he killed in war, with the last death in 1969. That year plus each year for twenty-six tributes brings the present day to 1995. In addition, the reader is told that Socrates was convicted in 1960 and then spent twenty-seven years in prison. A 1987 release date plus eight years of freedom would, once again, bring the date to 1995. However, Mosley also employs poetic license in his manipulation of time. The "History" chapter opens with the indirect reference to the civil unrest following the 1992 verdict of the Rodney King trial. Clearly, then, the text is not "fixed" in time; rather, it flows along a somewhat relaxed continuum of the mid-1990s.

Also, either via recollection or in disturbing nighttime dreams, Socrates revisits moments from the remote past. He recalls some of his more horrifying experiences while in prison, snippets that provide insight for the reader into the unusual strategies the prisoner had to adopt simply to survive. Socrates has periodic dreams about his childhood and his mother. Because she was the only person who remained loyal to him after his conviction (dying while he was imprisoned), Socrates yearns once again for her love and devotion. These recollections place the novel, if only temporarily, in a previous decade, whether it is a 1970 prison memory or a 1940-something childhood reminiscence.

Even though the novel is composed of distinct stories, it still maintains narrative unity. Such cohesion is achieved primarily with three characters:

Darryl, Right Burke, and Socrates himself serve as catalysts. The novel opens, of course, with Socrates's introduction to Darryl. The young boy's ensuing development structures the novel. A few chapters after he first meets Socrates, he moves in with the older man. No longer the hardened boy who responded to Socrates defiantly, Darryl willingly accepts the ex-con's instructions and even seeks out his counsel. The novel is propelled further when Darryl must then leave Socrates's house to ensure his own safety. The sadness he expresses upon his departure is evidence not only of his maturity into manhood, but also of the novel's development. Right Burke's rapid deterioration also serves to chart the novel's movement forward. In the beginning of the novel, Right can still visit Socrates's house. Later, he can visit, but he must spend the night before he can muster the energy to depart (inebriation notwithstanding). In the latter stages of the novel, Right, afflicted with unrelenting pain, is cloistered in his room at Luvia's. Only when Socrates secures for him unauthorized pain suppressants is he able to venture out one last time.

Without a doubt, Socrates's development provides the most significant means of charting the novel's movement. Starting out as a mere collector of discarded bottles and cans, Socrates emerges as a respected supermarket employee. After contending for the right to have gainful employment (without violence), Socrates has improved his station in life. With the ability now to afford just a few luxuries (things that others consider necessities), he can even offer modest support for his friends. He willingly commits to supplementing Darryl's upkeep, and he supplies Luvia with money to complement Right's meager funds. Socrates has transformed from a recently released prisoner who had to monitor himself closely in his interactions with others and grade himself accordingly (i.e., whether or not he resorted to violence). He now maintains emotional attachments to others. This emerging character unifies each of the fourteen stories (chapters).

A POSTCOLONIAL ANALYSIS

Postcolonial criticism examines a work using the oppressor-oppressed model whereby a colonizing group encroaches on the physical and cultural space of another group, the colonized, and forces the latter group to adopt the value system, language, cultural practices, and sensibilities of the colonizer. The postcolonial theorist is concerned with the oppressed group's rejection of previous subjugation and the restoration of its own agency and purpose, hence the term *post*colonial. These critics focus on issues of cultural difference in literary works. Instead of ignoring the tensions these differences may create, the postcolonialist will analyze such tensions to learn more about each cultural position. Concerning matters of imperialism, this process often involves initiating discussions on difference that have often remained unvoiced.

For example, one might read an American novel that chronicles British colonists' gradual expansion across North America from the seventeenth century on, as it also celebrates the promise, hope, and reward of America's growth. The postcolonial critic would challenge the omission of key concerns, like the widespread genocide of Native American communities. Or the critic might question the assumption that British culture is somehow superior to other cultures and "civilizing" (taking control over and ultimately suppressing) other cultures is thus justified.

The postcolonial critic is concerned not just with distinct cultural spaces and positions but also with hybridity, that is, the circumstance whereby individuals or groups belong to more than one culture. Perhaps most importantly, the postcolonialist deliberately acknowledges the "other" (oppressed, colonized) as a source of energy, or an agent of change, and not merely as an object, especially when the "other" awakens to his or her oppressed condition.

Granted, the African American experience differs slightly from the typical colonial experience in that African Americans were removed from their land and then placed in a foreign environment. Nevertheless, many of the phenomena felt in the colonizing moment impacted African life in America: forced abandonment of language, cultural suppression, severance of family bonds, and so on. And like the typical colonized group, African Americans must decide at some juncture to "decolonize" themselves and try to recapture a positive sense of themselves. While a standard ploy in the decolonizing effort might be to regain land holdings and government rule, for the African American, who is no longer an inhabitant of the former cultural or physical space, this effort involves reclaiming one's own mind and securing equity in a political and economic system originally designed to suppress even the slightest inkling of agency and resistance.

Mosley addresses colonization on several occasions in the novel. One of the more compelling observations is presented early in the text when Socrates encounters the thief Wilfred in Iula's café. The misguided younger man takes pride not only in his acquisitions, but also in the methods he has adopted for securing those acquisitions. Boasting how he disguises himself as a lower-class thug to rob affluent nonblacks, Wilfred thinks he is a better person because he does not mug any black people. Sporting a fancy car and designer clothes, Wilfred thinks he has bested whites at their own game. Socrates, however, in an uncompromising response to the braggart, criticizes him for his slave (colonized) mentality. For Socrates, the very fact that Wilfred would exploit the worst stereotype of blacks (as being ruffians) in his robbery attempts suggests that Wilfred has accepted and internalized such a negative portrait of blacks. Moreover, his exploitation of this image perhaps jeopardizes the life of poorer black males who cannot afford to dress any better than they do. As Socrates reminds Wilfred, now whites will look at someone like Socrates and identify him as a criminal (irony notwithstanding) just because of his dress. Anyone like Wilfred who would deliberately imperil the lives of other blacks suffers from the worst form of self-hatred that grounds colonized thinking. In addition, Socrates reminds Wilfred that his fine clothes and flashy cars are only the mere trinkets and gewgaws of the white establishment. According to Socrates, the more Wilfred acquires (especially given his methods), the more he becomes indoctrinated in the colonial mindset: "You hatin' them an' dressed like the ones you hate. You don't even know who the hell you is" (49). Though Wilfred thinks he has deceived the white colonizer, Socrates argues that he has simply done the colonizer's bidding when he emulates the colonizer's value system.

Socrates advocates the importance of constant and deliberate critique of the colonizer's (the white majority's) agenda. In a heated discussion about propaganda and the media with Roland and others in the Minettes' bookstore that takes place years earlier, Socrates argues that the black man is engaged in a war against the men who own everything, from the newspapers to the police. As a result, the black man cannot believe any assertion voiced by the colonizer's media or other mouthpieces, because most of what is broadcast is delivered only to maintain the strategically planned agenda of the majority. Minty Seale, one of the patrons of the store, recalls that during the Vietnam War, even honest-faced news anchor Walter Cronkite told half-truths and lies about America's military successes. The very debate that Socrates and others engage in defines postcolonial maneuver, and the fact that such discussions occur in the Capricorn Bookstore is significant. From the very first time he enters the store, Socrates knows that it is a different world, where he can browse through African American literature and read about black cowboys, black scientists, black war heroes, and even black con men. In other words, Socrates learns that his people have contributed to society, that they have not been the stereotypical parasites on society as presented in the colonial media. For Socrates, the bookstore is a revolutionary place, and the Minettes, who have devoted their whole lives to enriching the intellectual lives of blacks, are the ultimate postcolonial thinkers. Socrates himself serves as the quintessential model of someone who has awakened out of a colonial slumber. He who has served time for killing two black people now understands that his purpose in life should be to protect and nurture black life, not destroy it. He even explains to Oscar Minette that he was the best kind of colonized person because he killed two of his own people and then allowed himself to be captured. In essence he, serving the colonial agenda, destroyed three black lives at once.

Years later, Socrates is even more committed to his postcolonial perspective. When he and Roland are rifling through the remains of the store, Socrates admits to the more conservative Roland that he wanted to join the rioters, looting and burning the neighborhood. But he knows that he would have been responsible for police retaliation on his own community and further black casualties. And while there will be these casualties anyway, Socrates does not want to shoulder the blame for any of them. The only rules Socrates now wants to breach are those that define black people, men in particular, as being worthy of oppression. In true postcolonial clarity, Socrates appreciates the fact that every future decision he makes, major or minor, will impact not just him, but his larger cultural, racial, and economic community as well.

8

Blue Light
(1998)

With *Blue Light* Mosley enters the realm of science fiction writing while still employing strategies from his detective fiction. Largely an allegorical novel (an allegory is a work in which abstract entities are given concrete form, most often personified), *Blue Light* assesses human potential when positioned against forces, both abstract and real, that seek to destroy it. Set in the turbulent 1960s, when many Americans, especially young people, began to question the very social structures that previous generations took for granted and accepted as right and proper, the novel proposes a more enlightened way of viewing one's world and oneself. The Oakland/ Berkeley, California, setting provides the perfect backdrop for exploring unusual phenomena. *Blue Light* showcases the sacrifices that must be made in the interest of defiance and progress.

PLOT DEVELOPMENT

The novel opens (after the prologue) with Orde, one of the Blues (those who have been visited by the blue light) delivering one of his regular sidewalk sermons. Standing in the crowd, captivated by Orde's various pronouncements, is acolyte Chance (also the narrator of the novel) who, though not a blue himself, has been a follower of Orde in recent weeks. The Close Congregation believe that Orde holds special powers and possesses wisdom and insights beyond the grasp of normal beings. Chance also worships Orde. When he is questioned about Orde's practices at the beginning of the novel by Miles Barber, a local police detective, Chance refuses to betray his leader. Barber believes that Orde is responsible for several recent murders, the victims of which were members of the Close Congregation. Even when Chance discovers the body of Mary Klee (one of the victims) in Orde's apartment, he still remains loyal to Orde.

Orde insists that Mary died only as a result of Orde trying to feed her a mixture of his blood and hers in the hope that he could bestow upon her some of the powers of the Blues. Orde, knowing how difficult it is to reproduce with a non-Blue, thought that he could begin to remake "normal" humans into Blues by mixing Blues blood with that of non-Blues. Unfortunately, Mary and a few others die as a result of these attempts. Unwilling to abandon his friend, Chance refuses to divulge his knowledge to Barber. Coming to understand that he might never succeed in transforming a normal woman into a Blue, Orde solicits Chance for his assistance in helping to populate the small community of Blues. Again preparing a mixture of blood, this time from himself and Chance, Orde prods his follower to imbibe the concoction. Upon drinking the blood, Chance suffers convulsions; he feels as though worms are tussling in his stomach. Fleeing Orde's apartment like a crazed animal, he is later struck by a car. Unfazed, he continues running while experiencing bizarre visions and abnormal feelings. Eventually he is arrested and held for suspicion of drug use. Unaware of his actual surroundings at his time, he wakes up three months later in a mental hospital.

Orde is pleased to discover that Chance survived the potion. He now expects Chance to return to the Close Congregation and assist with developing more potions that others can take and be transformed, if not into complete Blues, into partial Blues. Soon after Chance is released, however, Orde sequesters himself in his apartment and refuses either to receive visitors or to come out. In the meantime, Chance, with the help of young Reggie (a Blue), discovers that Phyllis Yamauchi, one of the Blues, has been brutally murdered. As the other victims were mere followers (the Close Congregants), Phyllis is the first Blue to die. Chance knows now that Orde had nothing to do with this death (it was not the result of Orde's trying to mix his blood with that of a weaker partner). Returning to Orde's, Chance and Reggie insist that Orde receive them. They take some of Phyllis's blood for Orde to examine, and he ingests all of it. As a Blue, he can read the blood of others, especially other Blues. Phyllis suffered at the hands of Gray Man (or Death).

Pricking his own finger, Orde has Chance taste the blood. As a result,

Chance, envisioning Orde's memories, learns Gray Man's history. In a dreamlike state, Chance sees back a few years earlier. Horace LaFontaine, a terminal patient suffering from lung cancer, finally succumbs to the disease. As the human components of life depart his body, the now-ethereal corpse returns to nature, making its way through dense foliage and ultimately approaching desert land. Gray Man (or Death) begins to stalk Horace's corpse. Gray Man introduces himself to Horace as Grey Redstar when he assumes control of Horace's body. Now fully intending to use Horace's body to wreak havoc on the world, Gray Man forces Horace to return to his old home (now inhabited by a young woman and her uncle) while Gray Man threatens to harm the innocent Joclyn Kyle. Finally, Horace tries to poison himself in the hope of destroying Gray Man, but he fails in the attempt. Chance witnesses all of these actions in his visions, and he ultimately views Phyllis's untimely death. Upon awaking from his dreamlike state, Chance finds himself alone, a bit more courageous, yet unsure of what he must do next.

Chance returns to the location where Orde delivers his sermons so that he might question his friend about the visions. Though he does not find Orde, he does meet Adelaide, Orde's former girlfriend, who also introduces him to her daughter, Julia, whom she had had with Orde. Chance is amazed to learn that Orde has successfully fathered a child. Adelaide informs Chance that she too is looking for Orde so that he can help her with Julia. Suggesting that they accompany him home, Chance escorts mother and child to his ramshackle apartment. Upon arriving they discover an intruder (moments later to be known as Gray Man). The interloper, having sniffed another Blue in Julia, has come to claim his next victim. Immediately fleeing the apartment, Chance and his charges run to save their lives. Losing both Adelaide and Julia in flight, Chance is suddenly accosted by Miles Barber, who brings in the confused and slightly disoriented man for questioning.

Barber accuses Chance of killing Phyllis. Along with his fellow officer, Harlan Castro, Barber interrogates Chance in detail about Phyllis's death. Later, he is released because the police have no probable cause for detaining him. Chance once again returns to the park where the Close Congregation meets. There he finds Orde speaking before his flock. Orde introduces them to his daughter, whom he now calls Alacrity. Orde warns the congregants that an evil presence is presently among them, a Gray Man who wants to harm all of the Blues. In the middle of Orde's sermon, Gray Man approaches the rear of the crowd. Soon the scene erupts into pandemonium when Gray Man attacks the congregants. Many flee, but

Gray Man manages to kill a few, including Orde. Miles Barber survives but is left permanently disfigured and embittered. Chance runs away with Adelaide (Addy), Alacrity, Reggie, and Wanita (Reggie's younger sister). The police label the Close Congregation a cult and blame the group for the multiple deaths. Fearing that an arrest would make them more susceptible to Gray Man's vengeance, as he would more easily find them, Chance and his new group assume a nomadic life into the indefinite future.

For a while, the unlikely collective (Chance and Addy are non-Blues while Reggie, Wanita, and Alacrity are full-blooded Blues) live in the northern California woods, remaining close enough to the Bay Area to learn of any news about Gray Man and the Blues. After some time there, at Reggie's urging, the group departs in search of a safer place. After several days of travel by car and then more on foot, they finally arrive in what purports to be paradise, a place called Treaty. Warmly welcomed by their host, Juan Thrombone, Chance and the others prepare to acclimate themselves to this most unusual place. Juan has a special relationship with the natural environment, befriending animals and even vegetation. He encourages his new guests to relieve themselves of their troubles and to enjoy the peace and solitude of Treaty. Though Chance is initially leery of Juan, especially after he and Addy initiate a relationship, he ultimately warms to the philosopher/horticulturist.

However, everything changes after Chance has an unnerving dream about Gray Man. He is at once in the mind of both Gray Man and Horace LaFontaine. Upon awaking, at Wanita's urging, Chance realizes that Gray Man is coming to Treaty to wreak havoc on the enchanted place. Juan declares that Treaty is now transformed into War, and he urges all non-Blues to leave so that the Blues can collectively battle Gray Man without worrying about the weaker non-Blues. Addy declares that she must remain with her daughter, Alacrity, and her companion, Juan. Though Chance does leave, he soon returns.

Upon approaching War, Chance spies Gray Man attacking a couple of animals. When Chance fires gunshots at Gray Man's head, the evil one merely shrugs off the attack and fells Chance in return. By the time Chance recovers enough to follow him to War, Gray Man has kidnapped Addy and is dragging her away. Now facing a standoff with Juan and the other Blues, Gray Man offers to release Addy if Juan will order his humanlike trees to drain the life from the Blues. In the midst of the negotiation, Chance tries once again to attack Gray Man, again to no avail. Gray Man, now in possession of a defeated Chance and Addy, relishes his success, though not for long. Juan rushes Gray Man and engages him in hand-to-hand combat. Fearing his friend might be defeated this time by Gray Man, Chance enters the fray.

In the midst of the struggle, the threesome fall into the grove of trees, whereupon the trees begin to attack Gray Man. Suddenly, Chance is thrust from the commotion; he can now only witness the battle between Gray Man on one side and Juan and the tree on the other. Seemingly out of nowhere comes Miles Barber, wielding a torch of some kind. He hurls the flame toward the tree grove, setting afire Gray Man and Juan. Both perish in the blaze; Chance, however, manages to rescue the other Blues and Addy. He then lapses into unconsciousness. Upon awaking, all the others are gone, and Chance wanders aimlessly in the woods. Later, some hikers find him and take him to a hospital, where he spends his initial days drifting in and out of consciousness. Accused of setting fire to a national forest, Chance is placed under arrest. But because he is ultimately declared incompetent, he is taken to a state mental institution, where he remains at the end of the novel.

CHARACTER DEVELOPMENT

Several major characters populate the novel. Foremost is the main character and first-person narrator, Lester Foote, also known as Chance, who becomes a member of the Close Congregation as a result of his mental instability. Frustrated by his difficult graduate school studies as well as confused about his mixed heritage, Chance attempts suicide. A Ph.D. candidate in ancient studies at Berkeley, Chance does not understand why he has always been persecuted by a racist society. Painful memories, along with the fact that he is now mistreated in academic circles, largely because of his race, have made Chance susceptible to drug abuse. By the time he joins the Close Congregation, he is practically at his wit's end, wandering the streets aimlessly with his book in progress in tow.

Most of the other major characters are Blues—people who have been visited by the strange blue radiance and given special powers of perception. William T. Portman, or Orde, is in reality a homeless hippie whose mental state has been compromised by an overindulgence in hallucinogens. Though strikingly handsome, he is a college dropout and compulsive liar. Not satisfied with simply rendering his sermons in the park and increasing his spiritual flock, Orde wants to populate the earth with more of his kind. As a Blue, Orde is the natural enemy of Death (who despises human beings with advanced powers), and as a result he must be sacrificed. Because Orde is a leading Blue, his death alerts the others of Death's intent to destroy all Blues.

All of the Blues in the novel experience the blue light on the same day: Reggie Brown and his sister, Wanita; Winch Fargo; Claudia Zimmerman; Horace LaFontaine; Nesta Vine; Alacrity; and Juan Thrombone. Reggie, a thirteen-year-old black youth when the novel begins, is already a precocious child before he is imbued with blue. In fact, he is caring for his twin toddler sisters, Wanita and Luwanda, on the night that the blue light descends. By the time Chance and the others arrive at Treaty, Reggie has advanced to age sixteen. And he is as much a leader for the group as is Chance. Without question, Reggie serves as a role model for his sister Wanita. Because Luwanda dies on the night of the blue illumination, Wanita is now Reggie's only sibling. Very childlike in her demeanor, she often regales the group with fantastical stories about her imaginary excursions. Her presence preserves a modicum of innocence for the often troubled group.

Winch Fargo, "long-haired, self-tattooed" (5), is a troubled inmate who has been convicted of several murders. He receives the blue light just at the moment that he is robbing an elderly couple. Once he experiences the thrill of blue, he runs amok and shoots many in the crowd as he tries to recapture the pleasure of the blue feeling. A poor white man from Missouri, Winch is incarcerated and left to fend for himself.

Perhaps the most bizarre Blue is wealthy socialite Claudia Zimmerman, also known as Claudia Heart. Because she is in the act of making love when the blue light strikes, Claudia is transformed into a nymphomaniac. She is successful at seducing almost any man with whom she comes in contact. Though she is a member of the Close Congregation, Claudia also maintains a separate commune in San Francisco. After the massacre in the park when Gray Man kills Orde, Claudia flees with some of her acolytes to an abandoned gold mine in the desert. There she engages in various sexual escapades until the authorities locate her and try to pin the massacre on her.

Horace LaFontaine, an aging black man who grew up in the slums of Houston, is dying of lung cancer when he is approached by the shaft of blue light. Resting in the bedroom of his sister Elza's house, Horace is at the end of a troubled life. A former thief and rapist, Horace also killed in war and in prison. Still, when his body is inhabited by Gray Man, Horace is horrified at the prospect of being used by absolute evil. Frightened that he (or Gray Man in him) might inflict harm on his host (Joclyn Kyle) and plagued by his own sullied past, Horace suffers constant mental duress.

Ultimately referred to as the Teacher in Treaty, Nesta Vine begins her story as a lowly public library employee. An avid reader of all kinds of books, Nesta works at the library solely to gain access to these treasures. Unsure of life's possibilities for a young black woman, Nesta is, for a time, content simply to expand her mind. On the night of the blue intrusion, Nesta is home reading Aristophanes's *The Birds*. She is immediately transfixed, and she seems to divide into two personalities. She decides that she needs to travel to advance the knowledge she has gained from reading. Upon returning to California, she is a changed woman. This transformation prepares her for the teaching she must do while in Treaty.

The only naturally conceived Blue, Alacrity is introduced as a child of three or four, but soon after her arrival in Treaty, she is changed into a full-grown woman. Emerging as a great warrior as well, she is fearless in her interactions with nature. Even the strongest beasts in the forest do not frighten her. The indomitable strength she has acquired is the result of constant one-on-one battle with bears. While she is physically strong, her purpose in the novel is to bring happiness and joy to those around her.

Juan Thrombone is working as a gardener in Berkeley when he experiences the phenomenon of blue. At the time he is known as Hidalgo Quinones, but after witnessing the light, he is changed to Juan. Using his gardening skills, Juan works to create the paradise that becomes Treaty. Determined to keep all evil away from his new home, Juan plants great trees that are possessed of supernatural powers. The fifty-year-old is a man of superior wisdom and abiding patience.

Other major characters who are non-Blues like Chance include Miles Barber, Gerin Reed, Adelaide, and, of course, Gray Man. Barber, the police detective initially charged with investigating the deaths of four of Orde's followers, becomes obsessed in his determination to find and destroy Gray Man. Described by Chance as a fair cop, even if meddlesome, he never relents in his objective. Badly disfigured during the park massacre, Barber is ultimately relieved of his official duties. Still, he conducts his own private investigation into the history of the Close Congregation and its followers.

Gerin Reed is the warden at Folsom prison, where both Winch Fargo and Mackie Allitar are incarcerated. Very devoted to his duties at the prison, Reed is shaken when Winch suddenly escapes, and does so with the help of one of the guards. Realizing that he has become disenchanted with the world, Reed simply leaves the prison in the middle of the day, the first irresponsible action he has ever taken. No longer striving for professional fulfillment, he wishes only for personal harmony. Taking daily walks in the forest with Juan, Reed spends the greater portion of his time philosophizing and seeking intellectual insights, drawing from the curiosity of his Kentucky childhood.

Adelaide (or Addy) meets Orde when she is nineteen. Hailing from a traditional white Christian family, Addy, an attractive woman with flaming red hair, has always been slightly rebellious. Once Addy produces a Blue child, she is empowered with certain advanced senses. Though she does not have the Blues' powers of perception, she can intuit feelings from others, especially the children. Her inner strength inspires all who encounter her.

Rounding out the list of major characters is Gray Man, the personification of Death. While he ultimately assumes control over Horace La-Fontaine, Gray Man (or Grey Redstar) is presented as a separate entity. More of an abstraction than a tangible figure, Gray Man emerges with only one objective in mind: the complete and utter destruction of all Blues. Disgruntled that mere mortals are enhanced with almost supernatural skills, Gray Man is threatened by any other forces that approach his advanced status.

Several minor characters enhance the storyline, some who are Blues and others who are non-Blues. Among the Blues is Eileen Martel. A humane and compassionate woman, Eileen spends the greater portion of her time either caring for Reggie and Wanita (easing their mother's responsibilities) or visiting Winch Fargo in prison. That she would extend herself to Winch, her husband's killer, is a testament to her humanity and goodwill. And though she is an elderly white woman, she is still willing to defy social mores and assist with black children. Her death at the park massacre is a loss to all who knew her.

Minor non-Blue characters who become residents of Treaty are Trini and also Mackie Allitar. A sixteen-year-old runaway from Tennessee, Trini finds her way to Claudia's commune with her boyfriend, Lloyd. Becoming enamored of Claudia, Trini is her most ardent devotee. Upon Claudia's sudden departure, Trini, like all of Claudia's followers, is left in the commune with no apparent direction or purpose. Finally, Nesta, who has learned of Claudia's commune, rescues the impressionable young woman and ushers her to Treaty. Soon Trini, a white girl, finds deep love with Reggie. She brings stability to Treaty because she is quiet and cooperative. When she realizes that it is no longer safe to remain in Treaty, she willingly departs. Mackie, Winch Fargo's cellmate from prison, is incarcerated for multiple homicides. A physically imposing black man, Mackie assumes control over Winch, selling his blood to other inmates and ingesting it himself. When Winch escapes, Mackie, sorely missing the blood drug, is left depleted of energy and purpose. Reed ultimately has him transferred to a hospital, whereupon he escapes and ultimately finds his way to Treaty with Miles Barber.

Two final but very significant minor characters are Max and Coyote. Max is Claudia's dog as well as her sidekick and fellow Blue. On the night she encounters the blue radiance, Claudia is accompanied by Max. On several occasions in the novel, Max finds himself in confrontation with Gray Man. As a Blue, Max, though not human, is still a threat to Gray Man. Coyote, who has also experienced the blue light, appears throughout the novel in an attempt to forewarn others about Gray Man's imminent presence. Coyote even stalks Horace LaFontaine when he departs for what will be his four-year hibernation. She tries to warn Horace that he will soon be overtaken by Gray Man. At the end of the novel, when Chance returns to Treaty/War to assist in the battle with Gray Man, he first spies the evildoer in combat with both Max and Coyote. Within seconds, unfortunately, they perish in Gray Man's grip.

THEMATIC ISSUES

As a science fiction novel, *Blue Light* presents as its most dominant theme, quite obviously, the struggle between reality and the fantastical. The novel asks that the reader suspend disbelief about the seemingly impossible and to consider alternative notions for determining and receiving knowledge. In much the same way that the Blues, or those (like Chance) who are familiar with the Blues, are compelled to view their world beyond "normal" senses, the reader is challenged to consider the environing reality with greater flexibility. This theme is juxtaposed with another significant theme, that of imprisonment versus freedom. People who are more receptive to these new alternatives are less likely to feel entrapped by the oppressive forces imposed by an uncompromisingly restrictive and rigid society. Those who must cling to the more traditional methods of approaching "reality," however, are left vapid and incapable of emotional and intellectual growth. In short, fantasy (or imaginative freedom) leads to emotional, spiritual, and intellectual freedom, whereas reality (or what is considered reality) merely sustains ignorance and the mundane. That the celestial dispersal of blue light was, in fact, a democratic affair (that is, persons of all races, classes, and ages and both genders are affected), leads to greater appreciation of the novel's most pressing impulse of enlightenment and liberation. The blue light is, after all, called "God's tears";

hence the light is superior in all ways to humankind. Chance declares, however, that this God is "[not] the God of organized religion, but the amazing vitality of existence" (339). While organized religion is obviously dismissed as an oppressive force, the blue light's "vitality" is presented as affirming and liberating. It is no surprise, then, that almost all of the other subthemes are linked in some way to these two dominant themes.

Racial oppression versus liberal enlightenment is one of those subthemes. The issue is addressed both in the characterization of Chance and in the racial representations showcased in Treaty. Before Chance is aware of the imaginative and liberating possibilities brought about by the blue light, he feels trapped in a racist society that despises him for his apparent blackness and for his biracial status. That his white mother chooses to plunge forward with her life (and to prod Chance to do likewise) perturbs Chance even more because he feels ill equipped to battle this ubiquitous and ultrapowerful society. On the one hand, society relegates him to a certain lowly status because of his blackness. On the other, this same society chooses to ignore him, suggesting that he, in fact, has no status and no identity. In other words, society makes him painfully aware of his existence while at the same time, and paradoxically, insisting that he does not actually exist after all. Like Ralph Ellison's famous unnamed protagonist, Chance exists, but only in a state of invisibility. Because he has tried so desperately to belong, Chance is confused about why society fails to accept him: "I spoke the white man's language. I dreamed his dreams. But when I woke up, no one recognized me" (20). Chance is trapped because he struggles to fit in a world that is inherently designed to alienate him. Because Chance is prevented from finding a suitable niche within the social construct, he is, ironically, suited for the freedom promised by the blue light. Though he is never transformed into a full Blue, Chance does become more receptive to the unorthodox knowledge consistent with blue light. Had Chance been like those whites who "fit inside their clothes and behind their desks [and who] came from places where they were recognized as members and relatives and citizens" (20), he would have been considered a part of the norm. However, as such, he would have blindly accepted this norm as reality because he would not have had the prickly status of alienation (caused by racism) to keep him poised for keener insights. Traditional reality, sanctioned by the racist society, ensures intellectual and spiritual imprisonment, while the majesty inherent in alienation, along with a fantastical urgency, leads to newfound freedom. Once he positions himself to honor and embrace the blue light, Chance inclines toward such freedom.

The idealized society highlighted in Treaty also works to combat racism. The multiracial group functions in part to support the argument that a diverse society can also be a harmonious one. From the Mexican Juan Thrombone to middle-American Addy to white Gerin Reed to black Reggie Brown to the biracial Chance, the inhabitants of Treaty, upon suspending the various belief systems that plagued them back in the city (the so-called real world), discover the humanity that binds each one to the other. The residents are "freed" in terms of not only race, but also gender. Inasmuch as everyone looks up to the wise Juan (a man), they also respect Alacrity for her strength and courage. And they happily defer to Nesta for her comprehensive knowledge and for her facility with many languages. No one is denied his or her potential simply because of race, former social status, or gender. In addition, everyone is allowed to choose a mate according to individual preference, not as a result of some predetermined opinion (or prejudice). And the various emergent relationships are treated matter-of-factly. When black Reggie pursues white Trini, or when young Alacrity pursues forty-something Eric Beauvais, no one responds negatively. Treaty, a place of fantasy (and thus possibility and freedom), rebukes all forms of socially constructed oppression.

The struggle to broaden one's personal horizons is another subtheme. To challenge oneself intellectually, emotionally, spiritually, or any combination of these, is to seek understanding and wisdom beyond current notions of knowledge. Gerin Reed, the usually responsible prison warden, is keenly aware of this struggle. He achieves his awareness in part because of the imaginative faculties he sharpened as a child. Unable to afford real toys, a young Gerin created a fire engine from a squared-off piece of kindling and an air force squadron from fallen autumn leaves. Such an imagination would lead him to look up to the stars and ask his father, with deep philosophical intent, "if there was ever an end to all that way out there" (135). In considering the limitless horizon of the heavens, the young Gerin was also considering his own limitless possibilities. Unfortunately, Gerin finds himself having to militate against the suppressive tendencies of the mundane represented by this same father, who responds, "I don't have time to think about questions like that, Gerry, and neither do you" (135). In his practicality, Gerin's father almost undermines his son's curiosity. And though Gerin does suspend this impulse in the ensuing years, he does not completely destroy it. Later, as an adult, he fantasizes running as fast as he can down a beach until he can fly. Even though he knows he cannot fly, somehow running no longer provides even a modicum of fulfillment. In other words, once he even conceives of a different kind of existence, the known one no longer suffices. Once Gerin recaptures some of his childhood wonder, he is no longer trapped by adult restrictions. On the day he simply walks away from his job, Gerin feels a renewed sense of liberation. And even when he goes home to discover his first wife in the embrace of another, younger man, he is unfazed. He appreciates the fact that his wife, for whatever reason, needed to journey beyond the boundaries of their marriage, discover new horizons, and perhaps restore some of her own imaginative magic. Ultimately, Gerin's seeing himself elsewhere (beyond those stars of his childhood or hovering over that beach) will result in his seeing himself in Treaty, and with a new wife. To fulfill himself personally, he has to reject that which is "real" and do the unexpected. To free himself, he walks away, quite literally, from the prison, where, even though he was in charge, he felt (ironically) even more trapped than did the actual prisoners.

Still another minor theme issuing from the dichotomy between the real and the fantastical is the relativity of normalcy. Without question, the whole concept of normalcy is questioned in a science fiction novel such as *Blue Light*. What may be normal in one context (or culture) is abnormal in another. The ability to acclimate oneself to different normalcies is tantamount to achieving freedom. Seeing oneself in different contexts provides the imaginative fortitude that grounds a person's further development. Chance and his group are given the opportunity for such growth soon after their arrival in Treaty. Initially leery of their chances for survival there, Chance questions the wisdom of remaining in Treaty, even stating that Juan has survived there only because he is crazy. Interestingly enough, young dreamer Wanita declares that maybe they will survive if Juan shows the group "how to be crazy like him" (259). Wanita implies that once they learn how to live successfully (crazily) in Treaty, they will then be "normal." Clearly, this child (still connected to her imaginative self) has no fixed concept of normalcy. Rather, she is free enough to adjust to any exigencies required of her, and she reminds Chance that they must all be receptive to change and adjustment. Once one appreciates the relativity of normalcy, then one is less likely to feel unduly alienated and inadequate. Even Miles Barber, obsessed and disfigured detective that he is, understands this concept. In colorful language that echoes the cliché "one man's superstition is another man's religion," Miles states to Chance: "Blue light, white elephant, or Christ on a fuckin' cross. It's all the same nonsense" (152). Miles declares that he will not be dominated by any philosophy or belief system, because each is disputable.

This notion of relativity is developed even further in regard to perception and point of view—that is, one's definition of normalcy is determined not only by one's context (i.e., place) but also in terms of one's angle of vision (or how one sees himself or herself in that place). Though this issue is raised in Wanita's determination to see herself as "normal" (crazy like Juan) in Treaty, it is also slightly different here. The point of view in this instance concerns the overall presentation of events about the blue light, Gray Man, and the experiences in Treaty. Two different explanations are given in regard to these occurrences. Somewhere within this discrepancy lies a truth, but it is never fully realized. The explanation given by the authorities (the real, the practical, the traditional and accepted authorities) is that the Close Congregation is a cult, the members of which are strung-out drug addicts who participate in bizarre rituals. The park massacre is considered the "culmination of a series of sacrifices" by the group. This explanation, of course, squares with the need of the police to explain rationally all events leading up to the park incident. Because these authorities function only with the use of their five senses, they cannot fathom any other possible explanation; in fact, all other explanations are impossible. Concerning the final events in Treaty/War, authorities simply declare the inferno a forest fire set by the crazed Lester "Chance" Foote. And the more animated Chance becomes in his attempt to provide alternative details about the fire and preceding events, the crazier the authorities believe he is. Society's perception is that any behaviors deemed antisocial must be suppressed and restricted. When Chance declares at the end of the novel, "I am sane but I know more than the fools who keep me here. I know too much" (370), he indicates his awareness of conflicting points of view. Unfortunately for him, those who have the muscle to defend their point of view are deemed right. From Chance's point of view, however (and from the reader's, since the reader has journeyed along with Chance), there must be, in the words of English Romantic poet Samuel Taylor Coleridge, "a willing suspension of disbelief." While one might simply dismiss the Close Congregation and the Blues as drug-obsessed lunatics, the fact that the reader has "witnessed" all events makes such a declaration less than plausible. To further cloud the issue of truth, Mosley paints all scenes in the "real" world with a surreal brush, whereas the scenes in Treaty are presented with clarity. This contrast between the descriptions of Treaty and the final descriptions of Chance's post-Treaty world is especially striking. Recalling his feelings in the courtroom where he is being tried for arson, Chance states, "At one moment I faded into consciousness, finding myself dressed in an ill-fitted tan suit and talking to a middle-aged woman, a judge I believe . . . " (369). The scene is presented as though

Chance (and the reader as well) is seeing it through a haze. And the fact that Chance says he "faded" into consciousness suggests that he is "falling" (or descending) from a place of clarity and entering a cloudy, or surreal, realm (an ironic realm of consciousness).

Just as Chance is compelled at the end of the novel to search for some sign of blue light (some alternative to the world of regular people), even though he insists he wants to be "regular" again, the reader is left to question normalcy and reality. Both fear that to return to "normal" is to surrender to confinement.

HISTORICAL CONTEXT

Blue Light is set, for the most part, in the four-year span from 1965 to 1969. The blue radiance strikes on August 8, 1965, and four years later the Blues find themselves under attack by Gray Man. Following 1969 are, of course, those immeasurable years the group spends in Treaty. The backdrop of the late 1960s as well as the northern California cultural landscape provides the appropriate context for the kind of exploration and interrogation the novel highlights. Since the novel questions reality (or the traditional status quo), Mosley's situating the story in the Oakland–Berkeley–San Francisco corridor is appropriate. The Bay Area of 1965 was a place of transformation and upheaval. And certainly by 1969, the Berkeley campus, like many college campuses across the country, was embroiled in ongoing protests against the Vietnam War and other matters of social discontent. One of the more telling examples of such change was the student protest movement at the University of California–Berkeley during the 1964–1965 school year. Students engaged in an infamous year-long battle to protect their right to promote political activity on campus. What started as the United Front made up of a few students eventually evolved into the Free Speech Movement involving thousands. By July 1965, UC-Berkeley's policy gave students limited rights of advocacy and public political engagement.

Those in positions of authority viewed such student resistance with disdain. The free-love and free-spirit doctrines, along with the nonchalant drug use, of hippie types were considered a threat to civilized society. And certainly, the unlikely union of these mostly white hippies with young liberal black students was frowned upon. It is within this historical context that Mosley crafts his story. As Chance, Addy, Reggie, Wanita, and Alacrity wend their way through the northern California woods after Gray Man's park attack, they embody the stereotypical interracial group perceived as a disgrace by "normal" Americans. Even the Volkswagen van they drive is a symbol of this iconoclastic era. From Chance's regular attendance at rallies and love-ins to Claudia Heart's free-love (promiscuous) commune, *Blue Light* captures the spirit of the day. Labeled a cult, Chance and his fellow travelers are dismissed as dangerous drug addicts. Their highly questionable mental stability, then, provides the almost-perfect circumstance for considering the alternative realities represented by the Treaty experience. Given that Chance admits to regular drug use, his role as a reliable narrator is problematic, and hence appropriate for a fantastical novel. In other words, the transition from the real to the imaginative is made more plausible by the very real historical moment. One could easily consider the Treaty phenomenon merely a drug-induced hallucinogenic occurrence.

The historical framework for *Blue Light* is seamlessly linked to the literary backdrop. Because Chance fancies himself a budding Thucydides, he is engaged in writing his own history. Believing the Bay Area of the late 1960s to be a space ripe with the kind of change unknown since the time of Thucydides, Chance wishes to link the 1960s to that earlier historical moment: "It was the first time since the ancient city-states that a city was the center of change for the whole world. I was going to document that change" (19). The story of blue light, then, becomes Chance's equivalent of the history of the Peloponnesian War, especially since Chance has been dismissed from the doctoral program at UC-Berkeley for making no progress on his dissertation on Thucydides and the war. Just as Thucydides's work is history made literature, so is Chance's emergent document.

Athenian historian Thucydides was a general during the Peloponnesian War who was exiled from Athens for twenty years after failing to defend the city of Amphipolis. During his exile, he wrote his famous history of the war, objectively discussing contemporary events in a direct and descriptive style. Chance also hopes to be as objective and descriptive as Thucydides was by using various sources: eyewitness accounts, newspaper articles, lyrics from songs, and even impressions from political speeches. Just as Thucydides was a part of the history he wrote, Chance relishes experiencing the events that he, too, records. Chance's magnum opus evolves just as events evolve. If he is writing in the midst of a great transformation, he must accommodate rapid and immediate changes. Initially, he is writing *The History of Love*, but he changes the title to *History of the Coming of Light* to reflect both his awareness and his flexibility in regard to these changes.

In addition to being a fictional history, *Blue Light* also satisfies criteria for being a Utopian novel (a futuristic work about an ideal imaginary world). After Chance and the others arrive in Treaty, they form a congenial group of residents who work in harmony to survive and thrive. Former petty concerns disappear in favor of the commonwealth. Chance, who began this journey suspicious of Juan, now trusts his fellowman. Even the despicable Winch Fargo he does not hate; he only pities the man for his ignorance. At one point Chance finds himself farther in the woods with Juan, Gerin, Mackie, and Miles as they prepare to plant more trees, returning to nature its offerings from which they have benefited. Chance, in particular, delights in the camaraderie established among the men as well as the spiritual uplift from communing with nature. Never has he enjoyed a more idyllic existence. Treaty is a place where bears befriend humans and trees sing or bellow in order to entertain or protect. And though Treaty, like all Utopias, is ultimately destroyed, it offers the possibility that humankind might strive for the kind of serenity found there.

Blue Light can also be classified as an allegorical novel (one in which places, people, and objects have highly symbolic meanings; personification is most often used to give concrete form to abstract concepts). Perhaps the most obvious example of the novel's allegorical bent is the name of the mystical setting, Treaty. Chance makes note of the allegorical implications in the name when he questions what Juan means by the term when Chance and the others first arrive. Chance is left "to wonder if [Juan] was jokingly asking for a truce or informing [him] of the name of our destination" (254). Treaty is, in fact, both: the name of the place and the atmosphere sedulously maintained there. Once Gray Man, emblematic of gloom and darkness, threatens the place, the name immediately changes to War. Various characters in the novel are also given allegorical names. Chance, whose every move (risks and rescues) has been by chance, is renamed Last Chance once Juan knows that Gray Man's return is imminent. Chance is, in fact, the last chance for survival that any of Treaty's inhabitants have. Julia, of course, becomes Alacrity because she pursues everything eagerly and quickly. Nesta Vine becomes Teacher when she willingly shares her knowledge with others, though her original name underscores the fact that she is both rooted—connected to place (like a nest)—and wandering—she travels far and wide (like a vine). Reggie is the Pathfinder, because he is instrumental in leading the group to Treaty, while his sister Wanita is the Dreamer; her visions both entertain and forewarn.

As a history, a Utopian novel, or an allegory, *Blue Light* evolves as a rich, multilayered work that challenges the reader's understanding of reality and truth.

NARRATIVE STRUCTURE

Blue Light is narrated from the first-person perspective of Lester "Chance" Foote, whose voice unifies the overall text even when he discloses details from the lives of several other characters. The novel is made up of four major sections (the prologue and three other narrative components), each of which addresses specific stages in Chance's unusual journey.

The prologue presents the events that occur on the night that the blue light descends. Referred to as "God's tears" in this section, the blue light settles in on August 8, 1965. While other characters are being transformed into advanced Blues, Chance attempts to commit suicide by slitting his wrists. And when Reggie is bemoaning the death of his sister Luwanda and Eileen is identifying Winch as the murderer of her husband, Philip, Chance is being delivered by ambulance to a psychiatric hospital. The prologue serves to lay the foundation for the rest of the novel. Most of the major Blues, from young Reggie to Horace LaFontaine to William "Orde" Portman, are introduced. The rest of the novel serves to tell the story of how these Blues try to adjust to their new identities in the face of misunderstanding and adversity. The prologue also establishes that Chance is writing a book and that the book is *Blue Light,* even though Chance refers to his manuscript by different titles. Understanding this fact, the reader is reminded that *Blue Light,* while still a work in progress, is the deliberate and calculated effort of a very intrusive narrator (Chance constantly reminds the reader that he is in the background narrating). To justify the inclusion of details to which he would have had no firsthand access, Chance explains to the reader that he "gleaned [them] from conversations, newspaper articles, interviews, [and] obituaries . . . " (3). The nonlinear structure of the book is consistent with Chance's attempt to record events as they occur to him. As Chance admits, "I was writing a history about something I was seeing unfold. But now it came to me that I was a piece of that history" (102).

Section one, following the prologue, is set four years after the 1965 blue light visitation, with Chance informing the reader that he has been a member of Orde's Close Congregation for four years. While this section establishes the (very tenuous) chronological movement of the novel, it is still punctuated with various flashbacks. Soon into this section, Chance recalls an event three and a half years earlier when Orde reveals to him the death of one of the congregants. Even though Mary Klee dies as a result of Orde's trying to mix his blood with hers, Chance remains faithful to Orde and is still devoted in 1969. Other chapters in section one return intermittently to the lives of Blues, revealing details from the intervening four years. The most revealing flashback addresses the emergence of Gray Man. Upon Horace LaFontaine's death on the night he is imbued with the blue light, the corpse of the ex-con removes itself to a desert cave. Three years later it emerges, now overtaken by the spirit of Gray Man, who spends the next several months adjusting to this new form. Gray Man finally makes his presence known, first when he murders Phyllis Yamauchi, and then when he initiates the massacre in the park. Again, in this "Gray Man" chapter in section one, Chance links events from 1965 to those in 1969. In maneuvering back and forth between 1965 and 1969, Chance underscores the simultaneity of life's events. Rather than employing a rigid linear order, Mosley (via Chance's perspective) presents a more flexible continuum of time; past, present, and future are one.

With the park massacre completing section one, the next section, after establishing the flight of Chance, Addy, Reggie, Wanita, and Alacrity, serves to chart the ensuing actions of Claudia Heart, Winch Fargo, Miles Barber, and Gray Man. In addition, section two introduces key characters Gerin Reed, Nesta Vine, Mackie Allitar, and Juan Thrombone. While the novel does move forward in this section, the narrative still alerts the reader to its simultaneous, or circular, quality. Pages after Chance has revealed that Miles has begun (and has spent some time on) his search for the culprit of the park massacre (a detail that suggests forward movement), and pages after Chance has provided more details on Winch Fargo's escape and Gerin Reed's abrupt departure from the prison (with the reader now understanding that much time has elapsed since the park incident), suddenly the reader is thrust in the middle of a conversation between Gray Man (or Grey Redstar) and Joclyn Kyle, wherein Joclyn asks Redstar whether he has heard of "yesterday's" tragic event in the park. Once again the ostensible linear movement is suspended in favor of the aesthetically appropriate structure (meaning pertinent to the novel at hand) of simultaneity.

Section three is devoted almost entirely to the events in Treaty. Once in Treaty, the new residents find that time functions mysteriously and inconsistently. Soon after their arrival, Reggie and Alacrity (who was only four at the time of the massacre) mature practically overnight. Wanita supposedly remains childlike for much of her time there, even though by the end of the Treaty experience, Chance declares her to be twenty-six (she was only just past two in 1965). Chance notes that by the end of their time in Treaty, Woolly (son of Gerin and his wife, Preeta), the only one born there and the only one who "aged at a normal rate" (340), is fifteen. As the reader tries to establish an accurate time frame for the very end of the novel, Woolly's age may provide some indication. Upon exiting the woods, Chance is remanded to the custody of authorities and placed in a mental hospital, where he still remains. He states that he has been there for years since his time in Treaty, mentioning that his estranged mother passed away in 1976 and that his mental diagnosis changed in 1988. If the reader recalls that the massacre occurred in 1969 and that Chance and his charges spent months living a nomadic life before arriving in Treaty, then one can assume that they arrive in Treaty some time in 1970. While the length of time actually spent there is debatable given Treaty's ethereal quality, the reader is prompted to rely on Woolly's age. If Chance departs Treaty soon after Woolly's fifteenth birthday, then he returns to the "real" world in 1985. Then, if one relies on the truth of Chance's words, that seven years have elapsed since his return, then Chance is narrating from the present moment of 1991. And given that he is now using a computer to compose, one can assume that some time beyond the mid-1980s has passed. The reader comes to understand, then, that while he or she was thrust into events ostensibly occurring in the late 1960s, the narrative is projected some twenty-plus years forward. Time, as a fixed concern, is ever elusive.

The flexible narrative structure of *Blue Light* reinforces imaginative principles that are thematically underscored. In this way, form (structure) and content (theme) function to create a work that is seamless in its aesthetic order.

ALTERNATE READING: A POSTMODERNIST ANALYSIS

Postmodernism, as a form of critique, emerged in the very late 1970s and blossomed in the early 1980s. Two seminal works that solidified postmodernism's place in the academy are *The Postmodern Condition: A Report on Knowledge,* written by Jean-Francois Lyotard in 1979, and *Simulations,* written by Jean Baudrillard in 1981. These critics, and others that followed, consider postmodernism to be the theoretical principle that challenges the concepts put forth by modernism in the first half of the twentieth century. While modernism strove to address emergent social and aesthetic chaos, to challenge old norms, and then to establish (or at least suggest) new ways of seeing and understanding, postmodernism admits its inability (or even unwillingness) to create new unity. Instead, postmodernism maintains that true artistry should reflect the ongoing, never to be fully resolved, philosophical, social, and intellectual battles that consume all human interaction. Whereas modernism would blur old boundaries to establish new ones, postmodernism would question the boundaries themselves: caste (or class), gender, race, politics, aesthetics, and so on. In short, postmodernism destroys the former center or norm and in so doing reconsiders those entities previously defined as marginal or alien. Modernism bemoans the psychological fragmentation that accompanies stress-ridden human existence, while postmodernism celebrates, to some degree, such fragmentation as a phenomenon that potentially democratizes human experience. Social harmony is defined as the acceptance of warring perspectives. From a literary perspective, a novel might end by posing questions instead of answering them. Or a given literary work might defy categorization (in terms of "high art" or "low art," or in terms of genre identity) in an attempt to prod the reader to reconsider the very notion of definitions.

Blue Light, as a work of science fiction, participates in the postmodernist challenge. The novel dissolves the boundary between the real (or what was thought to be real) and the imaginary. Though Treaty is seen as a fantastical place (with its humanlike trees, friendly bears, and oversized butterflies), it is also a place that promotes the best of human potential. In true postmodernist fashion, Treaty suspends known reality (which is fixed and restrictive), liberating both the human mind and spirit and welcoming new possibilities. Important to note as well is Mosley's deliberate effort to blur the line between fact and fiction. Though *Blue Light* is, by traditional definition, a novel (and a highly imaginative one), it is also masked as a legitimate history of the blue light phenomenon. At the same time, then, that the reader is engaged in a compelling story, he or she is also perusing a chronicle of events based in fact. Mosley questions reality not only in a cosmological sense (what are the possibilities in the larger universe?) but also in one's daily concern with truth and myth (who is the authority and with what agenda?).

The very structure of *Blue Light* pays homage to postmodernism. Initially, the novel seems to be structureless, suggesting that there is actually no true structural standard for a literary work. The reader is thrust into an unknown space, with no established rules or script. As a consequence, the reader must simply depend on the individual and immediate context and pick up whatever cues there are along the way. This structureless style is created by Mosley's obscuring somewhat the narrative voice in the prologue. The initial "I" narrator (whom the reader later discovers is Chance) is removed after only a few lines when a different "I" narrator takes over (this time Orde, but he is not identified until later). After the unnamed Orde narrates for several paragraphs, Chance (still unnamed) returns, but only briefly. Chance indicates that the long story he is about to relate will be a combination of conversations, newspaper articles, interviews, obituaries, and his newfound ability to read blood. For the next several pages, the narrative voice, recounting details from the aforementioned sources, seems to be a detached third person who is simply reporting several events concerning the Blues. By the end of the prologue, Chance returns as narrator, but he remains unnamed until the first chapter. By confusing the reader early on about the actual narrator, Mosley, in true postmodernist fashion, suggests that there is no true authority; instead, there is only a conveyer of information, and the reader is ultimately left with the task of discernment. In this way, then, the novel is not a fixed, sacred text, but rather a fluid, ever-evolving text that changes along with the individual reader.

In this work, Mosley also disrupts the boundary between so-called "high art" and "low art," in both the novel and the crafting of the novel. Early in the novel Chance presents himself as being in the throes of writing a very important history, or chronicle (a scholarly work), yet notwithstanding his recent work as a doctoral student, he appears to the outside world to be anything other than scholarly. "A big black man in his twenties with a mane of matted and kinky hair," Chance writes his book "while standing on street corners or sitting on the sidewalk" (19). Because this seemingly "low" person is engaged in "highly" intellectual activity, Mosley argues, fixed definitions of high and low are ultimately useless. And in terms of crafting his novel, Mosley makes a similar disruption. What might be perceived as a "low art" science fiction work is elevated when it is linked to the great work of Thucydides. Not only does Chance refer to himself as a contemporary Thucydides, but Mosley also bows to Thucydides in the epigraph to *Blue Light*, wherein Mosley writes, "This history is dedicated to Thucydides, the father of memory." Calling this science fiction novel a "history" ostensibly thwarts any attempt to degrade the work. Mosley also confuses the line between high and low when he mixes literary genres within this one novel. While *Blue Light* is mainly science fiction, it is also a hybrid thriller, a detective novel, and an epic, and the reader must accept it in all of these manifestations.

9

Fearless Jones
(2001)

In his eleventh novel, *Fearless Jones*, Mosley returns to detective fiction, this time creating a new sleuth, Paris Minton. The owner of a used book-store, Paris is satisfied enjoying the easygoing intellectual life that his official occupation allows, but he is soon immersed in a complex situation from which he must actively extract himself. Along with his sidekick, the inimitable Fearless Jones, Paris will comb the streets of 1954 Los Angeles trying to avert danger and even death. This novel, however, differs from those in the Easy Rawlins series in that Mosley attains a level of narrative complexity previously unseen in his other detective novels. With all of its plot twists and detailed political and historical allusions, *Fearless Jones* demands of the reader careful focus and concentrated analysis.

PLOT DEVELOPMENT

Protagonist Paris Minton has been enjoying the life of an independent businessman for three months. However, his carefree lifestyle is abruptly interrupted when a stranger, Elana Love, enters his store. Elana has come in search of Reverend William Grove and Father Vincent la Trieste, leaders in a storefront church once housed just down the street from Paris's shop. Before Elana can explain exactly why she needs to locate the men, a burly and imposing man, Leon Douglas, enters the store and asks for Elana, who has secreted herself in the back room. When he cannot find Elana,

Leon threatens Paris and then assaults him. After Leon leaves, Elana emerges and confesses to Paris that Leon accompanied her there in search of William Grove. Elana has convinced Leon that Grove is in possession of a bond that Leon is eager to have. Though Grove does not have the bond, Leon, now Elana's boyfriend, thinks that he does because Grove and Elana were once lovers.

Elana begs Paris to help her, though he is reluctant to get involved in a situation that has already brought violence to his otherwise ordinary life. Vulnerable, however, to the wiles of a beautiful woman, Paris succumbs to Elana's charm. Over dinner and drinks Elana explains to Paris that Leon was recently released from jail. While incarcerated, he befriended an older Jewish man, David "Sol" Tannenbaum. Agreeing to defend Sol against other interlopers, Leon is rewarded with a bond of deposit (from a Swiss account) that Elana secures from Sol's wife, Hedva (also called Fanny). Sol is in prison for embezzling funds from the accounting firm that employed him. Now that Leon has been released, he wants his property. Elana claims that she hid the bond among Grove's possessions, without the minister's knowledge, and that is the reason she is desperate to find Grove.

Paris agrees to hide Elana away at a motel. In the middle of the night, the manipulative woman seduces Paris. By the time he awakes a few hours later, he finds Elana gone, along with his money and his car. Taking a bus back to his neighborhood, Paris is met with the greatest horror of his life: his store and home are reduced to smoldering embers. Left with no livelihood and no home, Paris is in desperate need of help. The only person who can assist in this dilemma is his longtime friend, Tristan "Fearless" Jones.

Because Fearless is incarcerated, Paris must first bail him out of jail. Their first stop is the Tannenbaum house. When they arrive there, they discover a frazzled and distraught Fanny and a seriously wounded Sol, the victim of a brutal stabbing. In the midst of offering aid to Sol, Fearless and Paris are arrested by the police. Sergeant Bernard Latham seems especially eager to convict the two; however, when Fanny refuses to identify them as the culprits, Fearless and Paris are released. And Fanny is now indebted to them for saving Sol's life.

With Sol recuperating in the hospital, Fanny offers the men accommodations at her house. Using the Tannenbaum residence as their headquarters, Fearless and Paris proceed with their investigation. They locate Elana Love's address and search her apartment, finding a lead on a man named Conrad Till. When they go to Conrad's apartment, however, they find him wounded, though not fatally. Conrad tries to attack Fearless; the ex-con only subdues Conrad without rendering further harm. Before departing, Fearless and Paris call for an ambulance. They leave without learning very much about Conrad. They learn later that Conrad has died. On another occasion, while Paris is alone in the house, he receives an odd phone call meant for Fanny. John Manly, who says he is a real estate agent, calls to inquire whether Fanny is interested in selling her house. Promising only to relay the message, Paris refuses to release any other information to the odd caller with the foreign accent, but he does obtain Manly's phone number for future reference.

Joining forces again, Fearless and Paris learn that some members of Grove's church, Messenger of the Divine, were involved in illegal activity: trafficking in stolen merchandise. Grove has recently wrested authority away from Father Vincent, founder of the church, and assumed sole control of the congregation. They also learn that Conrad was in good health just two hours before he died. He was pronounced dead just moments after Sergeant Latham left his room. That this particular policeman keeps showing up in the strangest places causes Paris much concern.

Venturing out on his own, Paris decides to visit the relocated church in the middle of the night. Conducting his own private surveillance, Paris observes two black men and one white man standing outside the church huddled in conversation. One he recognizes as William Grove; the other black man and the white man are unknown to him. Soon Grove and the mysterious white man leave, and the third man enters the church. Though it is three o'clock in the morning, Paris decides to pay the church a visit. Greeted at the door by Father Vincent la Trieste, Paris recognizes him as the third man. Sharing with Father Vincent only a minimal amount of information about his interaction with Elana, Paris tries to elicit a response from the elder man. Though reluctant to reveal too much, Father Vincent does agree to have Grove contact Paris by the next day.

Upon returning to the Tannenbaum house, Paris discovers Fanny's body. After being questioned by the police, Paris is left alone in the house. While rummaging through Fanny and Sol's belongings in search of clues, Paris receives a visit from Zev Minor, who claims to be a friend of the Tannenbaums. When informed about Fanny's death, Minor appears saddened. Paris learns that Minor and Morris Greenspan (the Tannenbaums' nephew-in-law) have been conducting some kind of business together in recent months.

After receiving a call from Grove, Paris agrees to meet him in the evening at a local diner. With Fearless in tow, Paris keeps this scheduled appointment. Grove informs the two that Elana still has the bond, regardless of what she told Paris previously. Grove also insists that the bond is worth much more than Elana realizes. Urging Paris and Fearless to find Elana, Grove promises them a substantial reward if they return the bond to him.

In the meantime Milo Sweet, bail bondsman and friend to Paris, has learned that the formerly incarcerated Leon Douglas has one of the city's best law firms working on his behalf, a firm that does not usually handle cases for black clients. Waverly, Brightwater, and Hoffman work only for the very wealthy and the very corrupt. If Leon has this kind of backing, someone with substantial clout is involved in this case. According to Milo, a significant amount of money is connected to this case, and he maintains that he, along with Fearless and Paris, ought to gain some of those funds. The three decide that even though this case has become extremely dangerous, they must complete their investigation in the hope of reaping quite a financial benefit.

After arranging new living accommodations, Paris and Fearless go in search of Leon Douglas. Locating his apartment, they spy Paris's car in the driveway; still, they are surprised to find Elana Love there. Elana explains to Paris that she tried to return his car on the day following her theft, but when she went to the bookstore, she found it in ruins. Unfortunately, Leon Douglas had also returned to the store and was lying in wait for Paris and Elana. Finding only Elana, of course, he forced her to leave with him. Now, according to Elana, Leon has the bond, which he intends to redeem with some powerful men who are willing to pay top dollar for it. While the three are in the middle of this conversation, Leon suddenly appears in the doorway. A scuffle ensues, which ends with Fearless subduing Leon and taking the bond from him. Deciding to take a frightened Elana with them, Fearless chauffeurs her in Paris's car while Paris drives his friend Layla's car.

Along the way to Milo's office, Fearless is stopped by several police officers. After being fully searched, he is detained, but Elana is escorted away with Sergeant Latham. Keeping a low profile, Paris, leaving Fearless behind for the moment, follows Latham and Elana to an exclusive hotel. After waiting an hour for them to exit the establishment, Paris finally sees them, this time accompanied briefly by another white man. Latham and Elana then drive off, and Paris follows them to a cheap motel. Paris calls Fearless to come and join him while they await Latham and Elana's next move. Well into the night, both Fearless and Paris have fallen asleep when they are awakened suddenly by gunshots. Fearless rushes from the car toward the alley where the shots were fired, while Paris maneuvers the car around for the benefit of the headlights. They discover a dead William Grove and a rapidly expiring Latham. Only seconds before, Elana Love had screeched away in Latham's car. Fearless also notes that someone fled away on foot up the alley.

After returning to Milo's to recap all events to date, Fearless and Paris agree to separate and conduct individual investigations. Milo also decides to snoop around a bit more. Fearless pays a visit to Sol at the hospital, while Fearless returns to the church. In the meantime, Paris learns from Sol's niece, Gella, that Morris has suddenly taken off after engaging in very strange behavior. While visiting with Father Vincent, Paris discovers that Grove had gone to the accounting firm of Lawson and Widlow, Sol's former employers, and apprised the businessmen that he had a bond that represented money allegedly stolen from them. Soon three white hoodlums show up at the church (at that time, still in its location near Paris's store). Refusing to let them in, Grove and Father Vincent decided in that moment to stealthily move the church to a different, undisclosed location (where it is now). Greedy, however, Grove placed another call to the accountants to give them yet another opportunity to act in good faith. This time, they sent over a man named Holderlin, who informed Grove that Leon Douglas had been working for him to secure the bond but that Douglas had lost Elana. He also stated that he worked for the interest of Israel to return to the Israeli government the funds that Sol Tannenbaum stole. Holderlin is, in reality, an enemy of the Jewish government. Paris now realizes that this case is more complex than he initially thought.

By the time Paris gets to the hospital to retrieve Fearless, Sol has died. Sending Fearless home, Paris goes to the Greenspans'. In addition to worrying about Morris, Gella is upset at the news of Sol's death. In the hope of easing her mind somewhat, Gella convinces Paris to accompany her on her search for Morris. When they arrive at Morris's office, Paris convinces Gella to stay in the car, lest she discover something unbearable. Soon after entering the building, Paris locates Morris's corpse. The strange, rude man has hanged himself, leaving a suicide note in which he confesses to the murder of Fanny. Without revealing his discovery, Paris returns Gella home and goes to reunite with Fearless.

In conversation with Fearless, Paris discloses other sketchy details from the suicide note. He also draws further conclusions about Morris's questionable activities. It seems that Morris had participated in some shady deals for Zev Minor (a.k.a. Abraham Zimmerman), a man who claimed to be a friend of the Tannenbaums but is actually a former Nazi operative who betrayed his fellow Jewish people during the Holocaust. Paris suspects that Minor is involved in Sol's attack and ultimate death.

Now trying to piece together other odd details, Paris decides it is time to talk to John Manly, the self-proclaimed real estate agent who called the Tannenbaum residence soon after Sol's hospitalization. Paris and Fearless meet Manly and his two assistants (acting as a kind of Israeli secret service) at the same hotel where Latham took Elana, and Paris immediately recognizes Manly as the white man who escorted Latham and Elana out of the hotel. Manly and his men, truly representing Israel, have come to America to reclaim stolen wealth from their people. According to Manly, Minor/Zimmerman, at the insistence of the Nazis, forced wealthy Jews to give up their liquid assets as well as other prized possessions such as jewelry and valuable art. Subsequent to these thefts, Minor used the Lawson and Widlow accounting firm to convert these properties to cash. When Sol discovered these machinations, he began embezzling funds and hiding them with the intention of one day returning the wealth to Israel. That is why both Minor (the criminal) and Manly (an Israeli agent) have been on Sol's trail. Latham gets involved when Manly and his crew hire the corrupt cop to assist them in scaring the Tannenbaums and others. Manly admits, however, that Latham became more of a liability than an asset. Because he now fears that Minor has left the country, Manly agrees to offer Paris and Fearless a sizable reward if they can locate the lost funds. He also reveals that the "prized" bond is practically worthless. The real money is still hidden.

Paris and Fearless reunite with Milo, who has been engaged in some investigations of his own. Milo has made a visit to Lawson and Widlow, informing them (and deceiving them) that he has the bond that they desperately want (neither the firm nor Milo knows the bond is useless). Widlow agrees to meet with Milo to discuss the matter. When Milo, along with Fearless and Paris, goes to the scheduled appointment, he finds, instead of either Lawson or Widlow, the man whom Paris immediately recognizes as Zev Minor. Along with Minor/Zimmerman are Mr. Christopher (later to be identified as the Nazi boss Holderlin, the man Paris saw with Grove and Father Vincent outside the church), Leon Douglas, and Douglas's sidekick, Tricks. The tension in the room is palpable, and Fearless decides to use it to cause friction among these criminals. Informing them that the bond is worthless and then informing Leon that he is, therefore, of no use to these Nazi sympathizers, Fearless initiates a shooting match. Within seconds Minor, Douglas, Christopher, and Tricks are all dead.

Paris ultimately finds Elana, who offers him the opportunity to become a partner and to split the bond with her. Appreciating that she is a dangerous woman (and knowing, of course, that the bond has no real value), Paris declines. Soon thereafter, Paris is arrested, but not for the reasons he expects (conspiracy, theft, or even murder). Instead, he is charged for arson (for burning down his own business). Paris has already learned, however, that Theodore Wally (an employee at a neighboring market) committed this crime. After spending a few weeks in jail, Paris is finally released because authorities cannot build a case against him.

Upon his release, Paris learns from Fearless that Sol had hidden all of the money in Gella's name in an account in Montreal. Gella has secured her funds and gone to Israel to return much of the stolen money to the Jewish people. As well, she rewards Fearless, Paris, and Milo with thirteen thousand dollars each. By novel's end, Paris has used his money to reestablish his business.

CHARACTER DEVELOPMENT

A self-proclaimed bookworm, major character and protagonist Paris Minton is proud of his bookstore. He has the leisure to read as many books as he wishes, and most of his days are spent sitting in his swivel chair passing away the time with a good book. His is not the kind of personality that attracts trouble. He even admits, when Leon Douglas attacks him early on in the novel, that he has never defended himself against a bully. A "transplanted southern boy who learned manners before he knew how to talk" (13), Paris would rather attempt diplomacy than fight. Even when the police harass him about the success of his business, Paris simply responds politely, concentrating instead on his loftier goal of independence and self-determination.

Second to Paris as the most significant major character is Tristan "Fearless" Jones, whose nickname describes his personality perfectly. Afraid of no one or no circumstance, Fearless proudly attracts trouble. That he is incarcerated at the beginning of the novel is evidence of his repeated flirtation with danger. Arrested for felony assault and charged for a lesser crime, Fearless is sentenced to nine months in jail. Instead of trying to reason with the three crooked mechanics he is accused of assaulting, Fearless reacts violently. As Paris maintains, "[Fearless] couldn't even spell the word *compromise*" (14). Still, Fearless is a very complex man. Though he is an unapologetic killer, he is also a kind man and generous beyond his means. His interest in the Tannenbaum case results not just from his loyalty to Paris (and the troubles Paris has suffered with his bookstore), but also from his newfound loyalty to the Tannenbaums themselves. Fearless promises Sol that he will protect the vulnerable Fanny while the injured man is in the hospital. And when Fanny is murdered, Fearless, in his allegiance to Sol, redoubles his efforts to find her killer(s). His intrepid style makes him the ultimate survivor.

Functioning quite superbly as the *femme fatale*, Elana Love is a threat to all who come in contact with her, because her loyalty extends only to Elana. Paramour of both Leon Douglas and William Grove, Elana tries to manipulate both in order to gain the greatest financial reward. That she would involve herself with Nazi sympathizers, via both Leon and Grove, is a testament to her depravity.

Worse than Elana Love, however, is Leon Douglas. Like Fearless, Leon attracts trouble and violence. But unlike Fearless, Leon seems to lack a tempering humanity; instead, he is evil throughout. Though he offers to protect Sol in jail (a seemingly humane gesture even if performed for compensation), he and his henchman Tricks are responsible for brutally beating Sol (in the minutes just before Fearless and Paris first arrive at the Tannenbaums'). Ultimately, however, Leon will discover that he, just a common hoodlum, is no match for the international outlaws who view him only as a disposable tool in their sophisticated game of espionage.

One of the more colorful major characters is Milo Sweet. A lawyer who was disbarred and jailed a few years back for undisclosed reasons, Milo has had a series of occupations since his attorney days. An extremely intelligent man, Milo is always entangled in some shady enterprise. Unfortunately, his impatience prevents him from enjoying any longstanding success. Nevertheless, Milo drives a hard bargain when he negotiates with Fearless and Paris about the assistance he can offer in their pursuit of the Tannenbaums' assailants; he insists on an equal share of whatever profits may come their way.

Presented as the most independent of the characters, Sol and Fanny Tannenbaum are different from most other whites whom Fearless and Paris encounter. Once they are assured that Fearless and Paris have come to them as friends, the Tannenbaums treat them with respect and dignity. As Jews, Sol and Fanny are sensitive to issues of victimization, and they refuse to mistreat Fearless and Paris simply because the men are black. Though her actions are unusual, Fanny welcomes the men into her home while Sol is hospitalized. As an American white woman, she is not supposed to harbor a black man (much less two black men) in her home. Still, she is unfazed by social expectation; she responds to everyone on an individual basis. The Tannenbaums' humanity and compassion are their dominant attributes, evident in the fact that they intend to use the money Sol has "embezzled" (in reality, he has simply restored money previously pilfered from the Jewish people) to strengthen Israel and assist in the Jewish cause.

Morris and Gella Greenspan are a study in contrast. While Gella seems to be a considerate and gentle person whose only concern is her aunt and uncle's welfare, Morris is a weak, insecure, and overbearing man (evident in the rude behavior he directs toward Paris and Fearless) whose naïveté has resulted in his involvement with the enemy. Like Sol and Fanny, Gella begins to trust Paris and Fearless once she knows they mean no harm to her family. Because she yearns for the kind of love and emotional support lacking in Morris, Gella finds herself vulnerable to any kindness bestowed on her.

Zev Minor/Abraham Zimmerman emerges as the major villain in the novel. Introduced just after Fanny's murder, Minor presents himself to Paris as a family friend who is shocked to learn of Fanny's death. However, Minor has worked for years in the interest of the Nazis, betraying his fellow Jewish people. Minor never once exhibits any sign of remorse for his actions.

Rounding out the list of major characters is Bernard Latham, the corrupt police sergeant whose unchecked greed results in his rampant abuse of power. Ironically, Latham is hired by the "good guys," John Manly and his associates, who have come to restore the stolen wealth to Israel. Still, Latham attempts to double-cross everyone in his path to secure the wealth for himself, completely undeterred in achieving his goal.

Several minor characters also complete the narrative. Theodore Wally is presented early in the novel as a seemingly loyal friend to Paris. An employee at the convenience store adjacent to Paris's bookstore, Theodore, a young man in his early twenties who acts like a sixty-year-old, is very concerned about Paris after Leon's initial visit and attack. After Paris's store is burned down, Theodore even offers a distraught Paris money to help in his recovery. Later, however, Paris learns from the guilt-ridden Theodore that Theodore's employer, Antonio, had forced Theodore to commit the arson on Paris's store in the hope of securing the lot where the bookstore stood. Theodore is transformed into a questionable character because of his action here and because of his (later to be disclosed) friendship with Elana.

Another important minor character is Conrad Till, a friend of both Elana and Leon who is unfortunately caught in the crossfire of his friends' misdeeds. When Fearless and Paris locate Conrad (after they discover his name while snooping around in Elana's apartment), he has been wounded, though not fatally. When Latham murders him in his hospital bed, Conrad becomes the most unfortunate of victims. Conrad's only involvement has been in helping Leon locate Elana when she flees with Paris at the beginning of the novel. But he is not a threat with regard to the bond or the other money.

William Grove, head pastor of Messenger of the Divine church, is all but reverential. Brought in from Arkansas as Father Vincent's head deacon, Grove assumes control of the church after only one year. Not even ordained, he forces Vincent into semiretirement. In addition, he carries on a scandalous affair with Elana Love. Like the other villains, his sole concern is improving his own financial standing.

Father Vincent finds himself in the middle of a scandal simply because he allowed the slick Grove to usurp his power. But once he is enmeshed in the evil doings, he is affected by them. Jealous of Grove's rise to power and fame, Vincent orchestrates Grove's murder. Paris figures out that Vincent apprised Latham of Grove's intent to steal the bond from Elana and Latham.

Initially John Manly and his cohorts, Ari and Lev, seem to be ruthless villains as well. That they have employed Latham on their behalf contributes to this portrait. And though they are acting in the interest of Israel (in attempting to recover stolen wealth), because they are not authorized by their homeland to conduct the business at hand, they must operate surreptitiously. Such stealthy maneuvers also lend mystery, and thus suspicion, to these characters.

On the other hand, Otto Holderlin (a.k.a. Christopher), former Nazi overboss of Zev Minor, is the quintessential ruthless villain. Though he and his ilk are responsible for stealing from and murdering scores of Jewish people, Holderlin deceives Grove and the Messenger of the Divine group by insisting that he is acting on behalf of Israel to recover the money supposedly stolen by Sol Tannenbaum. Though Holderlin appears only intermittently in the novel, the evil threat he represents is a palpable element throughout *Fearless Jones*.

THEMATIC ISSUES

Several major themes inform *Fearless Jones*. The most obvious of these is loyalty and fidelity versus betrayal and deceit. The plot, in fact, centers on this all-important issue. Paris, Fearless, and other heroic characters are burdened with the task of discerning between the trustworthy and the traitorous. From the very moment that Elana Love enters Paris's store, deception emerges as the most urgent of character motivations, and Paris and Fearless must unravel and avenge the repercussions of such deceptions and betrayals. As only a few characters exhibit the redemptive qualities of fidelity and loyalty, most in the novel, like Elana Love, embody treachery.

Deception personified, Elana Love makes a seductive impression, yet she is a dangerous woman. Though her physical beauty and her surname would suggest an innocuous presence, these characteristics instead mask her true nature. While the various men in her life (namely Leon and Grove) think that they can best her, she maintains control because she is devoted only to herself. Though Leon is responsible for her access to the bond, she in no way feels beholden to him. Had Grove been successful in cashing the bond, Elana would have abandoned Leon immediately. And soon after, she would have eluded Grove as well. That she is the first major character with whom Paris interacts is significant because she single-handedly establishes the ever-important conflict between appearance and reality.

Like Elana, Theodore Wally is a misleading figure. Though he is actually in his mid-twenties, he appears to be much older. He seems possessed of an aged and wise spirit, one motivated by compassion and selflessness. And while Paris has encouraged the young man to refer to him by his first name, Theodore insists on calling him Mr. Minton. When Paris is beaten by Leon Douglas, Theodore is among the first to offer assistance. Yet in a despicably offensive act of betrayal, Theodore burns down Paris's store. While appearing to be one of the most humane characters in the novel, Theodore ultimately reveals his more destructive potential. It is ironic that those characters who appear the most harmless in fact offer the greatest threat.

Morris Greenspan provides yet another example of shocking deception. When Morris first appears in the novel, he is presented as a rude, spineless annoyance. And because Fanny has little or no regard for him, Morris is made to seem powerless and dull-witted. That he is found to be involved not only in illegal activity but also in a collaboration with Zev Minor (the enemy of his wife's family) stuns the reader and stirs the narrative. By the point of this revelation, the reader has come to realize that no person or circumstance is as it seems.

Without a doubt, the vilest act of betrayal is enacted by Zev Minor and his cohorts. This group has wreaked havoc on the lives of Jewish people not only in the years leading up to World War II but also in the nine years since. Still reaping financial rewards from the stolen artifacts of wealthy Jews, Minor is greedy for even more money. He is even audacious enough to suggest that he is trying to recover the wealth of his fellow Jews. The very group to whom he should extend his greatest loyalty he instead abandons, abuses, and all but destroys.

While deception seems to be the ruling impulse in the novel, some characters do display redemptive behaviors. Walking definitions of loyalty and selflessness are Sol and Fanny Tannenbaum. In her brief appearance Fanny exhibits her loyalty to Gella and her newfound loyalty to Fearless and Paris, who have earned her trust. Sol's sense of loyalty has always extended to his entire Jewish community, in both the remote and recent past. When Gella and her father were forced to flee their homeland during the Holocaust, Sol assumed the responsibility of securing their freedom and bringing them to America. And after his nephew Schmoil's death, he (and Fanny) continued to care for Schmoil's daughter, Gella. And more recently, Sol and Fanny intended on restoring to Israel a substantial amount of formerly pilfered wealth.

Loyalty is exhibited as well in the friendship shared between Paris and Fearless. No matter the circumstances, these two ultimately support each other. Even though Paris does not bail Fearless out of jail until he requires his help, Fearless does not harbor any ill will toward his friend. Fearless understands the difference between loyalty and betrayal, and he knows that he has perhaps abused Paris's former kindness and that Paris's previous decision to leave him in jail was made to teach Fearless a lesson and caution him against taking the friendship for granted.

In addition to betrayal versus loyalty, the theme of fearlessness versus courage is highlighted. Though these concepts seem to be synonymous, they are presented as different in the text. Clearly, the title character, Tristan "Fearless" Jones, figures significantly in this discussion. Because of his friend's infamous boldness and intrepidity, Paris has come to exalt Fearless as the most courageous, and hence heroic, of all the men he has ever known. However, Fearless does not consider himself to be such. Given that he is simply unafraid in any circumstance (whether one of confrontation, pursuit, or endurance), he defines his behavior as unnoteworthy. On the other hand, maintains Fearless, a person who is fearful yet confronts the circumstance at hand is truly the courageous one. States Fearless, "Hero is just bein' brave when there's trouble. An' bein' brave means to face your fears and do it anyway. Shoot. You can't call me a hero 'cause I ain't scared'a nuthin' on God's blue Earth" (248). Such a definition would, then, position Paris as the hero. Admitting that he would rather avoid both physical and emotional pain, Paris thinks of himself as less noble than Fearless. However, Fearless reminds him that fearlessness and courage are really two markedly different concepts. Even the most mild-mannered person will exhibit courage when challenged at the very core of his or her being. This is evident in the fact that Paris commits to this dangerous case once his very livelihood (and in his case, his sole love—the bookstore) is practically destroyed. Because the attack on the store is an attack on his very essence, Paris invokes all courageous instincts and meets this new challenge.

Yet another compelling theme is the struggle for emotional and financial freedom in the face of opposition. Paris's sole motivation in life has been the attainment of independence. And the more his freedom is threatened, the more determined he becomes to preserve it. From his earliest remembrance, books provided Paris with emotional comfort because they allowed him to journey beyond his present circumstance. Having latched onto this resource, he was determined to secure it for himself permanently. When Paris was a thirteen-year-old boy in Louisiana, his newfound emotional foundation was almost threatened by a mean-spirited librarian who disputed Paris's right to enjoy literature. Teasing him by allowing him to enter the well-stocked library maintained for whites only, Celestine Dowling then informs him that he can access none of the books housed there, that in fact no books are meant for a black boy like him. Initially discouraged, Paris would determine within four years to move to a city where he could have access to as many books as he could digest. And because books initiated Paris's desire for emotional freedom, they are also instrumental in his desire for financial freedom, which inspires him to open the bookstore. Still, Paris is challenged as a black businessman in 1954 Los Angeles. The novel opens with Paris describing one of the routine visits made by policemen whose sole intent is to harass him and discourage his initiative. But Paris has come to understand that "[being] challenged by the law was a rite of passage for any Negro who wanted to better himself or his situation" (4). And he is willing to meet and exceed whatever challenge confronts him if the reward is self-determination and "self-ownership."

Completing the list of major thematic issues is the pursuit of racial harmony despite social indoctrination. When Fearless and Paris befriend a reciprocating Fanny and Sol, their action defies acceptable social behavior. Nonetheless, the Tannenbaums respond to sincerity and good intent. Unaffected by America's obsession with race and free of racist influences and stereotypes about bloodthirsty and libidinous black men, Fanny accepts individuals. Because she has the capacity to think critically rather than emotionally and prejudicially, Fanny understands that Fearless and Paris have more to fear from her than she does from them. Were she to give even the slightest hint that these two posed her any threat, they would risk immediate physical harm. But because Fanny has the capacity to function as a humane being, she rises above petty racial differences.

In addition, Fanny's and Sol's personal awareness of oppression and persecution have conditioned them to be sensitive to others who have suffered similar fates. There is, then, not only generic human similarity among the different groups (black and Jewish) but also similar experiences with prejudice that align these groups. Just as Paris distrusts the police, so does Fanny. Just as Paris questions anyone operating in an official position of authority, so does Fanny. The Tannenbaum–Minton/Jones alliance challenges the status quo in its insistence that human beings have the capacity to see each other beyond the imposed identities placed on them by an agenda-laden society whose sole intent is to divide and conquer.

HISTORICAL CONTEXT

Though *Fearless Jones* is set in 1954, the novel is positioned in a considerably broader context, namely the decade preceding World War II (1939–1945) when the Holocaust occurred. From 1933 to 1945, this barbaric event sanctioned the persecution and extermination of European Jews and other so-called undesirable groups in Nazi Germany. With Adolf Hitler's rise to power in 1933, Jews were sent to concentration camps, where they were tortured and systematically murdered. By the end of the war in 1945, over six million Jews had perished. The most infamous camps were at Auschwitz in Poland and Dachau in Germany. The Nazis, or National Socialist German Workers' party, was established in 1920 and gained a mass following because it appealed to the hurt pride of German nationals who had suffered defeat in World War I. Nazism was marked by a virulent anti-Semitism (hatred of Jews) and anti-Communism (disdain for the notion of a classless, egalitarian society). The movement attracted capitalist-inspired bankers and industrialists who sought to rebuild Germany's economy following World War I. In the throes of the Holocaust and World War II, these unscrupulous capitalists stole Jewish property and succeeded in holding the assets in Swiss banks and European insurance companies for years following the end of the war. In 1953, German legislation sought to compensate survivors, but as late as the 1990s further repayment was solicited from these fund holders.

Both Fanny and Gella provide a brief lesson about this period in history. Fanny relates that she and Sol were from Estonia, a former Russian Baltic province. After World War I, they left and moved to America, while Gella's family (including her father, Schmoil, Sol's nephew) moved to Germany. Successful in Germany, Schmoil owned three newspapers, but when he suspected the emergent Nazi dominance, he sold his businesses, put all of his money into his art collection, and moved his property to Switzerland. He then took his family to Vienna, Austria. Unfortunately, persecution followed the family there, and only Schmoil and Gella survived. The Tannenbaums and the Greenspans are integrally involved in this notorious historical moment. Even as late as the 1954 setting, Zev Minor is acting as an insurance agent for priceless art collections as he still attempts to reap the benefits of Nazi plunder. In reality, the Jewish people are being robbed repeatedly with every transaction Minor authorizes.

Yet another historical event is referenced in the novel: the establishment of Israel as a separate country. Following World War II, the United Nations divided Palestine into Jewish and Arab states, and in 1948 Israel was proclaimed as the official Jewish nation. Though conflict between Jews and Arabs ensued immediately and has been sustained ever since, Israel remains a distinct national entity. For dedicated Jews like Sol and Fanny, Israel represents a Jewish victory over the strife and persecution that preceded and helped to initiate World War II. Their desire to travel there and return wealth to their global community underscores the pride they have in having survived one of the most villainous crimes ever visited upon humanity. The determination and resolve of John Manly and his associates confirm this post-Holocaust sense of agency and emotional fortitude as well.

In addition to the Holocaust and related incidents, the historical plight of the black American is also addressed. The 1954 setting marks an important year for civil rights in general and for black Americans in particular. On May 17, 1954, the Supreme Court proclaimed its landmark *Brown v. Board of Education* decision, which declared the doctrine of racial segregation unconstitutional. This case would change forever black-white interactions in America. That *Fearless Jones* is set in October of that year is significant; the novel is placed in the throes of monumental transformation. The modern Civil Rights movement is ushered in with the Brown decision, and black demand for social equality would give rise to a renewed sense of purpose and promise. Much like the Jews in their recently established nation, American blacks began to feel a previously unknown connection to this strange homeland known as America.

The black American relationship with America has always been paradoxical. On the one hand, America's touted belief in liberty and freedom ostensibly attracts and inspires all American citizens regardless of background. But on the other, those who have not always benefited from America's promise have often maintained an emotional detachment from the country. Paris highlights this contradiction with regard to America when he describes his relationship with the South. Though he acknowledges the horrors often visited on blacks in this particular region, he has always felt a special love for the place: "A lot of colored people tell me that they hate the South; Jim Crow and segregation made a heavy weight for their hearts. But I never felt like that" (115). Still, Paris is forced to confront the South's inhumanity when he encounters racist librarian Celestine Dowling. No doubt, then, he is both connected to and horrified by America's (as represented by the South's) projected character.

This love-hate feeling has resulted in certain migratory practices by black Americans as they strive to improve their station in life as well as America's treatment of them. Following World War II scores of blacks fled the South (in the second wave of the Great Migration that succeeded World War I), hoping that a new life in the north or in the west would offer them both economic and social advancement. By the time of the novel's 1954 setting, such migration had become a substantial sociological concept. Mosley presents this nomadic phenomenon to provide texture and accuracy in the novel. Several characters hail from different regions of the South. Though only indirect references are made to the characters' backgrounds, the novel is made more realistic by such details. Paris, of course, moved several years earlier to California from New Iberia, Louisiana. Elana Love found her way there from Georgia, while Leon Douglas traveled from Alabama, and William Grove once trekked along the dusty country roads of Arkansas. For different reasons and with different intentions, each comes to California to stake a claim to a better life.

NARRATIVE STRUCTURE

Fearless Jones is presented from the first-person perspective of Paris Minton. That the novel is narrated by someone other than the title character creates an obvious narrative tension. Before even reaching the first word of the novel, the reader is already focused on Fearless by virtue of the title, yet the narrative journey begins with an immediate introduction to Paris. The reader's curiosity about Fearless (and hence the narrative tension) is heightened when Fearless's appearance is delayed until the fifth chapter. The reader eagerly awaits the confirmation of the bold and brave atmosphere that he or she has anticipated since considering the book's title. Because Paris has admitted in the first four chapters that he is all but brave and self-assured, the reader requires the presence of Fearless to affirm the courageous intent of the novel.

This difference between Paris and Fearless also provides a means of charting the novel's progress. Paris continuously compares himself to Fearless, and in such comparisons, he exposes a desire to be more like Fearless. At the same time that Fearless is bold and defiant (capable of violence), he is also kind, considerate, and honorable. And while Paris is the more conservative of the two, Fearless willingly takes risks. In this way, each is a foil character (one who by contrast, similarity, or both highlights the traits of another) to the other. In terms of narrative structure (tension), however, Paris's increased willingness to engage in direct confrontation and to initiate further involvement in the case showcases not only his personal development but also narrative movement. In other words, Paris moves ever closer to the thematic impulse (fearlessness) represented by the title. The tension created in the narrative at the beginning of the novel by the explicit difference between Fearless and Paris is methodically eased as the novel progresses.

The immediate timeline established for the novel is approximately one week during the month of October in 1954, from the moment Elana Love enters Paris's bookstore until Paris meets her again at the end when previously unanswered questions are resolved. However, this foundational plot is also set within an extended frame; the basic plot is connected to key details that occur both before and after the main time frame of the novel. Prior to the novel's opening, Paris's store has been in operation for three months, during which time he has had to endure subtle harassment by the police and redouble his commitment to success. This detail reminds the reader of Paris's particular circumstances as a black man trying merely to survive in the 1950s. At the end of the novel, the details fast-forward, initially nine weeks (beyond Paris's final exchange with Elana Love) and ultimately several months. Ironically, these subsequent details also involve the police. Paris is charged with arson regarding the destruction of his store. And for six weeks he is held in custody until an informal court hearing takes place, after which he is held for another three weeks. Then he is simply released. Several months beyond his release, he is sitting in his new bookstore, still being harassed periodically by the police. This extended narrative (occurring before and after the major plot) serves to reinforce the narrative tension by reminding the reader of the especial burden under which a black man like Paris must try to function in what often amounts to a police state for minority citizens. Quite obvious as well is that this observation links Paris's plight to that of the Tannenbaums and other victimized Jews. In short, the extended narrative is integrally connected to all aspects of the narrative proper. To confirm this point, Mosley makes a direct link between the main narrative and the extended narrative with a comment expressed by Paris when he tries to understand a particular mystery in the throes of the main plot. Paris states, "A few weeks later, when I was taking a forced vacation, it came to me that . . . " (266). When first reading this passage, the reader is unaware of the true nature of this "vacation" but will later discover that it refers to Paris's forced incarceration highlighted in the extended narrative. This passage serves, then, as a significant narrative device integrating and unifying the entire narrative construction.

As is true of any mystery or detective novel, certain questions posed early on intrigue the reader and compel him or her to read further. These questions also involve primary plot twists designed especially to both seduce and frustrate the reader. Several key questions presented in *Fearless Jones* are as follows: What is the value of the bond Elana Love has? Who sets fire to Paris's store? Who attacks Sol Tannenbaum, and why? Who murders Fanny Tannenbaum, and why? The reader is led to believe that the first question is inextricably linked to the other three, especially since the bond originated from Sol and since the reader assumes that the same persons who attack Sol and Fanny are responsible for the destruction of Paris's business. However, Mosley makes this connection seem important in order to confuse the reader and heighten the mystery. As the reader will discover later, the crux of the plot is the money that Sol has embezzled from his employers, and the greed for these sizable funds has ultimately resulted in Sol and Fanny's deaths. Though the bond (and its assumed importance) leads Elana to enter Paris's store (and thus set the plot in motion), it is, in fact, only a red herring used to distract and mislead. Later, of course, the reader discovers that the arson exacted on the store has absolutely no connection to the bond (Theodore Wally has simply acted out of a sense of misguided loyalty to his employer). Though Elana is discovered to be acquainted with Theodore, she does not even befriend him until after he commits the crime. Throughout much of the novel, however, the reader is encouraged to link the arson to all of the other concerns and mysteries.

ALTERNATE READING: A POSTCOLONIAL READING

Postcolonial critique examines the relationship between the oppressor and the oppressed and admonishes the oppressed to find their own voice, that is, to establish agency in their lives instead of accepting the imposed object status. Postcolonial criticism can be reasonably traced to Frantz Fanon's *The Wretched of the Earth* (1961), wherein the psychiatrist from Martinique espouses a cultural resistance to France's African empire. The first step in this process for the oppressed (or colonized) is to reclaim their past. And the second is to eradicate the colonialist perspective that has devalued the culture (or past) of the colonized.

This mode of criticism examines a text using this oppressor-oppressed model, whereby a colonizing entity or group encroaches upon the physical and cultural space of another, the colonized, and forces the latter group to adopt the value system, language, cultural practices, and sensibilities of the colonizer. The postcolonial theorist, as noted previously, is concerned, of course, with the oppressed group's rejection of previous subjugation and the restoration of its own agency and purpose—hence the term *post*colonial. These critics focus on issues of difference in literary texts. Instead of ignoring the tensions these differences may create, the postcolonialist will analyze such tensions to learn more about each cultural position. This process challenges the long-held belief of colonizers about the inferiority of the colonized. When the colonizer acknowledges difference, it is presented as exotic, strange, or bizarre. The colonized are defined as homogeneous masses rather than as individuals, as instinct-driven animals rather than as intellectual beings. The postcolonialist seeks to recognize and celebrate difference while also acknowledging individual talent, potential, and achievement in members of the oppressed (or colonized, or "othered") group.

The postcolonial critic is concerned not just with distinct cultural spaces and positions but with hybridity as well, that is, the circumstance whereby individuals or groups belong to more than one culture. And perhaps most importantly, the postcolonialist deliberately acknowledges the other (the oppressed, the colonized) as a source of energy (i.e., as an agent of change) and not merely as an object, especially when the other awakens to his or her oppressed condition.

Both the Tannenbaums' saga and Paris's conflicts lend themselves to a postcolonial critique. Though Sol and Fanny were fortunate enough to have left Europe before Hitler's Nazi rule emerged, they are still positioned to militate against the vestiges of this oppressive power. Because Sol, in particular, is sensitive to the Nazi attempt to demean, belittle, and destroy Jewish culture, religion, and pride in the time before and during World War II, he commits himself to restoring agency to the Jewish people in the postwar era. Though Sol cannot restore the various artifacts and art collections pilfered from the Jews by the likes of Otto Holderlin and Zev Minor (Abraham Zimmerman), he can regain the wealth that emanated from the stolen property. Such wealth will assist in Israel's reclamation of an independent Jewish past. The Jewish spirit and culture are validated in this heroic gesture.

Upon learning that Zev is using the Lawson and Widlow accounting firm to transfer illegal funds from the art collections, Sol decides to embezzle money from the company. While his actions might be defined as unethical, Sol has consciously decided to reject the colonialist notion of inherent colonial righteousness and superiority. He has eroded colonial indoctrination. Though he is "stealing," in reality he is diminishing the impact of the colonial power that Minor and his associates represent. Because Sol considers the Jewish plight to be worthy of greater consideration, any efforts to defend the global Jewish community are justified. Inasmuch as Sol is spared from colonial brainwashing, Zev Minor has accepted the colonialist belief. Of Jewish descent himself, Minor willingly participates in his own victimization—ironically so—when he condones the victimization of his community. Working in support of Nazi interests (represented in the novel by Holderlin/Christopher), Minor assumes his role as colonialist lackey. In this regard, Sol and Minor have fixed themselves in opposite stations on the colonial paradigm. Whereas Sol claims the pre- and postcolonial positions, Minor is inextricably bound to the colonial moment.

Like Sol, Paris also learns to make a postcolonial attack on oppression. Granted, the African American experience differs slightly from the typical colonial experience in that the African was removed from his land and then placed in a foreign environment. Nevertheless, many of the phenomena felt in colonization impacted African life in America: forced abandonment of language, cultural suppression, severance of family bonds, and so on. And like the typical colonized group, African Americans must decide at some juncture to decolonize and try to recapture a positive sense of themselves. While a standard ploy in the decolonizing effort might be to regain landholdings and government rule, for African Americans, who are no longer a part of the former physical landscape, this effort involves reclaiming their own minds and securing equity in a political and economic system that was innately designed to suppress them.

Though white librarian Celestine Dowling tries to dissuade Paris from reading and expanding his intellect, he, after experiencing an initial period of despondence, rejects her attempts to subvert his dignity and self-respect. Innate in him is a postcolonial impulse that steels him against her oppressive tendency. When Dowling states, "These books were written by white people for white people. This is literature and art and the way our country is and should be" (117), she suggests that only whites are civilized enough to produce cultural artifacts, that only they are, in fact, cultured. But when Paris rebukes her position, he is, in essence, verifying and defending black cultural agency. If he, a black person, can aspire to read and intellectualize, then certainly persons who resemble him are capable not only of similar aspirations but also of artistic and aesthetic (i.e., cultural) expression. Upon regaining his composure and confidence, Paris commits to reading one book each day. In confirming his own intellectual superiority, Paris undermines the colonial superiority of Celestine Dowling and her ilk.

The ultimate colonial power that the Tannenbaums, Paris, and Fearless confront is the police force. Given her experience with official power as represented by the police, Fanny is suspicious of all such authority. When Sergeant Latham arrives to question Fanny, Paris, and Fearless about Sol's attack and he deliberately insults her, she demands that the "Cossack" (a reference to peasant soldiers in the Russian military) leave. Latham, in quintessential colonizer style, impugns the relationship between Fanny and the black men, suggesting that theirs is a suspect friendship because white women should not consort with black men. Obviously, though, Fanny, Paris, and Fearless have resisted this colonial belief when they treat everyone as individuals rather than as members of a stereotypical group. This same police force thinks that Paris should not be a successful and independent businessman; Paris challenges their belief and authority here, too.

10

Bad Boy Brawly Brown
(2002)

Mosley's first Easy Rawlins novel in six years, *Bad Boy Brawly Brown* resumes the saga only three months following the end of *A Little Yellow Dog*. Easy now balances the various aspects of his life: fatherhood, business, and romance. Happy to have a new love interest, he hopes to bring stability to his home, especially after being shaken by the death of Mouse. This novel enjoys the same fast-paced action of the previous installments. And once again, Mosley addresses important social issues and historical truths while also providing an engaging story.

PLOT DEVELOPMENT

Easy's investigative skills are tapped once again when longtime friend John McKenzie asks Easy to do a favor for both John and John's girlfriend, Alva. Brawly Brown, Alva's son from a previous marriage, is involved in what Alva believes to be a radical organization, the Urban Revolutionary Party (also known as the First Men). Alva wants Easy to locate Brawly, find out how he is doing, and possibly return him to safety.

Easy decides to visit Isolde Moore, Alva's estranged cousin, with whom Brawly lived during his teen years. Upon approaching Isolde's front door, Easy discovers the body of a dead man, later revealed as Aldridge Brown, Brawly's father. Easy snoops around Isolde's otherwise abandoned house, paying particular attention to some photographs, and then departs when he observes the police arriving.

Having learned that Brawly frequents Hambones, a popular soul food establishment, Easy goes there. Proprietor Sam Houston confirms Brawly's association with the First Men. Sam also reveals to Easy the meeting schedule of the First Men, and Easy decides to attend a meeting in the evening. When he arrives, some members of the group immediately express their suspicions about the newcomer. Though Xavier Bodan and Christina Montes ultimately warm to Easy, Conrad (no last name) does not. Easy spies Brawly across the room, in attendance with Clarissa, the waitress from Hambones and one of Sam's relatives.

At this particular meeting, one of the supposedly celebrated leaders of the movement, Henry Strong, is slated to speak. But as soon as he assumes the podium, police rush in and raid the meeting. Easy flees with Christina (Tina). Outside, they are spirited away in a car with Conrad, Strong, and Xavier. After they drive a considerable distance, both Henry and Conrad agree that Easy's presence is problematic, so Conrad forces Easy from the car. Fending for himself, Easy makes his way back to his car and then home.

Early the next morning John comes to Easy's house to disclose more information. Isolde has called Alva and John and has accused Brawly of killing Aldridge Brown. Though she admits that she didn't witness the killing, she fears Brawly is the culprit because of the hard feelings he harbored about his father. Discovering that Isolde is holed up in an apartment, Easy goes to interview her. Isolde provides Easy with a brief history of Aldridge and Brawly's strained relationship, explaining why she thinks Brawly may have killed his father.

Continuing his investigation, Easy confronts Brawly at Clarissa's apartment. Brawly seems genuinely stunned by the news of his father's death. But as Easy continues to press Brawly about his alibi, the young man balks. Finally, he stalks out of the apartment, leaving Easy and Clarissa miffed. At that moment, Easy decides that he has fulfilled his promise to Alva and John. Brawly, a fully grown man, is satisfied with his First Men affiliation, so Easy sees no reason for further intervention.

Unfortunately, Easy's relationship with the First Men is not so easily relinquished. On the following day, he is approached by Detective Vincent Knorr, who oversees a special investigative unit that spies on "subversive" groups. Knorr believes that the Urban Revolutionary Party is planning a violent attack, and he wants Easy to help thwart the mission.

Easy searches for Conrad (whose real name is Anton Breland), whom he finds at home in a heated discussion with an unknown man. The stranger beats Conrad and threatens him about a gambling debt. Concerned that the man may inflict extraordinary pain on Conrad, Easy manages to overtake him and rescue a shocked Conrad. Easy drives him away while asking questions about First Men, Brawly, and some potentially illegal practices. Conrad admits only to gun trafficking, though Easy suspects the group has more underhanded dealings. Finally, in retaliation for what Conrad did to him two nights ago, Easy forces the crook from his car without shoes or wallet, comforted in the belief that a now frightened Conrad will flee.

In the middle of the night Easy receives a phone call from Henry Strong, who asks Easy to meet him at a coffee shop. There the two men talk while Easy tries to learn more about the First Men. Finally, Strong agrees to take Easy to Brawly. Upon approaching the dark house where Brawly is supposedly holed up, Strong and Easy are ambushed; Strong is fatally shot while Easy manages to escape without harm.

Now with two murders to solve, Easy knows that he must penetrate the First Men organization even further—by talking to Tina and Xavier. After interrogating them, Easy is confident that they have no criminal leanings—their affiliation with First Men is honorable. Easy, having earlier discovered a stash of guns at the home of one of Brawly's high school friends (a white woman, BobbiAnne Terrell), urges Tina and Xavier to go with him there.

Finding the apartment empty, the three are looking around when they are suddenly rushed by police, who immediately arrest them. After being questioned and harassed by Lieutenant Pitale, Easy places a call to Knorr. Seconds later, a stunned Pitale is instructed to release Easy, who returns to Alva for more answers about Brawly's past.

In his interactions with Tina and with the police, Easy has learned that Strong had maintained two homes for the past year. His official address was the Colorado Hotel and Residences, and his secret hideaway was an apartment. At the hotel, Easy befriends the head bellman and discovers that while Strong was a resident, he was visited only by white men, who also paid the tab. At the apartment, Easy finds almost six thousand dollars, which he takes. Uncovering such a substantial amount of money leads Easy to realize that this case is quite complex.

Clarissa informs Easy that Brawly, Strong, and Conrad were party to a special, more radical force within the First Men. Instead of just building schools and feeding the hungry, this special group is poised for revolt. As a friend to Brawly, BobbiAnne simply supplied a place to warehouse the arsenal, and she allowed Conrad to stay with her to escape various gamblers and ruffians.

Easy questions John about one of his workers, Mercury Hall, a man whom Easy helped to secure the job with John. A former thief, Mercury, who has also recently come into a significant amount of money, has suddenly quit. Now Easy is very suspicious, especially since Strong was killed not far away from this construction site.

Easy reunites with Tina and takes her on a drive while posing further questions. The day before, she rented a house for Brawly and Conrad. Because she is still unsuspecting about their true designs (she thinks the guns are merely for self-defense), Tina naively trusts the two men. Suddenly Tina changes her attitude and pulls a gun on Easy. Fully aware that Strong was on his way to meet Easy on the night he was killed, Tina thinks that Easy is not to be trusted. Waiting for the right moment, Easy overpowers Tina and knocks her unconscious.

Easy then goes to the rented house where he spies Conrad, Brawly, BobbiAnne, an unknown man, and later Mercury. He waits in his car until they leave, then scopes out the inside of the premises. There he discovers some of Brawly's belongings, and tacked to the wall is what seems to be a skeletal burglary plan. Looking around the place, Easy is somehow reminded of some pictures he had seen during his first visit to Isolde's house, when he discovered Aldridge's body.

Returning to Isolde's hideout, Easy presses her for more answers by presenting to her his theory: Isolde was involved with Strong, who promised to flee with her out of the country once he had secured more funds from the robbery planned by Brawly, Strong, Conrad, and Mercury (with whom Isolde had a secret relationship). Easy has realized that the pictures he noted at Isolde's were taken at Strong's apartment. When Aldridge (another of Isolde's paramours) threatened to stop Brawly from committing this crime, Mercury decided he needed to be silenced. And when Isolde told Mercury that Strong intended to flee, Mercury killed him, too. Isolde betrayed Strong because he would not marry her.

Because he now knows (and has suspected for quite some time) that Strong was a spy for the authorities, Easy must prevent Brawly from participating in the upcoming robbery. In a moment of revelation, Easy realizes where Brawly is hiding out. Planting himself in a building adjacent to John and Alva's apartment building (Brawly is hiding there in a different apartment), Easy has concocted a strategy to force Brawly (and whoever might be with him) out of the building at a certain time. At the appointed hour, Brawly emerges, whereupon Easy, having secured a pellet gun, shoots the young man and attempts also to strike Conrad. Because he manages to injure Brawly, the would-be robber is prevented from executing his mission. However, Conrad, Mercury, BobbiAnne, and the still unidentified man are killed during the robbery attempt the next day.

CHARACTER DEVELOPMENT

Easy is plagued with guilt following the death of his longtime friend Raymond "Mouse" Alexander. He is so confused when he awakens after another of his disturbing dreams that he immediately prepares to go to work, even though it is Saturday and not a workday. When John asks for his assistance, Easy is thankful to get involved in a case that will distract him. As he states, "As long as I moved forward trying to unravel the trail of Brawly Brown, I was in a kind of safety zone where guilt couldn't touch me" (114). Though his life feels a bit unsettled because of his confounded emotions, Easy still manages to be a good father and a diligent employee at Sojourner Truth Junior High School. Taking his duties as supervisory custodian very seriously, Easy is happy to have a secure job that allows him to care for his children. Now forty-four, Easy has begun to slow down somewhat. He no longer drinks, and he tries to stop smoking, especially upon realizing how winded he becomes when performing some of the tasks that at one time gave him no pause. And as always, Easy works to better himself professionally and economically; he spends his spare time studying for the classified building supervisor's exam. Because he prods his children to seize educational opportunities, he wants to present himself as a worthy example.

Another important figure is, of course, the title character, Brawly Brown. At twenty-three, Brawly is described as "a beefy brown man" with an imposing presence. Brawly has joined the First Men not only because he wants to fight for equal rights for blacks, but also because he yearns to be a member of some kind of family. Over the past ten years he has had a difficult life, one that even his mother admits robbed him of his childhood. When he is sent away to be raised by his father (after his mother and father separate), Brawly feels as though his mother abandons him. When his favorite uncle, his mother's brother Leonard, is killed when he and Brawly's father, Aldridge, attempt a robbery, Brawly feels betrayed by both his mother and his father. Acting out by becoming a thief himself, Brawly spends three years in a juvenile detention center. By the time he comes to John and Alva's he is restless and dissatisfied.

Alva Torres, Brawly's mother, is a tormented woman. From the time her marriage to Aldridge failed to the present day, she has been an emotional wreck. Feeling abandoned when her philandering husband spent considerable time away from home, Alva had no alternative but to dissolve the relationship. Unfortunately, its end left her with sole responsibility for Brawly. For a brief time, she could depend on her brother Leonard to provide assistance (a level head and discipline) with the boy, but after he died, both she and Brawly were left dazed and confused. Harassed by the police, who were sure that Leonard's accomplice (Aldridge) managed to escape with money, Alva ultimately succumbed to a nervous breakdown, this after she had already sent Brawly to Aldridge. Her emotional troubles further harm her relationship with the boy. Her need to save him now is also an attempt to redeem herself for the trauma she believes she helped to visit upon the adolescent Brawly.

Alva's companion and Easy's longtime friend, John McKenzie, is perhaps the most stable character in the novel. A bartender since he was sixteen, John now dabbles in real estate and construction. Because he has always come to Easy's aid without question, Easy has no choice but to help him and Alva. John is "taciturn with a mean temper" (253), but one can always count on him, and Easy has the greatest respect for him. Though John offers to pay Easy for his troubles, all Easy requests is a meal and camaraderie for him and his family.

Another major character is Alva's cousin, Isolde Moore, who is linked to almost everyone else in the novel. Years ago, when Brawly was fourteen, Isolde took him in after he and Aldridge had a fight. According to Isolde, Brawly needed her both emotionally and physically. She fulfilled all of these needs, insisting, however, that she never initiated the contact. When he turned sixteen, Isolde tried to end the relationship, much to Brawly's dismay. Given the kind of woman Isolde later proves to be, the reader is doubtful about Isolde's version of the story. Isolde ultimately becomes involved with Aldridge, Henry Strong, and even Mercury Hall. She will attach herself to any man who she thinks will offer her a better life, no matter how unethical his methods.

Mercury Hall, the novel's villain, initially seems to be a minor character. One of two men for whom Easy secures a job with John, Mercury owes his very life to Easy. Some time before, Easy and Mouse prevented Mercury and Kenneth Chapman, former robbers, from being assassinated by mob bosses when they mistakenly stole from them. Since then, Mercury has seemed to be quite appreciative of Easy's efforts on his behalf. However, once he becomes involved with the likes of Anton Breland (Conrad) and Henry Strong, all Mercury can see is fast money and an easy life.

When he kills both Aldridge and Strong, his fate is sealed, and not even Easy can save him then.

In addition to Brawly, major characters who are also members of the Urban Revolutionary Party include Clarissa, Christina Montes, Anton Breland (Conrad), and Henry Strong. Clarissa, Brawly's devoted and protective girlfriend, is very sensitive to Brawly's various frustrations. Because she is fully aware of his past, including the disturbing affair with Isolde, Clarissa defends Brawly against any perceived enemies. Unaware of the criminal plans that Brawly and the others have, Clarissa remains an innocent bystander. Christina (Tina) Montes is completely devoted to the mission of the Revolutionary Party. Wanting only to educate and feed the poor, Tina has no interest in violent activity. Her mistake is, of course, trusting that all the others in the organization have the same goals. Even when she learns that Brawly and Conrad have stockpiled guns, she accepts their explanation that they are merely preparing for self-defense. Also falling prey to the charms of Henry Strong, Tina is made vulnerable to the machinations of the inner circle. Conrad is simply a greedy individual whose only interest in "revolution" is to pad his own coffers. From the reader's introduction to him, Conrad is presented as a villainous figure. He is suspicious of Easy from the beginning, and he does everything within his power to discredit Easy. A chronic gambler, he is desperate for funds to offset his various debts. Perhaps his most despicable act is the way he uses women (Tina and BobbiAnne) to achieve his unsavory goals. Second to Mercury in true villainy is Henry Strong. A spy for the police, Strong has infiltrated the organization supposedly to prevent its violent overthrow of the public peace. In reality, he has joined the group not only to betray his own people but also to pilfer funds for his own aggrandizement.

Several minor characters flesh out the narrative. Those who have a prominent role in Easy's life, and who have recurring roles from previous novels, are Bonnie Shay, Jesus, Feather, Jackson Blue, Odell Jones, and, in spirit form, Mouse. Bonnie, the international flight attendant with whom Easy became romantically involved in *A Little Yellow Dog*, has now moved in with Easy and the children. Easy describes her as the first woman whom he truly feels to be his equal. She challenges him while also allowing him space to do his work. Jesus, now seventeen, is progressing rapidly toward manhood. He is responsible enough to care for young Feather whenever Easy and Bonnie are away. Jesus, initially to Easy's consternation, has decided that he wants to quit high school because the teachers are not interested in him. Articulating his feelings very clearly, Jesus explains that he has more important goals in life, goals that he can easily pursue if Easy will allow him to leave school. Unlike Jesus, Feather, still in elementary school, adores her academic setting, evident in the pride she takes when she twice brings home B-plus papers. Easy and Bonnie encourage Feather in her efforts as they come to realize that each child must pursue his or her goals in different ways.

Jackson Blue, now forty-two, is still the conniving, rather indolent person he always was. Though he remains the smartest man Easy knows, Jackson refuses to live up to his intellectual potential, at least in terms of pursuing gainful employment. Odell Jones, Easy's oldest friend in Los Angeles, helps Easy in driving Brawly out of the building in the novel's climax. Odell calls Brawly's apartment and purports to warn the young man that the police are on their way to conduct a raid. Brawly rushes from the building only to meet Easy's gunfire. While Mouse Alexander has been a major character in all of the other Rawlins mysteries, in *Bad Boy Brawly Brown* he is a minor character by virtue of his spiritual presence. In Easy's dreams, Mouse continues to instruct and guide his friend.

Other minor characters who have appeared in earlier novels include William "Mofass" Wharton, Jewelle MacDonald, and Hiram Newgate. Mofass and Jewelle continue to manage Easy's real estate properties while also building their own empire. They, along with John and some other investors, are financing the houses that John's work team is constructing. Easy continues to depend on the loyalty of Mofass and especially Jewelle. The principal of Sojourner Truth Junior High School and Easy's nemesis, Newgate attempts again in this novel to showcase his illusory power. Still, Easy thwarts his every attempt and continues to befuddle the man. Two of Easy's employees, Ace and Helen, are his staunchest allies; they are diligent in their efforts and they always cover for Easy whenever he is absent on other business.

Newly created minor characters include Kenneth Chapman, Aldridge Brown, Sam Houston, BobbieAnne Terrell, Xavier Bodan, and Liselle Latour. Chapman is the other robber whom Easy and Mouse saved from mobsters. Unlike Mercury, however, Chapman has honored his promise to lead a model life. Only because he is dead from the beginning of the novel is Aldridge Brown a minor character; both his presence in (and absence from) Brawly's life has affected the young man deeply. On the one hand, Brawly wants to emulate his father (evident in his willingness to commit a robbery), while on the other hand, he wants to distance himself from the man and prove his own manhood. Even though his actions (his infidelity) destroyed his family years ago, Aldridge has always cared for his son. He is killed because he intended to intercept Brawly's robbery plans. Sam Houston, proprietor of Hambones, is initially presented as a loudmouthed, overbearing braggart with whom Easy interacted only when forced to do so. By the time Sam has traveled around with Easy and witnessed his skill, however, he becomes more reserved, especially when Easy warns Sam that his life might be jeopardized if he discusses any of the details of the case. Brawly's high school friend, BobbiAnne Terrell, is so committed to her confidant that she risks and ultimately sacrifices her life for him. Because she is white, her association with the First Men is suspect. The fact that both her parents are dead allows her some latitude in her interactions. In some ways, she and Brawly are alike; she has no family, and Brawly feels as though he does not have one. Like Tina Montes, Xavier Bodan is committed to the original mission of the Urban Revolutionary Party. A decidedly nonviolent man, Bodan is kept ignorant of any of the inner circle's plans, because he never would condone, overtly or tacitly, their actions. His presence in the novel makes the behaviors of the villains all the more heinous. Liselle Latour, proprietor of the boardinghouse where Tina Montes lives, is one of Easy's oldest friends from Houston. Formerly a prostitute and madam back in Texas, Liselle now leads an upstanding life. She rents rooms only to single women, and she forbids any male visitors. When Easy wishes to question Tina, Liselle, very protective of her tenants, warns him not to bring any harm to the young woman.

Rounding out the list of minor characters are members of the police force or special investigative unit(s): Detective Vincent Knorr and Colonel Lakeland (the no-nonsense military man). Both men try to persuade Easy to assist them in their surveillance of the First Men. Though he is not eager to betray fellow black citizens for the largely white police force, Easy leads them to believe that he will help them if they agree to cover for him and provide him with the information that he requests. Of course, he never intends to give them any real information; his only objective is to ease Brawly out of this situation fairly unscathed.

THEMATIC ISSUES

Without a doubt, a significant theme in the novel is the human response to the inextricable link between betrayal and guilt. This theme serves as the catalyst that not only sets the narrative in motion, but also propels it to the end. One of the reasons Alva asks Easy (a man she has formerly despised) for his assistance in locating her son is that she is racked with guilt about the troubled life she helped to create for Brawly. As a mother, she believes that she should have been strong enough and insightful enough to protect him. She indicts herself for betraying his trust when she sent him away ten years earlier to his father. Alva is especially troubled because her failings resulted in Brawly's falling prey to another woman, one who should have also been a better (surrogate) mother. That Isolde engages in sexual activity with Brawly is the ultimate act of betrayal, and Alva suffers painful guilt because she thinks she set the stage for this encounter. In addition, she feels guilty about the loss of her brother Leonard. Though she had nothing to do with his death, the fact that it had a detrimental effect on Brawly leaves Alva consumed with self-condemnation. Alva's emotional pain results in her being hospitalized not only during Brawly's childhood, years ago, but also in the present day, when near the end of the novel Brawly's circumstances become too much for her to bear.

In addition to Alva, Easy is also plagued with guilt as a result of what he believes to be his betrayal of Mouse—that if Mouse had not been involved in Easy's last investigation, he would not have died so suddenly. Easy's guilt is so intense that he questions his very manhood. Though he is still physically and sexually a man, Easy feels increasingly bankrupt emotionally. He feels as though he lost a substantial part of himself when he lost Mouse. Now faced with the challenge of saving young Brawly, Easy thinks he can possibly redeem himself if he returns the misguided youth home alive. While Easy's desire to help Brawly is commendable, the veteran detective knows that he will ultimately have to face his inadequacies directly regarding the Mouse incident. Perhaps what is most interesting about this dilemma is that Mouse, via one of Easy's dreams, sends him a message regarding their final moments together. In a dream conversation, Easy apologizes for letting Mouse down (i.e., betraying him). Mouse responds, "You let me die." One could argue, on the one hand, that Mouse confirms Easy's betrayal. But on the other hand, given Mouse's often cryptic, ambiguous messages, he might be saying quite simply that Easy allowed him to depart. The latter interpretation is not far-fetched when one recalls that in this same "conversation," Mouse tells Easy to kill Brawly and just end this entire nightmare, so that John and Alva can begin to heal. Whatever Mouse's intent, Easy's struggle with the memory of his friend will be ongoing. As a result, then, this theme provides a narrative tension that is sustained throughout the novel.

As is true of the other Rawlins novels, a recurring theme in *Bad Boy Brawly Brown* is the struggle of black manhood to survive. A premise stated in earlier novels that Easy echoes here is that black men in America need to have multiple skills so that they can always be prepared for every contingency. In a world where black men's efforts have often been thwarted, they have had to sharpen other skills to provide a stable life for themselves and their families. When Easy was a boy (as he recalls in this novel), his father impressed upon him the importance of versatility. The older Rawlins insisted that no matter what happens in one's life, a true man is never defeated, because he learns from every incident, and from every incident good flows. Easy challenges his father, in typical childlike wonder, by hypothesizing the loss of a limb. The older man insists that even the loss of one's arm is a positive circumstance if one accepts the loss like a man and strengthens the arm he has left. After all, "a real man will know that he has to overcome anything that gets in the way of him caring for his family" (149). In his adult life Easy has come to accept this lesson without further debate. He even has to teach it to the white police, who question his authority as an investigator. When they refer to him as merely a janitor, Easy responds by asking them a series of questions: if they know how to sew, if they know how to bake, if they know how to lay bricks, if they know how to tan leather, or if they can tell in an instant when and if a man will go crazy. As they stand there stunned, Easy then informs him that he knows how to perform all of these tasks, and even more. His very life (survival) has depended on these capabilities. Later, Easy will insist that any black man's successes result from his willingness to take a risk, even beyond those risks involved in day-to-day living. Easy understands the reality that as a black man, he must employ whatever skills are at his disposal (and whatever methods, ethical or not). He verifies this point when commenting on Alva's change-of-heart: he declares that she had not made a mistake about the kind of man he was; instead, she made a mistake in believing that she would never require his brand of assistance. Here Easy maintains that at some point, most (if not all) black lives (with black men acting as the agents) will need unique survival tools.

The most engaging theme in the novel is the right to individual pursuit, or the right for self-reliance, against societal expectation. When Jesus first discloses his desire to quit school, Easy is horrified at the possibility that yet another minority male will not achieve the highest education that his skills might allow. Ultimately, however, Easy accepts that individuals should have the right to pursue their own dreams and not be restricted by the demands of the larger society. Jesus believes that he is wasting his time in the company of fools (teachers) who have no concern about his intellectual or emotional well-being. Jesus has even realized that the supposed facts these teachers impart are most often erroneous; in fact, their actions have locked the gates of knowledge, argues Jesus. He decides, then, to journey down a life road less traveled. Easy is confident that Jesus will construct his sailboat and that he will be successful in his seafaring life. Moreover, Easy is pleased with the man that Jesus has become (though he is only seventeen): sensitive, humane, and practical. When Easy considers many of the formally educated persons he has encountered over the years, he is reminded that their degrees did not render them any smarter than anyone else. The smartest person Easy knows is Jackson Blue, a self-educated man. Every time Easy encounters Jackson, the otherwise trifling man shares with his friend some rich philosophical thought. Even though Jackson has not translated his knowledge into the lucrative career one expects of a grown man in a capitalist culture, he is still possessed of a knowledge base that no one can take from him. Easy's decision to leave Jesus to his own devices (to allow the boy to find his own way in the world) is validated when Mr. Tai, proprietor of the neighborhood market, shares with Easy his own response about his son's dubious academic standing. Mr. Tai, no longer worried that his son is failing in school, has decided to wait until the boy is sixteen and then have him come to work at the market. If that intense labor does not send him back to school, says Mr. Tai, then the business will simply become Tai and Son. The practical and easygoing Mr. Tai is not burdened by societal expectations; rather, he will give his son (this individual) the opportunity to succeed, whatever course he chooses. As a means of echoing this point, Easy even mocks the mob pursuit of the American dream. While sitting in a diner and observing the customers, many of whom are factory workers at a local plant, Easy declares them citizens of a nation that has triumphed in every major war. As a result, says Easy, these citizens enjoy the fruits of victory: "mindless labor and enough of anything they wanted to buy" (129). Clearly, he questions the mindless nature of capitalist engagement. By contrast, then, the intrepid independence and individuality espoused by Jesus is celebrated.

HISTORICAL CONTEXT

Bad Boy Brawly Brown is set in February 1964, three months after the November 1963 setting of the last Rawlins installment, *A Little Yellow Dog*. The national and fictional atmosphere of this interim period has been marked by both shock and change. Easy's mild depression about the death of Mouse is emblematic of America's sadness about President John F. Kennedy's assassination. The sudden death of both men brings to *Bad Boy Brawly Brown* a sense of urgency with regard to effecting positive change and a new stability for all Americans.

The year 1964 is an important one for social progress in America. The long-awaited Civil Rights Bill was passed, and it lay the foundation, of course, for passage of the Voting Rights Act of 1965. Both pieces of legislation offered hope to black Americans that they would finally benefit from all rights offered in the Constitution. That *Bad Boy Brawly Brown* is directly concerned with these advances is evident in the fact that Mosley employs a ten-year window to establish a more comprehensive context. Early in the novel, 1954 is invoked when the reader is told that Brawly was sent away at age fourteen to live with his father. In the annals of American history, 1954 is an important year. With the Supreme Court's decision in *Brown v. the Board of Education of Topeka, Kansas*, America ostensibly ended segregation. However, during the ensuing ten years (up to the present context of the novel), de facto (actual) segregation ruled the land. The reality of early 1964, then, is that the promises of 1954 have not been honored.

By 1964 black Americans were even more anxious to gain all of their rights. Increasingly, groups like the vocal, and often controversial, Black Panther Party enjoyed a mass following as they attempted to force social change. Mosley's Urban Revolutionary Party is quite obviously a fictional representation of the Black Panthers. Though this group did not organize until 1966, Mosley presents his Revolutionary Party in the 1964 setting in anticipation of the actual group and to allow creative latitude in the depiction. Organized in October 1966 in Oakland, California, by Huey Newton and Bobby Seale, the Black Panthers advocated black self-defense while seeking to restructure American society for economic, political, and social betterment. Influenced by the teachings of social activist Malcolm X, the Panthers stressed racial dignity and self-reliance. They urged blacks to seek control of their communities and to defend and protect the vulnerable among them, particularly the elderly and children. The Panthers are credited with initiating nutrition programs and sponsoring African-centered schools. Still, the media projected the Panthers to the American public as a threatening body. When Panther members, especially the men, patrolled their neighborhoods sporting their signature black berets and shouldering rifles, they presented an ominous picture to some. As a consequence, the reputation of the Panthers was often conflicted.

Mosley quite credibly re-creates this ambiguous portrait with his Urban Revolutionary Party. This group of First Men is comprised of persons who have the best interest of community in mind as well as those whose motivations are guided purely by self-interest. While Tina and Xavier want better education for black children and proper nutrition and political clout for the neighborhood, others, like Conrad, use the organization as a front for their own selfish machinations. And then there are those like the young, impatient Brawly, whose frustrations make him easy prey for corruption. In presenting this comprehensive exposé, Mosley fairly objectively historicizes Black Panther politics. The purer goals of the group are highlighted at the same time that human imperfections are noted. Unfortunately, as Mosley not-so-subtly implies, the behaviors of a corrupt few provide authorities with the perfect political ammunition for discrediting the entire organization.

To reiterate to the reader that this period marks significant change, Mosley (via Easy) mentions the recent upset in the boxing world in a reference to the "recently deposed champion, Sonny Liston" (278). On February 24, 1964, Cassius Clay (who later called himself Muhammad Ali) bested Liston for the heavyweight championship. And he retained his title the following year in another bout with Liston. That Easy mentions Liston and not Clay is significant, because by doing so, he highlights that an end of an era is rapidly approaching. The sentiment that Clay represents will follow in the upcoming months and years. The different worlds that Liston and Clay represent are also depicted in the Easy-Brawly dichotomy. As Easy states, "Brawly came from a very different generation than mine. He was intelligent and ambitious, where I had been crafty and happy if I made it through the day. I never questioned the white man's authority—that was a given" (287). The world that Brawly and Clay inhabit is one of defiance and revolt.

Soon after assuming the heavyweight championship Cassius Clay joined the black Muslims and became a disciple of Malcolm X. He defied white authority when he refused to accept second-class citizenship. His most controversial move, which came much later, was his refusal to fight in the Vietnam War. During this time, Ali became symbol of pride for the black community in his representation of a different style of black manhood, unapologetically defining himself as "The Greatest." The subtle elegance with which Easy's generation identified rapidly faded in this era. Revolution and confrontation became the clarion call of the new day.

NARRATIVE STRUCTURE

Like all of the Rawlins novels, *Bad Boy Brawly Brown* is narrated from the first-person perspective by Easy himself. By virtue of this point of view, the novel is not just a detective saga; it is also a character analysis of the detective. Therefore, Easy's development, even before the novel begins, reinforces the narrative structure. Soon into the narrative, the reader is made aware that Easy has chosen for the first time in his life to tell the truth to the various people he initially interviews about the Brawly situation. Because of this transformation, the reader quite naturally wonders how this plot might be different with a different Easy. Better still, the reader wonders how long Easy will be able to refrain from lying, especially as the case develops more complexities and as Easy must become more circumspect about those he can trust. In short, this aspect of Easy's personality provides the reader with substantive narrative tension.

This novel benefits from a very tightly wrought plot, resulting in part from the exact time lapse that frames it: the book opens up on a Saturday, and it draws to a conclusion one week later, also on Saturday. The reader very easily charts the daily progress that Easy makes toward resolution. Because Easy is so dedicated to his family, he must return home each night to check on them. This precise schedule aids the reader in marking the passage of time.

As is true of any worthy piece of fiction, particularly a detective novel, certain minor questions are posed that are designed to sustain narrative tension, and consequently reader interest. Early in the novel, Easy informs the reader that he is studying for an exam that will yield professional advancement if he passes it. Immediately, the reader wonders if the result will be known by novel's end. Once again, Easy's development becomes a means of charting narrative movement.

Other questions that interest the reader and sustain narrative movement include whether Easy and his overbearing boss will have a major confrontation, whether details about Brawly's troubled life will be revealed, whether Easy and Bonnie will stay together, whether Mouse is dead, and whether Easy will allow Jesus to quit school and pursue a seafaring life.

The final two questions are concerns not just within this novel, but they also become intertextual (occurring between two texts). Throughout *Bad Boy Brawly Brown* Easy is troubled by the fact that Mouse never had a funeral. Thus he begins to suspect that perhaps his old friend might not actually be dead. By novel's end, Easy plans to go in search of Mouse's grave, an investigation that will take him, perhaps, into the next Rawlins installment. The Jesus situation also extends beyond the scope of this novel; the reader wishes to know if Jesus is successful in his goal, with regard not only to building his boat but also to satisfying his education. *Bad Boy Brawly Brown* unequivocally fits seamlessly into the Rawlins saga, and its structure clearly anticipates future installments.

A NEW CRITICAL APPROACH

New Criticism (also called the formalist approach) emerged as a distinct literary tool in the 1920s. It was defined by a group of budding critics at Vanderbilt University, including the teacher-scholar-poet John Crowe Ransom and a cadre of his brightest students: Allen Tate, Robert Penn Warren, and Cleanth Brooks. Each of these men would ultimately influence the direction of American literary study for many years to follow.

This approach to literature is perhaps the most natural of methods. It maintains that any given literary work exists in its own right—that is, argues the new critic, it has an inherent autonomy that is not determined by such peripheral concerns as the author's life or other sociological, political, economic, or psychological issues. With this assumption, then, the scholar is free to critique the form of the work: its shape and effect; the characteristics that unify it; and even the various tensions, ambiguities, or oppositions that ironically reinforce the unity. The critic first determines a unifying theme or message, and then he or she examines all aspects of the work in an effort to articulate how these parts help to highlight this theme. In other words, the scholar locates the skeleton of the work (its basic form, its core) and then investigates how the other body parts support that skeleton and assist in the proper functioning of the body (the entire literary work).

As noted in the *Thematic Issues* section, a dominant theme in *Bad Boy Brawly Brown* concerns black male survival and the importance of black male preparedness in the face of a hostile world. Certainly, with Easy (a black man) as narrator, this message is reiterated consistently. More curious, however, is that the theme is conveyed in more subtle ways. By juxtaposing certain scenes and moments in the novel, the reader comes to understand how these minor parts contribute to the overall unit.

For example, in a seemingly insignificant exchange with Tina, Easy questions why she does not read the local paper. When she responds that she is not interested in white men's lies, Easy reminds her that she might read something of considerable import to her own life (as a black person). In other words, Easy is confirming that black people must understand not only their own cultural or racial spaces, but also the world of the empowered (white society). Because there is an inextricable link between these two worlds, blacks cannot afford to be detached and nonchalant. The survival of the unempowered is dependent on such comprehensive knowledge. Easy's admonition to Tina, though quick and seemingly ancillary, is bound to the dominant theme.

This conversation (narrative part) is also linked to another conversation between Jackson and Easy wherein the same message is reinforced. Jackson proudly shares with Easy his knowledge of famed scientist Isaac Newton, but when Easy shows disinterest in this vast store of information, Jackson almost demands that Easy show interest. According to Jackson, if men like Easy and him try to understand and appreciate the accomplishments of Newton, they might have something significant to (re-) consider in their own lives—if they more fully understand Newton, they may better understand themselves. At the very least, if the white man's knowledge is ultimately going to affect their black lives, they had best take heed and learn as much as they can. Jackson's brief lecture clearly validates Easy's ongoing message about black male preparation and versatility. Of course, the irony here is that Jackson must teach Easy the very lesson that Easy has been imparting to others. Still, though, such irony provides the kind of narrative tension (noted in New Criticism) that strengthens the work's unity.

This point is made clear at the end of the Jackson/Easy chapter, when Easy is still pondering Jackson's rather complex lecture. Both Easy and the reader are left to consider what seems to be an elusive idea, but upon further scrutiny, the reader at least finds meaning. Jackson, noting Newton's interest in calculus, explains to Easy that mathematics is simply the language of how mechanisms work and "that that was the real secret men were always going for—to speak in the language of things" (268). On the surface, Jackson's words seem to be merely intellectual effusions with no real application. But on further notice, one finds that Jackson has simply reinforced earlier messages: to know another language (even the language of mathematics) is to exist more powerfully in another cultural space. Just as Easy has admonished Tina to know the language of the white man's newspaper, Jackson insists that black men know as many "languages" as they can.

Even one of the subplots of the novel shares this message. Jesus has decided that he wants to learn the language of sailing and to construct his preparedness in an unconventional way. Though Easy is initially opposed to his son's wishes, he ultimately realizes that Jesus is creating for himself a broader base of experience that will afford him more choices for survival. The message that Jesus conveys to his father and to the reader is consistent with the overall narrative objective.

Bibliography

Page numbers cited in the text refer to the hardcover editions of *Always Outnumbered, Always Outgunned; Fearless Jones;* and *Bad Boy Brawly Brown.* For *Devil in a Blue Dress, Black Betty, RL's Dream, A Little Yellow Dog,* and *Blue Light,* the page references are to the paperback editions.

WORKS BY WALTER MOSLEY

Novels

Devil in a Blue Dress. New York: Norton, 1990. Rpt. New York: Pocket Books, 1991.
A Red Death. New York: Norton, 1991. Rpt. New York: Pocket Books, 1992.
White Butterfly. New York: Norton, 1992. Rpt. New York: Pocket Books, 1993.
Black Betty. New York: Norton, 1994. Rpt. New York: Pocket Books, 1995.
RL's Dream. New York: Norton, 1995. Rpt. New York: Washington Square, 1996.
A Little Yellow Dog. New York: Norton, 1996. Rpt. New York: Pocket Books, 1997.
Gone Fishin'. Baltimore: Black Classic, 1997. Rpt. New York: Pocket Books, 1998.
Always Outnumbered, Always Outgunned. New York: Norton, 1998. Rpt. New York: Pocket Books, 1998.
Blue Light. Boston: Little, Brown, 1998. Rpt. New York: Warner, 1999.
Walkin' the Dog. Boston: Little, Brown, 1999. Rpt. New York: Back Bay, 2000.
Fearless Jones. Boston: Little, Brown, 2001. Rpt. New York: Warner, 2002.
Futureland. New York: Warner, 2001.
Bad Boy Brawly Brown. Boston: Little, Brown, 2002.
Six Easy Pieces: Easy Rawlins Stories. Boston: Little, Brown, 2003.

Other Works

"A Closed Book: The Publishing Industry May Talk a Good Game, But It Still Doesn't Hire People of Color." *Los Angeles Times* (May 29, 1994): E-2.

Always Outnumbered, Always Outgunned. (consultant for HBO film, 1998)

A Red Death. (adapted for the Chicago Theatre Company, 1997)

"The Black Man: Hero." In *Speak My Name: Black Men on Masculinity and the American Dream.* Ed. Don Belton. Boston: Beacon, 1997: 234–40.

"Black Woman in the Chinese Hat." *GQ.* August, 2000: 94.

"Culture Zone; Black to the Future." *New York Times* (November 1, 1998): 32.

Devil in a Blue Dress. (consultant for Hollywood film, 1995)

Editor, *Black Genius: African American Solutions to African American Problems.* New York: Norton, 1999.

"For Authors, Fragile Ideas Need Loving Every Day." *New York Times* (July 3, 2000): http://www.nytimes.com/library/books/070300mosley-writing.html

"A Message Louder Than a Billion Pleas." *Los Angeles Times* (May 5, 1992): B-7.

Middle Passage. U.S. version of French film, written and narrated by Mosley for presentation on HBO, February 2002.

"No Renaissance without Our Editors and Publishers." In *Defining Ourselves: Black Writers in the '90s.* Eds. Elizabeth Nunez and Brenda M. Greene. New York: Peter Lang, 1999: 9–14.

"Pet Fly." *New Yorker.* December 13, 1999: 90.

Since You Been Gone. (play performed in workshop at Harford Stage Company, 1999)

The Tempest Tales. (serialized stories for *Savoy* magazine, 2001 issues)

"Understanding the Riots." *Los Angeles Times* (May 14, 1992): special section 6.

Workin' on the Chain Gang: Shaking Off the Dead Hand of History. New York: Ballantine, 2000.

"The World of Easy Rawlins." *Los Angeles Times* (July 14, 1991): Home-1.

"Writing About the Universe." *Whole Earth* (Winter 1998): 8.

www.waltermosley.com

WORKS ABOUT WALTER MOSLEY

Interviews

Applebone, Louise. "Author of Popular Mysteries Visiting Dallas." *Dallas Morning News* (June 19, 2001): 1Y.

Bruckner, D. J. R. "Moral Questions via Mystery Stories." *New York Times* (September 4, 1990): C-1, 16.

Cannon, Margaret. "Crime Writer's Roots the Clue to His Fiction." *Globe and Mail* (Toronto) (October 3, 1992): C-1.

Carvajal, Doreen. "An Author Tells of His Frustrations in Trying to Promote Diversity in the Industry." *New York Times* (November 24, 1997): D-11.

Colker, David. "Easy Does It for This Novelist." *Los Angeles Times* (December 6, 2001): T-2.

"Crime and Prophecy." *Maclean's* (June 17, 2002): 68.

Cryer, Dan. "Talking with Walter Mosley." *Newsday* (February 2, 1997): G-11.

Cuza, Bobby. "Reading Q & A with Walter Mosley: Practical Words to Live By." *Los Angeles Times* (March 19, 2000): B-2.

Durrant, Sabine. "Easy Does It." *Times of London* (November 6, 1994).

"Eavesdropping: Conversation with Walter Mosley and Colson Whitehead." *Book* (May 2001): 44–46.

Eichenberger, Bill. "For a Writer, Mosley Has Some Mysterious Ideas." *Columbus Dispatch* (February 17, 2000): E-8.

Frisby, Michael K. "First Fan's Club: President's Attention Makes Writer Soar." *Wall Street Journal* (January 2, 1997): 1.

Frumkes, Lewis Burke. "A Conversation with Walter Mosley." *Writer* 112 (December 1999): 20.

George, Lynell. "Authors: The People Behind the Books We Read." *Los Angeles Times* (November 24, 1999): E-1.

———. "Walter Mosley's Street Stories." *Los Angeles Times Magazine* (May 22, 1994): 14–17.

Gleick, Elizabeth. "Easy Does It." *People Weekly* 38 (September 7, 1992): 105–6.

Gordon, Ed. "Interview with Walter Mosley." *BET Tonight with Ed Gordon*. Black Entertainment Television. July 2, 2002.

Halverson, Guy. "Mystery Writer Walter Mosley Tackles the Mean Streets of L.A." *Christian Science Monitor* (August 12, 1994): 14.

Hogness, Peter. "How Walter Mosley Discovered His Audience—and the Voice of His Fiction." *Writer's Digest* (March 1996): 8–9.

Holmes, Emory, II. "Writer (Not) in Residence." *Los Angeles Magazine* 43 (November 1998): 32.

Jaggi, Maya. "Easy Does It." *Guardian* (November 29, 1997): 26.

Johnson, Adrienne. "Looks Who's Coming Writing Jones." *News & Observer* (Raleigh, NC) (June 11, 2001): E-1.

Jones, Vanessa E. "Walter Mosley: From Mystery to Redemption." *Boston Globe* (October 14, 1999): D-1.

Joyner, Tom. "Interview with Walter Mosley." *Tom Joyner Morning Show*. July 19, 2001.

Lee, Felicia R. "Walter Mosley: Bracing Views from a Man of Mysteries." *New York Times* (April 3, 2000): E-1, 3.

McCullough, Bob. "Walter Mosley: The Crime Novelist Explores Black Life in Postwar America Through His Reluctant PI." *Publishers Weekly* (May 23, 1994): 67–68.

Moore, Steven. "Black and Blues." *Guardian* (October 13, 1993): 2, 4.

Mudge, Alden. "New Crime Fiction with a Twist." *Bookpage* (June 2001): http://www.bookpage.com/0106bp/walter_mosley.html

Nathan, Jean. "Easy Writer." *Esquire* (June 1994): 42.

Oxford, Esther. "Interview with Walter Mosley." *Independent* (London) (October 9, 1995): 2, 4.

Penkava, Melinda. "Interview: Author Walter Mosley Discusses His New Book, *Workin' on the Chain Gang*." *Talk of the Nation*. National Public Radio. January 18, 2000.

Peterson, V. R. "Living Easy: Talking with Walter Mosley." *People Weekly* (October 30, 1995): 42.

Porter, Evette. "*BIBR* Talks with Walter Mosley." *Black Issues Book Review* (July-August 2002): 30–31.

"PW Talks with Walter Mosley." *Publishers Weekly* (May 28, 2001): 54.

Rizzo, Frank. "A Conversation with Walter Mosley." *Hartford Courant* (June 6, 1999): G-1.

Salm, Arthur. "Thinking Paramount in Author's Life, Work." *San Diego Union-Tribune* (January 4, 2002): E-1.

Scott, Nancy. "Solving L.A.'s Mysteries." *San Francisco Examiner* (July 21, 1992): D-1.

Siegel, Joel, and Deborah Roberts. "Walter Mosley Interview: His Latest Book is His Oldest." *Good Morning America*. ABC News. February 9, 1997.

Snowden, Don. "There's No Easy Way Out." *Los Angeles Times* (May 5, 1992): Home-1.

Southgate, Martha. "Walter Mosley: A Man of His Word." *Essence* (February 1997): 72–73.

Stamberg, Susan. "Walter Mosley on His Favorite Work." *Morning Edition*. National Public Radio. June 26, 2001.

Steger, Jason. "The Mosley View." *Sunday Age* (February 11, 1996): 9.

Streitfeld, David. "The Clues to the City of L.A.; Walter Mosley's Gumshoe Tracks Decades of Despair." *Washington Post* (November 10, 1992): C-1.

Strickland, Darryl. "A Profitable Switch: Bestselling Author Uses His Success to Boost Black-Owned Publishers." *Seattle Times* (January 14, 1997): D-1.

"Walter Mosley: A Seat at the Table." *Locus* 47 (December 2001): 6–7, 75–76.

"Walter Mosley: The Books Interview." *Observer* (April 11, 1999): 13.

Wilenz, Amy. "Talking with Walter Mosley: L. A. Law, '50s Style." *Newsday* (June 30, 1991): 40.

Williams, Juan. "Interview: Walter Mosley Talks About His Political Views and His Writing Career." *Talk of the Nation*. National Public Radio. August 23, 2000.

Yates, Robert. "Easy Virtue." *Guardian* (October 10, 1995): 2, 15.

BIOGRAPHICAL INFORMATION

Bowman, Elizabeth Atkins. "Black Like Who?" *Black Issues Book Review* (January-February 2001): 24–27.

Brown, Dona. "Walter Mosley." *Bookcase* (September 1995): 18–21.

Foster, Frances Smith. "Walter Mosley." *The Oxford Companion to African American Literature*. Eds. William L. Andrews, Frances Smith Foster, and Trudier Harris. New York: Oxford University Press, 1997: 510–11.

Knotts, Kristina L. "Walter Mosley." *Contemporary African American Novelists: A Bio-Bibliographical Critical Sourcebook*. Ed. Emmanuel S. Nelson. Westport, CT: Greenwood Press, 1999: 350–54.

Lorenz, Janet. "Walter Mosley." *Cyclopedia of World Authors*. Vol. 4, 3rd edition. Englewood Cliffs, NJ: Salem Press, 1997: 1453–54.

Lyall, Sarah. "Heroes in Black, Not White." *New York Times* (June 15, 1994): C-1, 8.

McKanic, Arlene. "More Than a Man of Mystery." *Black Issues Book Review* (September-October 1999): 16–19.

"Walter Mosley." *Current Biography* 55 (September 1994): 382–85.

"Walter Mosley." *The Norton Anthology of African American Literature*. Eds. Henry Louis Gates, Jr., and Nellie Y. McKay. New York: Norton, 1997: 2594–95.

Werbe, Peter. "Hard-boiled: A Profile of Walter Mosley." *The Progressive* 64 (April 2000): 64–65.

Whetstone, Muriel. "The Mystery of Walter Mosley." *Ebony* 51 (December 1995): 106–9.

REVIEWS

Devil in a Blue Dress

Atlanta Journal and Constitution, June 17, 1990: L-9.

Cosmopolitan, June 1990: 32.

Dallas Morning News, September 6, 1990: C-2.

Essence, January 1991: 32.

Library Journal, June 1, 1990: 188.

Los Angeles Journal, August 15, 1990: 7.

Los Angeles Times, July 29, 1990: Home-3.

Milwaukee Journal, July 1, 1990: E-9.

Newsday, June 10, 1990: 18.

New Statesman & Society, April 19, 1991: 37.

Newsweek, July 9, 1990: 65.

New York Times Book Review, August 15, 1990: B-2.

Publishers Weekly, June 1, 1990: 46.

San Francisco Chronicle, July 8, 1990: Sunday-4.

Seattle Times, September 16, 1990: L-9.

St. Petersburg Times, July 22, 1990: D-7.

Voice Literary Supplement, October 1992: 23.

Washington Post, June 22, 1990: C-3.
Washington Times, September 2, 1991: E-8.

A Red Death

Cosmopolitan, July 1991: 28.
Kansas City Star, July 21, 1991: I-10.
Kirkus Reviews, May 15, 1991.
Library Journal, June 1, 1991: 200.
Newsday, July 1, 1991: 38.
New York Times, August 7, 1991: B-2.
Omaha World-Herald, July 28, 1991: 20.
Publishers Weekly, May 17, 1991: 57.
San Francisco Chronicle, July 7, 1991: Sunday-9.
Tulsa World, July 21, 1991: D-6.
Voice Literary Supplement, October 1992: 24.
Wall Street Journal, July 24, 1991: A-8.
Washington Post, August 18, 1991: Final-10.

White Butterfly

American Visions, February–March 1993: 34.
Booklist, May 15, 1992: 1665.
Boston Globe, July 2, 1992: City Edition-67.
California Lawyer, April 1993: 56.
Chicago Sun-Times, August 16, 1992: Final-13.
Cosmopolitan, July 1992: 30.
Entertainment Weekly, August 14, 1992: 52–53.
Globe and Mail (Toronto), July 18, 1992: C-15.
Kirkus Reviews, May 1, 1992.
Library Journal, June 1, 1992: 186.
Los Angeles Times, July 12, 1992: Home-2.
Newsday, July 9, 1992: 62.
New Statesman & Society (London), September 3, 1993: 41.
New York Times Book Review, September 6, 1992: 25.
Orange County Register, July 25, 1992: F-4.
Publishers Weekly, May 4, 1992: 43.
Salt Lake Tribune, August 16, 1992: E-9.
San Francisco Chronicle, July 5, 1992: Sunday-1.
San Francisco Examiner, July 21, 1992: D-1.
Time, November 23, 1992: 81.
Tulsa World, December 20, 1992: D-6.
Washington Post, August 16, 1992: Final-X6.

Black Betty

Booklist, May 1, 1994: 1563.
Christian Science Monitor, July 1, 1994: 10.
Dallas Morning News, July 31, 1994: J-10.
Entertainment Weekly, June 24, 1994: 94–95.
Fortune, August 8, 1994: 107–8.
Kirkus Reviews, April 15, 1994.
Library Journal, May 1, 1994: 141.
Newsweek, July 4, 1994: 66–67.
New York Times Book Review, June 5, 1994: 13.
People Weekly, June 20, 1994: 31.
Publishers Weekly, April 25, 1994: 60.
Reason, December 1994: 52.
Washington Post, June 20, 1994: C-2.

RL's Dream

Booklist, June 1, 1995: 1684.
Chicago Sun-Times, August 13, 1995: Late Sports Final-15.
Emerge, October 1995: 200.
Entertainment Weekly, August 18, 1995: 47–48.
Guardian, October 15, 1995: 15.
Hartford Courant, August 20, 1995: G-3.
Houston Chronicle, September 10, 1995: 24.
Kansas City Star, November 5, 1995: I-10.
Kirkus Reviews, June 1, 1995.
Los Angeles Daily News, August 17, 1995: L-12.
Los Angeles Times, August 6, 1995: Home-3.
Library Journal, September 15, 1995: 93.
Milwaukee Journal Sentinel, September 10, 1995: E-10.
Nation, September 18, 1995: 290.
News & Observer (Raleigh, NC), September 24, 1995: G-5.
Newsday, August 6, 1995: 32.
New Statesman & Society (London), October 13, 1995: 33.
New York Times Book Review, August 13, 1995: 11.
Plain Dealer (Cleveland, OH), December 28, 1995: E-8.
Playboy, October 1, 1995: 34.
Portland Oregonian, September 24, 1995: E-7.
Publishers Weekly, May 29, 1995: 65.
San Francisco Chronicle, August 6, 1995: Sunday-3.
San Francisco Examiner, September 3, 1995: B-7.
Seattle Post-Intelligencer, September 26, 1995: C-1.

Times (London) *Literary Supplement*, September 22, 1995: 24.
Washington Post, August 20, 1995: Final-X7.

A Little Yellow Dog

Atlanta Journal and Constitution, July 7, 1996: L-8.
Booklist, May 1, 1996: 1469.
Boston Herald, July 21, 1996: O-5.
Buffalo News, June 23, 1996: G-6.
Chicago Sun-Times, June 23, 1996: Late Sports Final-14.
Christian Science Monitor, July 25, 1996: B-1.
Dallas Morning News, July 21, 1996: J-9.
Emerge, July-August, 1996: 75.
Hartford Courant, July 14, 1996: G-3.
Kirkus Reviews, April 15, 1996.
Library Journal, June 1, 1996: 157.
Los Angeles Times, July 14, 1996: Home-2.
Milwaukee Journal Sentinel, July 21, 1996: 11.
New York Times Book Review, June 16, 1996: 18.
Newsday, July 14, 1996: C-32.
People Weekly, July 15, 1996: 37.
Publishers Weekly, May 13, 1996: 58.
School Library Journal, October 1996: 164.
Times Union (Albany, NY), June 30, 1996: G-10.
Wall Street Journal, July 19, 1996: A-10.
Washington Post, July 19, 1996: B-2.

Gone Fishin'

Atlanta Journal and Constitution, February 11, 1997: C-5.
Black Issues in Higher Education, April 3, 1997: 34.
Black Scholar, Summer 1997: 52.
Booklist, December 1, 1996: 621.
Boston Herald, January 19, 1997: O-1.
Chicago Sun-Times, February 9, 1997: Late Sports Final-17.
Denver Post, February 16, 1997: G-7.
Entertainment Weekly, January 24, 1997: 53.
Forbes, August 11, 1997: 28.
Houston Chronicle, February 9, 1997: 18.
Library Journal, December 1996: 146.
Los Angeles Daily News, January 26, 1997: L-24.
Los Angeles Times, February 2, 1997: Home-10.
Milwaukee Journal Sentinel, February 9, 1997: 11.

New York Times Book Review, January 26, 1997: 18.
People Weekly, March 3, 1997: 43.
Plain Dealer (Cleveland, OH), February 2, 1997: I-11.
Portland Oregonian, January 21, 1997: C-1.
Publishers Weekly, November 18, 1996: 65.
San Francisco Chronicle, January 12, 1997: Sunday-1.
Seattle Times, January 14, 1997: D-7.
St. Louis Post-Dispatch, January 26, 1997: C-5.
Time, January 20, 1997: 75.
Times Union (Albany, NY), January 26, 1997: G-10.
Washington Post, February 2, 1997: Final-X1.

Always Outnumbered, Always Outgunned

Baltimore Sun, November 2, 1997: F-5.
Booklist, August 1997: 1848.
Capital Times (Madison, WI), January 2, 1998: A-11.
Chicago Sun-Times, November 16, 1997: Late Sports Final-20.
Columbus Dispatch, January 29, 1998: Home-13.
Dallas Morning News, January 11, 1998: J-8.
Denver Post, November 23, 1997: G-5.
Houston Chronicle, January 11, 1998: 21.
Kirkus Reviews, September 15, 1997.
Library Journal, October 11, 1997: 124.
Los Angeles Times, November 9, 1997: Home-9.
Milwaukee Journal Sentinel, December 21, 1997: 11.
New York Daily News, November 16, 1997: 30.
New York Times Book Review, November 9, 1997: 11.
People Weekly, November 3, 1997: 40.
Pittsburgh Post-Gazette, January 18, 1998: G-9.
Publishers Weekly, October 6, 1997: 74.
San Francisco Chronicle, November 16, 1997: Sunday-1.
Seattle Post-Intelligencer, January 10, 1998: C-2.
Washington Post, December 21, 1997: Final-X1.

Blue Light

Analog Science Fiction & Fact, June 1999: 134.
Booklist, September 1, 1998: 6.
Boston Globe, November 8, 1998: K-2.
Emerge, November 1998: 73.
Entertainment Weekly, November 27, 1998: 78.
Kirkus Reviews, September 1998.

Library Journal, October 1, 1998: 134.
Los Angeles Times, November 25, 1998: Home-9.
New Statesman, April 9, 1999: 50.
New York Times Book Review, November 15, 1998: 20.
People Weekly, January 18, 1999: 37.
Plain Dealer (Cleveland, OH), October 27, 1998: E-3.
Publishers Weekly, September 14, 1998: 44.
San Francisco Chronicle, October 21, 1998: E-3.
Spectator, May 8, 1999: 35.
Times Literary Supplement, May 14, 1999: 24.
USA Today, November 5, 1998: D-8.
Washington Post, November 13, 1998: D-2.

Walkin' the Dog

Booklist, July 1999: 1896.
Boston Globe, October 22, 1999: C-15.
Chicago Sun-Times, October 31, 1999: 15.
Denver Post, November 11, 1999: G-5.
Emerge, October 1999: 68.
Houston Chronicle, October 31, 1999: 5.
Kirkus Reviews, August 1, 1999.
Library Journal, August 1999: 141.
Los Angeles Times, October 17, 1999: Home-1.
Milwaukee Journal Sentinel, October 17, 1999: 6.
Newsday, October 24, 1999: B-10.
New Statesman, May 29, 2000: 57.
New York Times Book Review, November 7, 1999: 9.
Publishers Weekly, August 9, 1999: 338.
Seattle Post-Intelligencer, October 26, 1999: C-2.
St. Louis Post-Dispatch, November 7, 1999: F-13.
USA Today, October 14, 1999: D-1.

Fearless Jones

Black Issues Book Review, July 2001: 28.
Book, July 2001: 71.
Booklist, May 1, 2001: 1636.
Buffalo News, August 26, 2001: F-5.
Capital Times (Madison, WI), June 29, 2001: A-9.
Chicago Sun-Times, October 28, 2001: 18.
Columbus Dispatch, July 5, 2001: Home-15.
Denver Post, July 29, 2001: F-4.

Essence, June 2001: 80.
Guardian, December 8, 2001: P-10.
Hartford Courant, July 1, 2001: G-3.
Houston Chronicle, July 8, 2001: 19.
Kirkus Reviews, April 1, 2001.
Library Journal, June 1, 2001: 224.
Los Angeles Times, June 10, 2001: E-2.
Milwaukee Journal Sentinel, June 10, 2001: E-6.
Newsday, June 3, 2001: B-9.
New York Daily News, June 17, 2001: Sports Final-15.
New York Times Book Review, June 10, 2001: 24.
New Yorker, July 30, 2001: 79.
People Weekly, July 23, 2001: 43.
Plain Dealer (Cleveland, OH), July 1, 2001: I-1.
Portland Oregonian, June 24, 2001: D-11.
Publishers Weekly, May 28, 2001: 53.
San Francisco Chronicle, June 24, 2001: Final-63.
St. Louis Post-Dispatch, June 10, 2001: D-9.
Village Voice, July 10, 2001: 44.
Washington Post, June 10, 2001: T-14.

Futureland

Black Issues Book Review, November-December 2001: 57.
Booklist, September 1, 2001: 4.
Ebony, January 2002: 18.
Library Journal, October 1, 2001: 145.
Kirkus Reviews, September 1, 2001: 1253.
Los Angeles Times, December 9, 2001: 11.
New Crisis, January-February 2002: 54.
New York Times Book Review, November 25, 2001: 18.
Providence Journal, January 19, 2002: J-6.
Publishers Weekly, September 10, 2001: 65.
San Diego Union-Tribune, December 9, 2001: 2, 3.
Washington Post, November 11, 2001: T-14.

Bad Boy Brawly Brown

Atlanta Journal and Constitution, June 30, 2002: F-4.
Black Issues Book Review, July-August 2002: 30.
Booklist, May 1, 2002: 1466.
Kirkus Reviews, May 15, 2002: 709.
Library Journal, May 15, 2002: 130.

Los Angeles Times, July 7, 2002.
Milwaukee Journal Sentinel, June 30, 2002: E-8.
New York Daily News, June 24, 2002: Sports Final-35.
New York Times, July 4, 2002: E-1.
Newsweek, June 24, 2002: 86.
Publishers Weekly, June 17, 2002: 45.
USA Today, July 2, 2002: D-4.
Wall Street Journal, July 11, 2002: D-10.
Washington Post, July 10, 2002: C-3.

CRITICISM

Berger, Roger A. "'The Black Dick': Race, Sexuality, and Discourse in the L.A. Novels of Walter Mosley." *African American Review* 31 (Summer 1997): 281–94.

Berrettini, Mark L. "Private Knowledge, Public Space: Investigation and Navigation in *Devil in a Blue Dress.*" *Cinema Journal* 39 (Fall 1999): 74–89.

Crooks, Robert. "From the Far Side of the Urban Frontier: The Detective Fiction of Chester Himes and Walter Mosley." *College Literature* 22.3 (1995): 68–90.

Fine, David, ed. *Los Angeles in Fiction: A Collection of Essays from James M. Cain to Walter Mosley.* Albuquerque: University of New Mexico Press, 1995.

Frieburger, William. "James Ellroy, Walter Mosley, and the Politics of the Los Angeles Crime Novel." *Clues: A Journal of Detection* 17 (Fall-Winter 1996): 87–104.

Lock, Helen. "Invisible Detection: The Case of Walter Mosley." *MELUS* 26 (Spring 2001): 77–89.

Lomax, Sara M. "Double Agent Easy Rawlins: The Development of a Cultural Detective." *American Visions* 7 (May-June 1992): 32–33.

Mason, Theodore O., Jr. "Walter Mosley's Easy Rawlins: The Detective and Afro-American Fiction." *Kenyon Review* 14 (Fall 1992): 173–83.

Mills, Alice. "Warring Ideals in Dark Bodies: Cultural Allegiances in the Work of Walter Mosley." *Palara* 4 (2000): 23–39.

Nieland, Justus J. "Race-ing Noir and Re-Placing History: The Mulatta and Memory in *One False Move* and *Devil in a Blue Dress.*" *Velvet Light Trap* 43 (1999): 63–77.

Smith, David L. "Walter Mosley's *Blue Light:* (Double Consciousness) Squared." *Extrapolation* 42 (Spring 2001): 7–26.

Wesley, Marilyn C. "Power and Knowledge in Walter Mosley's *Devil in a Blue Dress.*" *African American Review* 35 (Spring 2001): 103–16.

Young, Mary. "Walter Mosley, Detective Fiction, and Black Culture." *Journal of Popular Culture* 32 (Summer 1998): 141–50.

WORKS OF GENERAL INTEREST

Andrews, William, Frances Smith Foster, and Trudier Harris, eds. *The Oxford Companion to African American Literature.* New York: Oxford University Press, 1997.

Bailey, Frankie Y. *Out of the Woodpile: Black Characters in Crime and Detective Fiction.* Westport, CT: Greenwood Press, 1991.

Barry, Peter. *Beginning Theory: An Introduction to Literary and Cultural Theory.* Manchester, England: Manchester University Press, 1995.

Delamater, Jerome H., and Ruth Prigozy, eds. *The Detective in American Fiction, Film, and Television.* Westport, CT: Greenwood Press, 1998.

Douglass, Frederick. *Narrative of the Life of Frederick Douglass.* 1845. Rpt. New York: Signet, 1997.

DuBois, W. E. B. *The Souls of Black Folk.* 1903. Rpt. New York: Penguin, 1996.

Ellison, Ralph. *Invisible Man.* 1952. Rpt. New York: Vintage, 1989.

Gates, Henry Louis, Jr., and Nellie Y. McKay, eds. *The Norton Anthology of African American Literature,* New York: Norton, 1997.

Heglar, Charles. "Rudolph Fisher and the African American Detective." *Armchair Detective* 30 (1997): 16–22.

Hughes, Langston. "The Negro Artist and the Racial Mountain." 1926. Rpt. *The Norton Anthology of African American Literature.* Eds. Henry Louis Gates, Jr., and Nellie Y. McKay. New York: Norton, 1997: 1267–71.

Jablon, Madelyn. "'Making the Faces Black': The African-American Detective Novel." In *Changing Representations of Minorities East and West.* Eds. Larry E. Smith and John Rieder. Honolulu: University of Hawaii Press, 1996: 26–40.

Jacobs, Harriet. *Incidents in the Life of a Slave Girl.* 1861. Rpt. Cambridge: Harvard University Press, 1987.

Johnson, Robert. *The Complete Recordings.* CBS Records, 1990.

Jones, Malcolm. "It's Black, White—And Noir: Crime Writers Are Taking a Hard-Boiled Look at Race." *Newsweek* (June 24, 2002): 86.

Klein, Kathleen Gregory, ed. *Diversity and Detective Fiction.* Bowling Green, OH: Bowling Green State University Press, 1999.

Lock, Helen. *A Case of Mis-Taken Identity: Detective Undercurrents in Recent African American Fiction.* New York: Peter Lang, 1994.

Lynn, Steven. *Texts and Contexts: Writing about Literature with Critical Theory.* 2d ed. New York: Addison-Wesley, 1998.

Medina, Tony, Samiya A. Bashir, and Quraysh Ali Lansana, eds. *Role Call: A Generational Anthology of Social & Political Black Literature & Art.* Chicago: Third World Press, 2002.

Nickerson, Catherine. *Web of Iniquity: Early Detective Fiction by American Writers.* Durham, NC: Duke University Press, 1999.

Quashie, Kevin Everod, Joyce Lausch, and Keith D. Miller, eds. *New Bones: Contemporary Black Writers in America*. Upper Saddle River, NJ: Prentice-Hall, 2001.

Silet, Charles L. P., ed. *The Critical Response to Chester Himes*. Westport, CT: Greenwood Press, 1999.

Soitos, Stephen F. *The Blues Detective: A Study of African American Detective Fiction*. Amherst: University of Massachusetts Press, 1996.

Stevenson, Diane. "Landscape and Race in the Detective Novel." *Studies in the Humanities* 19 (1992): 145–57.

Thomas, Sheree R., ed. *Dark Matter: A Century of Speculative Fiction from the African Diaspora*. New York: Aspect, 2000. Rpt. Warner, 2001.

Van Dover, J. K., ed. *The Critical Response to Raymond Chandler*. Westport, CT: Greenwood Press, 1995.

West, Cornel. "Teaching the History of the Civil Rights Movement, 1865–1965." Lecture at the Summer Institute of the National Endowment for the Humanities. Harvard University. June 26, 1998.

Willen, Margaret M. "Saying Ourselves: Women of Color Writing Detective Fiction." *Clues: A Journal of Detection* 18 (Fall-Winter 1997): 43–57.

Woods, Paula L., ed. *Spooks, Spies, and Private Eyes: Black Mystery, Crime and Suspense Fiction*. New York: Doubleday, 1995.

Index

Helen Plates (*Bad Boy Brawly Brown, A Little Yellow Dog*), 110, 196

Hemingway, Ernest, 26

Henry Strong (*Bad Boy Brawly Brown*), 190, 191, 192, 194, 195

Himes, Chester, 21–22

Hiram T. Newgate (*Bad Boy Brawly Brown, A Little Yellow Dog*), 102, 106, 110, 111–12, 120, 196

Historical Context: in *Always Outnumbered, Always Outgunned*, 137–39; in *Bad Boy Brawly Brown*, 200–202; in *Black Betty*, 69–72; in *Blue Light*, 158–61; in *Devil in a Blue Dress*, 48–51; in *Fearless Jones*, 180–82; in *A Little Yellow Dog*, 115–19; in *RL's Dream*, 92–93

Historical reading: in *Devil in a Blue Dress*, 53–56

Hitler, Adolph, 55, 180, 186

Holland Gasteau (*A Little Yellow Dog*), 103, 104, 105, 107, 108, 112, 113, 122

Holmes, Hamilton, 71

Holocaust, 49, 55, 172, 178, 180

Hopkins, Pauline, 21

Hopkinson, Nalo, 31

Horace LaFontaine (*Blue Light*), 147, 148, 150, 152, 153, 161, 162

Howard Green (*Devil in a Blue Dress*), 36, 38, 39, 42, 52, 53

Howard Shakur (*Always Outnumbered, Always Outgunned*), 126, 127, 130, 139

Huck Finn, 50

Hughes, Langston, 11, 15, 28, 92

Human experience, interconnectedness of: in *RL's Dream*, 90–91

Hunter (Gault), Charlayne, 71

Huxley, Aldous, 29

Idabell Turner (*A Little Yellow Dog*), 101, 102, 103, 104, 107, 108, 109, 110, 112, 113, 114, 115, 118, 119, 120, 123

Identity crisis: in *RL's Dream*, 85; self-hatred in *Always Outnumbered, Always Outgunned*, 143

I Have a Dream, 116

Imprisonment versus freedom: in *Blue Light*, 153

Incidents in the Life of a Slave Girl, 69

Independence, financial and emotional: in *Devil in a Blue Dress*, 44, 45; in *Fearless Jones*, 179

Injustice: in *Always Outnumbered, Always Outgunned*, 131

Intertextuality: in *Bad Boy Brawly Brown*, 203; in *RL's Dream*, 96–97, 99

Invisible Man, 20

Irene Fortlow (*Always Outnumbered, Always Outgunned*), 136

Isaacs, Susan, 11

Isolde Moore (*Bad Boy Brawly Brown*), 189, 190, 192, 194, 195, 198

Israel: in *Fearless Jones*, 171, 172, 175, 176, 181

Iula LaPort (*Always Outnumbered, Always Outgunned*), 131, 142

Jackson Blue (*Bad Boy Brawly Brown, Black Betty, Devil in a Blue Dress, A Little Yellow Dog*), 37, 38, 43, 59, 64, 67, 103, 105, 108, 117, 195, 196, 200, 205

Jacobs, Harriet, 69, 70

Jamal Chesterton (*RL's Dream*), 85

Jessie Peckell (*RL's Dream*), 87

Jesus (*Bad Boy Brawly Brown, Black Betty, A Little Yellow Dog*), 57, 59, 62, 64–65, 73, 102, 105, 106, 107, 110, 111, 120, 195–96, 199, 200, 203, 205

Jewelle MacDonald (*Bad Boy Brawly Brown, Black Betty, A Little Yellow Dog*), 63, 111, 196

Jewish issues: in Mosley's life, 1, 2, 4; in *Devil in a Blue Dress*, 49–50; in *Fearless Jones*, 177–78, 180–81, 186

About the Author

CHARLES E. WILSON, Jr., is University Professor and Chair, Department of English, Old Dominion University, where he teaches African American Literature, Southern Literature, and American Literature. His previous publications include *Gloria Naylor: A Critical Companion* and articles on Ernest J. Gaines and Charles W. Chesnutt.

Critical Companions to Popular Contemporary Writers
First Series—also available on CD-ROM

V. C. Andrews *by E. D. Huntley*

Tom Clancy *by Helen S. Garson*

Mary Higgins Clark *by Linda C. Pelzer*

Arthur C. Clarke *by Robin Anne Reid*

James Clavell *by Gina Macdonald*

Pat Conroy *by Landon C. Burns*

Robin Cook *by Lorena Laura Stookey*

Michael Crichton *by Elizabeth A. Trembley*

Howard Fast *by Andrew Macdonald*

Ken Follett *by Richard C. Turner*

John Grisham *by Mary Beth Pringle*

James Herriot *by Michael J. Rossi*

Tony Hillerman *by John M. Reilly*

John Jakes *by Mary Ellen Jones*

Stephen King *by Sharon A. Russell*

Dean Koontz *by Joan G. Kotker*

Robert Ludlum *by Gina Macdonald*

Anne McCaffrey *by Robin Roberts*

Colleen McCullough *by Mary Jean DeMarr*

James A. Michener *by Marilyn S. Severson*

Anne Rice *by Jennifer Smith*

Tom Robbins *by Catherine E. Hoyser and Lorena Laura Stookey*

John Saul *by Paul Bail*

Erich Segal *by Linda C. Pelzer*

Gore Vidal *by Susan Baker and Curtis S. Gibson*